Betty Strudwick £4.50

KENT ARCHAEOLOGICAL SOCIETY

KENT RECORDS

VOLUME XXI

1979

KENT RECORDS

General Editor: A. P. Detsicas, M.A., F.S.A.

A

KENTISH

MISCELLANY

Edited by F. Hull, B.A., Ph.D., F.R.Hist.S.

PREPARED FOR THE

PUBLICATIONS COMMITTEE

OF THE

KENT ARCHAEOLOGICAL SOCIETY

1979
Published by
PHILLIMORE & CO. LTD.
London and Chichester
Head Office: Shopwyke Hall,
Chichester, Sussex, England

Typeset by COMPUTACOMP (UK) LTD.
Fort William, Scotland.
Printed in England by
UNWIN BROTHERS LTD.
at the Gresham Press, Old Woking, Surrey
and bound by
THE NEWDIGATE PRESS LTD.
at Book House, Dorking, Surrey

A KENTISH MISCELLANY

CONTENTS

GENERAL INTRODUCTION

The publications of Record Societies usually provide one or more of three services to their readers. They offer transcripts of basic medieval research material (the Feet of Fines is an obvious example); they record in print some highly significant manuscript which itself reveals a new dimension for the research of a particular period or topic; or, occasionally, they may be principally of interest to the members of the Society as of general local significance. In offering yet another Miscellany volume, it is hoped that the modesty of the individual items will be outweighed by their value for specific research and their general appeal.

It is, indeed, increasingly difficult to find editors who have both the scholarship and time to undertake mammoth tasks such as seemed possible in an earlier age and this fact, too, has influenced the Publications Committee in its decision. Even the book now published has passed through its vicissitudes—originally it was conceived as a collection of records of interest for burghal history, but its structure changed as suitable material came to hand and as some hoped-for contributions failed to materialise, so that what is now offered is a study of aspects of economic and social history in Kent from the thirteenth to the sixteenth century.

The first paper is in the nature of a revision. In volume XVIII, *Medieval Kentish Society*, published in 1964, Professor Sylvia Thrupp and Dr. D. B. Johnson prepared a text and commentary on the fine series of early rolls of freemen for Canterbury. The paper by A. F. Butcher now published, reveals errors in the transcription in the earlier article, and, still more important, examines critically the various propositions in Professor Thrupp's article and indicates where, and why, they are less than convincing. In a splendid piece of detailed research Mr. Butcher probes many of the problems which arise in using lists of names and indicates the dangers inherent in accepting traditional though unproven concepts. The importance of medieval Canterbury is well attested and this paper helps to establish that knowledge on a still surer basis.

Second, there is Mr. Sinclair Williams' study of East Malling in 1410 from a detailed rental which survives among the Twisden MSS. The close examination of a rural area in this manner reveals unexpected elements of continuity not only forward into our own age, but also back into the shadows of pre-Conquest Kent. The evidence concerns the much debated field systems of this county and portrays a society moving out of the medieval towards the modern though still firmly entrenched in the traditional.

If Canterbury represents the peak of urban society in Kent the chaotic memoranda concerning freemen of Queenborough and other matters surely represent the struggle of a small fishing community to achieve the greatness thrust upon it. Queenborough, a medieval "new town", suffered to an even greater degree than new towns of today the effects of governmental support and neglect and out of the latter probably developed a peculiar franchise, a "mystique" of its own, which is illustrated by these scribbled entries.

If Kent from an early date felt something of the conflicting loyalties of town and country illustrated in these three articles, yet any study of the late medieval period would be inadequate without some reference to the church. It can be estimated that before the Dissolution nearly half of Kentish land belonged to some ecclesiastical establishment and, if the small preceptory of Swingfield is representative of the fringe rather than the core of ecclesiastical property, this does not detract from the value of the study by Messrs. Grove and Rigold. Here is a detailed inventory taken shortly before the great dispossession, almost a sale particular for the future lay landlord; here, too, is valuable detail concerning one of the smaller historic buildings only recently saved after a long and difficult period of negotiation. The fact that the same document also provides valuable information on building construction in the early sixteenth century should not be overlooked.

As the glory departed so a newer, still more mercenary society emerged and one in which increasingly matters formerly of ecclesiastical interest became the concern of the civil authority. The Justice of the Peace and his clerk assumed ever greater significance as the parliament of the day passed new legislation and as more and more responsibilities came to rest on these lay shoulders. The sixteenth century saw the proliferation of records in the parish and the county and the growth of a new dispensation in which the central government represented by the Privy Council used the local gentleman as a means of enforcing the law, raising the militia and carrying out a social revolution. Small wonder that laws were codified and precedents recorded. By some strange chance two fragments of a Tudor precedent book of indictments compiled from Kentish cases reached the County Archives Office. One had belonged to the antiquary Dr. Cock, of Appledore, the other, received years later, was found in Gravesend and, indeed, other fragments may survive elsewhere. Dr. Poole has taken these and fitted them together to reveal a book possibly used by a Clerk of the Peace of the mid-sixteenth century. It essentially concerns Quarter Sesions, not Assizes, and therefore may be truly regarded as our earliest local record of Quarter Sessions in Kent. There are medieval records in the P.R.O. edited and published as vol. XIII of *Kent Records* under the title "Kent Keepers of the Peace, 1316–1317" by Dr. B. H. Putnam. The earliest County records in local custody date from about 1588.

Thus, in five brief papers, a period of three and a half centuries is glimpsed and so, too, consideration is given to agriculture, urban society and commerce, the monastic fringe and the world of law. Each reveals some new element in our county's history, each belongs to the same central tradition and continuity of English society. It is to be hoped that readers will find items of interest and significance within this compass.

Felix Hull.

EDITORIAL NOTE

While each editor has produced his own work in his own way and has indicated methods used, so far as possible English has been preferred to Latin in late texts of this kind and abbreviations have been extended and superscript letters eliminated. Where it seemed appropriate editors have prepared appendices or indices of persons named in their text with reference to the internal numbering of entries or paragraphs in each particular article.

CANTERBURY'S EARLIEST ROLLS OF FREEMEN ADMISSIONS, 1297–1363: A RECONSIDERATION

A. F. BUTCHER

The value of early records of freemen admissions is widely recognised. In such records may be discovered, for the later Middle Ages, the social and economic development of many English towns. Occasionally, it is only in such records that this evidence survives. From the numbers admitted to the freedom of the town, from a study of declared occupations and places of origin, and from an investigation of families and individuals revealed in these sources many aspects of urban society may be illuminated. It has been suggested, for example, that the numbers of new freemen indicate the size and economic vitality of particular communities; that the occupations of new freemen may be used to show social and trade structure and, over time, provide a guide to changing social composition and economic function; and that the relative local importance of a town may be related to the distance from which it is able to draw migrants aspiring to the rank of freeman. Until recently, however, this source has often been used uncritically. The close scrutiny to which it is now being subjected may force earlier generalizations to be qualified.[1]

For Canterbury just such early records survive for the period 1297–1363 in eleven parchment rolls.[2] In acknowledgement of the importance of this source for Kentish history an edition was published in 1964 together with a brief introductory essay.[3] If these materials are to be of benefit to local historians and others, then the need for an accurate printed text is clear. Unfortunately, the text provided is so inaccurate as to seriously impair its value.[4] The purpose of this essay is to provide an accurate description of the rolls of freemen admissions, to correct the more substantial errors of transcription, and to re-evaluate the evidence they contain for the economic and social history of Canterbury in the late thirteenth and fourteenth centuries.

I. THE MANUSCRIPTS

Roll 1. This roll is closely written, without error, on a single membrane measuring 21.9 × 43.8 mm., and has the appearance of a fair copy. Two later medieval additions are the date at the head of the *recto* and "Lib" against the name of John de Trendherst. The roll has two headings, the first "*Rotulus Novorum intrancium tempore Ade de Wald' et Ade Bele Ballivorum Cantuar' coram Johanne Holte Henr' Daniel. Regin' Hurel. Matheo de Eye. Adam de Bisshoppesgate. Simone Bertelot. Johanne Andreu clerico,*" and the second "*Nomina Novorum intrancium die mercur' proxima*

1

post festum sancti Botulphi Anno r r. E. fil' R. H xxvj[10] in presencia. H. Daniel J. Holte. Ade de Bele Simonis Bertelot Thome Chicche. R de Chelesfeud." No attempt has been made on this roll to distinguish between different types of admission and entries are mixed at random. The evidence of the later medieval heading and the second rubric given above is that the date of this roll is the regnal year 26 Edward I or 1297–98 and not 1298–99 as given by Thrupp and Johnson.[5]

Roll 2. This roll, again a fair copy, is made up of two membranes sewn end-to-end measuring in all 23.1 × 111.9 mm., ruled and written on the *recto* only. It has a single heading: "*Nomina Novorum intransium Tempore H. Danyel et R Hurel Ballivorum Civitatis Cant' Anno Regni R E. xxxj[0] In Presencia Ade De Waldis J. Holte Ade Bissoppesgate S Bertelmeu P de chelesfeld et R de chelesfeld.*" Once again no attempt has been made to distinguish between different types of admission but admissions have been recorded by wards, beginning (presumably, though not entered) with Westgate and then under the headings of Borgate, Newyngate, Worthgate, Northgate, and Redingate, in that order. The date of this roll is regnal year 31 Edward I or 1302–03.

Roll 3. This roll, comprising a single membrane measuring 22.5 × 60.3 mm. is written on both sides. Different in kind from those that precede it chronologically but embodying formulae employed in all subsequent rolls it has been transcribed at Appendix I. It has the appearance of a working document and, apart from the difference in its heading, is the first surviving roll to separate different types of admission. The date of this roll is regnal year 1 Edward III or 1327–28 and has been catalogued out of chronological sequence, more properly following what is now Roll 4.

Roll 4. This roll consists of two ruled membranes sewn end-to-end measuring in all 23.7 × 138.4 mm. and being written on both sides. The heading on the *recto* is in the same form as Roll 2 and, as there, no distinctions are made between types of admission but admissions are set out by wards (though Redingate is not included) with similar additional sections ("*Adhuc Burgate*", etc.). The *verso* bears various statements of account not noticed by Thrupp and Johnson and these have been transcribed at Appendix II. The evidence of the heading and the statements of account confirm a date for this roll of regnal year 5 Edward II or 1311–12.

Roll 5. This roll is a single membrane measuring 23 × 58.8 mm. and written on both sides. The headings on the *recto* are in the same form as that for Roll 3 and, as in that roll, distinctions are made between types of admission though divisions according to ward are absent. This is the first surviving roll to account for more than one year. The two years enrolled are regnal years 18–19 Edward III and 19–20 Edward III or 1344–45 and 1345–46. A heading on the *verso* gives "*Anno xviij[0]*" followed by a list of 13 freemen admitted by favour but this heading would seem to be inaccurate for at the foot of the *recto* under the heading indicating the regnal year

2

19–20 Edward III a sub-heading reads "*Memorandum de nominibus que admissi sunt ad libertatem civitatis Cantuar' racione xij jurati ut ex alia parte*", presumably referring to entries on the *verso*.

Roll 6. This roll is a single membrane measuring 23.5 × 69 mm., written principally on the *recto* but with some entries on the *verso*. Its heading is in the same form as that of Roll 3, divisions are made according to types of admission but not according to ward, and admissions by marriage and redemption are given specific sub-headings. The *verso* bears two indistinct entries—"(…) *faversham* (crossed out) *faber de schepeheye* (inserted above)" with the date "*a" xxxiii"*", and "(…) *Nichs* (?) *de meydestane*" with the date 23 Edward III. The date of this roll is regnal year 23–24 Edward III or 1349–50.

Roll 7. This roll is a single membrane measuring 20.9 × 64.4 mm. and written on both sides. The heading is in the same form as Roll 3 and divisions and subheadings as in Roll 6. The *verso* bears the date "*Rot de a" 25*" and the whole roll is dated regnal year 24–25 Edward III or 1350–51.

Roll 8. This roll is a single membrane measuring 21.1 × 51.1 mm. and written on both sides in the same form as Roll 7. The *verso* bears the date "*A" xxviij*" and the whole roll is dated regnal year 28–29 Edward III or 1354–55.

Roll 9. This roll is a single membrane measuring 20.4 × 47.6 mm., written on both sides and in the same form as Roll 7. The *verso* bears the date "*Anno xxix"*" and the whole roll is dated regnal year 29–30 Edward III or 1355–56.

Roll 10. This roll is a single membrane measuring 18.5 × 71.8 mm. and written on both sides in the same form as Roll 7 with an additional sub-heading for those admitted by favour. Two years are accounted for on this roll under the regnal years 30 and 31 Edward III or 1356–57 and 1357–58. The heading on the *verso* is indistinct but what may be detected seems to confirm this dating—"(…) *xxx* (…) *xxxj*".

Roll 11. This roll is a single membrane measuring 24 × 70 mm. and written on both sides in the same form as Roll 7 though without a sub-heading for those admitted by redemption. Three years are accounted for on this roll under the regnal years 34–35, 35–36 and 36–37 Edward III or 1360–61, 1361–62 and 1362–63. A note on the *verso* confirms this dating—"*Anno xxxiiij Et xxxv Et xxxvj Rotule de liber' hominibus Cant'* ".

II. ECONOMY AND SOCIETY

In their discussion of the social and economic significance of the rolls of freemen admissions Thrupp and Johnson used three principal methods of analysis. By comparison of the annual number of admissions they sought to establish trends which might have some bearing upon the prosperity of the community as a whole. By consideration of the place surnames of those admitted they attempted to indicate the changing pattern of immigration

3

and, by inference, the economic vitality of the city and the attraction of its privileges. By examination of the occupations of new freemen and their changing numbers over time they suggested an occupational structure and, in identifying change, drew further conclusions about the social and economic development of Canterbury in this period.

Their conclusions all pointed to the Black Death of 1348–49 as a watershed in the city's history. The trend in the annual number of entries was "upward between 1298 and 1327 and sagging by 1345, with the lowest dip a decade later."[6] Despite the possibility of political pressure, it was argued that the rising number of entries in the early period might be accounted for by prosperity.[7] "The fall in entries in the later years may in turn be related at first to a possible drain of Kentishmen to the French wars, and then undoubtedly to post-plague business stagnation."[8] The pattern of migration would seem to confirm this picture of contraction. It was suggested that "Canterbury became more markedly Kentish in the slack years from 1344–45 on than had been the case in the early years of the century",[9] and that "the radius within which Canterbury drew its non-Kentish freemen also shrank" in the later period.[10] Comparing the periods 1298–1328[11] and 1344–63 "The picture is one of falling demand for foodstuffs, leather and metalwork and yet of growing opportunity in the textile trades."[12] It is argued below that while the Black Death may have been a watershed the conclusions drawn by Thrupp and Johnson from the rolls of freemen admissions are all mistaken.

It is extremely doubtful whether *any* long-term trends may be deduced from a comparison of the annual numbers of the admissions to the freedom in these rolls.[13] Between 1297 and 1328 evidence survives for only 4 years and these are separated by gaps of 5, 9, and 16 years respectively. To assume an upward tendency from such evidence would be statistically naive and to argue from this to conclusions about economic prosperity would be unwise. During a period of severe economic difficulties and political unrest such as the early fourteenth century it may be that fiscal and political motives for enlarging the freeman body or more efficiently enforcing registration should be given serious consideration. To identify any sagging or slackness from the mid-1340s onwards would be dangerous from this evidence.

Statistical problems aside, the nature of Canterbury's franchise deserves further attention. It seems to have been assumed by Thrupp and Johnson that, apart from those admitted by virtue of marriage to a freeman's daughter, by patrimony or by favour, the franchise was open to all choosing to enter it, able to pay the fine, and proving acceptable to the supervisory committee. Thus, for the great majority, here as in many other towns, the purchase of freedom was the purchase of the exclusive right to practise trade or craft as well as the right to enjoy the other benefits of the franchise. From the 1390s, however, evidence from the first city account books[14] makes clear that the privilege of practising trade or craft was *not* confined to Canterbury's freemen. Two groups were permitted to pursue their chosen occupations, the first known as the *intrantes* and the second the freemen. The *intrantes* were required to pay an annual fine for their privilege and their names and fines were recorded annually, by ward, among the city accounts. Admission to the franchise implied freedom from payment of such fines. The implications of this arrangement for the interpretation of the rolls of freemen admissions are considerable.

Table 1
Numbers of Admissions to the Freedom of Canterbury, 1297–1363.

	Redemption	Marriage	Patrimony	Favour	Total	Roll No.
1297–98	35	4	3	—	42	1
1302–03	83	20	14	—	117	2
1311–12	89	46	27	2	164	4
1327–28	89	11 (+ 39)*	3	29	171	3
1344–45	1	16	1	—	18	5
1345–46	34	21	—	13	68	5
1349–50	30	31	—	10	71	6
1350–51	40	12	—	13	65	7
1354–55	9	7	—	2	18	8
1355–56	7	4	—	—	11	9
1356–57	9	4	—	4	17	10
1357–58	18	9	—	3	30	10
1360–61	18	6	1	1	26	11
1361–62	34	6	—	1	41	11
1362–63	17	4	—	6	27	11

* designation uncertain.

If such a system was in force throughout the fourteenth century, and the origins of the *intrantes* are obscure indeed, then the value of the rolls of freemen admissions as evidence of economic life must be further qualified. If such a system was introduced during the fourteenth century then no evaluation of the evidence is possible without some estimate of the date of its introduction. Ignorance of these matters bedevils the use of these rolls: do they provide evidence of the activities of an elite group or one more broadly based whose behaviour is more typical of the whole community?

The level of fines paid by those admitted to the freedom might possibly throw some light on this problem. Analysis of these fines may suggest some changes in the course of the century.

Table 2

Number and Level of Fines paid for Admission to the Freedom, 1297–1363.

	0–5s.	–10s.	–20s.	–30s.
1297–98	32	3	—	—
1302–03	56	23	3	—
1311–12	2	72	9	3
1327–28	—	78	9	2
1344–45	—	—	1	—
1345–46	—	32	1	1
1349–50	5	16	8	1
1350–51	1	38	1	—
1354–55	4	6	—	—
1355–56	1	6	1	—
1356–57	2	6	1	—
1360–61	—	13	3	—
1361–62	—	29	5	—
1362–63	—	12	5	—

Most notably there would appear to be a marked shift in the number of fines paid at the lower levels after 1303. Such suggestions must only be tentative but from 1311, at least, the level of fines paid seems to be predominantly between 5s. and 10s. as against the clear predominance at the lower level of 5s. and below in 1297–98 and 1302–03. The nature of this shift (if shift it be) raises the important question as to how the level of fines was decided. The range of payments made by incoming freemen is fairly wide. The lowest fine, recorded in 1297–98, was 1s. 6d., and the highest, recorded in 1327–28, was 30s. It seems probable that, given the acceptability of the candidate, fines were levied, within customary bounds, according to estimated means. If this is so then the significance of the suggested shift is that from 1311 onwards, at least, the average means of incoming freemen is markedly higher than that in 1297–98 or 1302–03.

The reasons for the change in the level of fines paid is difficult to determine. It might have been that there was a change in the basic level required for entry but the persistence of lower fines paid throughout the period, though reduced in number, tends to argue against this. It might have been that such was the prosperity of the candidates from the first decade of the fourteenth century onwards that the average means of all incoming freemen was substantially higher than it had been but this seems intrinsically unlikely. It might have been that some time in the early fourteenth century there was a change in the nature of the franchise which effectively restricted membership of the freeman body to the more prosperous immigrant but, though this is possible, it is little more than speculation.

6

Apart from the evidence of the fines themselves and the knowledge of the existence of the *intrantes* from the 1390s the format of the Rolls may indicate some change in the early fourteenth century. In two respects Rolls 1, 2 and 4, the earliest of the Rolls, are all similar: all three enrol the names of the pledges or "sponsors" of those entering by redemption and in their headings all three embody the phrase "*Novorum intrancium*". Otherwise Roll 1 is unlike any other roll in that it consists merely of an undifferentiated list of names. Rolls 2 and 4 are alike in one other important respect—while not separating different types of freedom they do divide the names recorded by wards. After 1311–12 the format of the Rolls changes to a format adopted in all of the remaining rolls and in the earliest city account books. Now the new freemen are differentiated by type of admission and not by ward and now the common heading speaks "*de nominibus que admissi sunt ad libertatem civitatis Cantuar'* ". Any argument from this to some far-reaching structural change is tenuous at best and perhaps does little more than emphasise how little is known about constitutional arrangements within the city at this time. But, for whatever reason, it does seem likely that the constituency of Canterbury's freemen did alter in the early fourteenth century and this alteration has direct bearing upon the interpretation of the evidence of freemen admissions for economic and social purposes.

Having considered general trends, Thrupp and Johnson turned to the question of the origins of Canterbury freemen. Though inaccuracies of transcription limited their investigation and lessen the value of the detail of their argument the general picture they draw is accurate enough. More recent work has confirmed the pattern of medieval rural-urban migration they suggest.[15] The arguments for change over time, however, are much less secure. For reasons argued above, it would seem that the surviving rolls of admissions give insufficient evidence to permit the establishment of trends in the fourteenth century. Furthermore, the simple numerical comparison of a 30-year period (1297–1328) for which there is evidence for only 4 years with a 20-year period (1344–63) for which there is evidence for only 11 years seems likely to be little more than misleading. When the place surname evidence analysed comprises only 124 of the *c.* 850 enrolled freemen then the exercise is of doubtful value. Nor is it clear that the enrolled form of a freeman's name is any reliable guide to the date at which the migrant left his community of origin. Perhaps all that can safely be said of the evidence from place surnames at this date is that it provides a rough, general picture of the pattern of migration. Thus, it is possible to talk in aggregate terms about the evidence of place surnames in these rolls but difficult indeed to come to more detailed conclusions.

Nonetheless, it is possible to go further than Thrupp and Johnson in this analysis. Careful consideration of the place surname evidence reveals some 312 names (about 35 per cent of all names enrolled) which give indication of origins. An analysis of these names appears below.

Table 3

*Origins of Canterbury Freemen from Place Surnames, 1297–1363.**

	Kent	Elsewhere	Unknown	Roll No.
1297–98	14	5	4	1
1302–03	28	9	5	2
1311–12	51	18	9	4
1327–28	49	23	6	3
1344–45	9	3	1 ⎫ 5	
1345–46	11	8	3 ⎭	
1349–50	21	6	4	6
1350–51	11	6	2	7
1354–55	2	—	—	8
1355–56	—	—	—	9
1356–57	5	—	—	10
1357–58	8	1	1	
1360–61	4	—	2 ⎫	
1361–62	7	1	2 ⎬ 11	
1362–63	2	1	— ⎭	

* Based on an analysis of the 312 place surnames among the names of the 886 freemen recorded in these years.

While even these figures permit no more than speculative generalisations, there would seem to be little grounds for the suggestion that Canterbury became more markedly Kentish from 1344–45 onwards. And there is insufficient evidence after 1351 for any conclusions as to the pattern of migration into Canterbury. The inference that the economic vitality of the city was in decline from the 1340s and especially after the Black Death, on the basis of these materials, will not do.

The discussion of the occupational structure of Canterbury at this time arouses statistical objections similar to those previously introduced. Once again, it must be said that the comparison of the periods 1297–1328 and 1344–63 is not valid. If the number of specified occupations is added to the number of occupational surnames then the 345 freemen considered represent only c. 39 per cent of all new freemen. If there was a change in the nature of the franchise, if the freeman body became more exclusive, then any attempt to identify changes in occupational structure from these freemen admissions becomes virtually impossible. Notions of falling demand or growing opportunity cannot be sustained.

A more detailed analysis of occupations based on specific declarations and occupational surnames is set out below.[16]

Table 4
Occupations of new Freemen, 1297–1362*

	Textiles	Clothing	Food & Drink	Distributive	Leather	Metal	Wood	Building	Misc.
1297–98	0	0	4	1	4	2	0	0	1
1302–03	4	1	6	2	5	9	3	2	8
1311–12	3	3	23	7	13	6	0	4	7
1327–28	2	0	10	6	8	6	1	2	10
1344–45	6	1	4	1	1	0	1	1	3
1345–46	10	2	6	2	11	2	2	1	6
1349–50	1	1	2	3	2	3	0	2	1
1350–51	0	1	8	3	3	3	1	0	3
1354–55	1	0	1	0	0	1	0	0	0
1355–56	1	0	1	0	3	1	0	0	0
1356–57	0	0	1	0	0	0	1	0	1
1357–58	4	0	1	2	0	0	1	2	1
1360–61	2	0	1	0	2	1	1	0	0
1361–62	4	2	2	2	0	3	1	2	4
1362–63	1	2	1	3	4	2	0	1	1

* This analysis is based upon the occupations and occupational surnames of 325 new freemen of the 886 who were admitted in these years.

The idea of post-plague business stagnation receives no support from this evidence.

Used in conjunction with the rich local archive of lay and ecclesiastical materials and the taxation records of central government Canterbury's earliest rolls of freemen admissions may prove a valuable source.[17] Taken in isolation the evidence of the freemen admissions seems little more than misleading. The impact of bubonic plague, signalled in these records in 1350, 1351 and 1361–62 by a surge in the numbers of new freemen, may not have been as disastrous for the late fourteenth century urban economy as Thrupp and Johnson supposed. If, in the long term, successive depopulations proved enervating to the economy, it may be that in the second half of the fourteenth century it stimulated a new vitality. Perhaps the city of Canterbury, too, experienced the Indian summer of prosperity known to its Cathedral Priory.

Notes

1. For a recent critical examination of the York Freemen's Register see, R. B. Dobson, "Admissions to the Freedom of the City of York in the Later Middle Ages", *Econ. Hist. Rev.*, second ser., Vol. xxvi, No. 1, February 1973, where many fundamental questions are raised concerning the nature of citizenship and urban "freedom".
2. MSS. Dean and Chapter Library, Canterbury Cathedral, Canterbury City Archives R/F 1–11. I am grateful to Miss A. Oakley, for producing mss. and for discussion of points of detail; and to Dr. W. G. Urry, for his interest and encouragement.
3. S. L. Thrupp, with the assistance of H. B. Johnson, "The Earliest Canterbury Freemen Rolls", in *Medieval Kentish Society*, ed. F. R. H. Du Boulay, Kent Records, xviii (1964), 173–214. Hereafter referred to as Thrupp and Johnson.
4. The inaccuracies arise largely from errors in transcription though some from problems of

legibility where rubbing has made sections indistinct. Use of ultra-violet light has enabled most of the indistinct sections to be recovered.

5. Thrupp and Johnson, 178.
6. *Ibid.*, 174.
7. *Ibid.*, 175.
8. *Ibid.*, 175.
9. *Ibid.*, 176.
10. *Ibid.*, 176.
11. *Recte* 1297, see above.
12. Thrupp and Johnson, 176.
13. See, Table 1.
14. MSS. Dean and Chapter Library, Canterbury Cathedral, Canterbury City Archives F/A 1 and F/A9.
15. A. F. Butcher, "The Origins of Romney Freemen, 1433–1523", *Econ. Hist. Rev.* second ser., Vol. xxvii, No. 1, Feb. 1974, 16–27.
16. The occupational categories used in Table 4 differ from those used by Thrupp and Johnson which seem too broad. Those used here are based on the categories used by J. F. Pound, "The Social and Trade Structure of Norwich, 1525–1575", *Past and Present*, no. 34 (1966), 49–69. Thus, under Textiles, the following descriptions have been included—tixtor, linenweaver, carder, chaloner, fuller, sherman, dyer, webbe; under Clothing—cissor and tailor; under Food and Drink—butcher, fisher, cook, carnifex, miller, brewer, taverner, baker, garleke; under Distributive—barber, mercer, chandler, merchant, draper, chapman, spicer; under Leather—girdler, cordwainer, currier, saddler, verrier, ganter, skinner, corveser, tanner, parmenter, sutor; under Metal—goldsmith, cutler, furbour, bladesmith, smith, plumber, faber, mareschal; under Wood—bowyer, wheeler, cooper, turner; under Building—tiler, painter, mason, carpenter, limeburner, sawyer; and under Miscellaneous—feliper, passour, heyward, hackneyman, roper, polentar, chalker, shyvyer, flaoner, clerk, harpour, selier, orfreyser, hettere, playtere, loder, porter, moner, straumonger, flokker, bolter, horner, disher.
17. An essay based upon these materials is currently in preparation and shortly to be produced. For a list of the names of the Canterbury freemen, 1297–1363, see below at Appendix III.

Appendix I

Roll 3 (R/F3)
Recto.

Me^d de nominibus subscriptis qui admissi sunt ad lib' Civitat' Cantuar' tempore . . . . tunc ballivorum dicte Civitatis p visū et consideracionem Simonis Bertelot thom' t . . . . Gillemyn Anselmy Partrych Willi Frenshe Elye de morton thome de Derham Steph' coupere et Johis de Wenchepe ad hoc deputatorum p coītatē dce Civitatis die sabti px an' fm Annc b M anno R R E III post conq' primo usque ad fm S Mich' px seqū

Quorum fines Patent inferrius videlicet

[column one]

D Ricō de thork'		D thom Slegh	x.s
lespicer	dj marc'	D Johē Sprot	x.s.
D Henr' de Tenham	xx.s.	D Roberto de Redynge	j. marc'
D Laur' de Westram	x.s	D Henr' de maydestañ	
D Willō Fankon de clar'	x s	tailour	dj. marc'

10

D thoṁ de Elmested	x.s.
D Robtō de prestoñ	x.s
D Jordano Wolmay	x s
D Robtō Godwyne	
Skynner'	x.s
.... de	
Wingeham	j. marc'
.... de Nelme	x.s
.... Criel	xx.s
... Johe de Elham	xxx.s.
D Gervas' le bolter'	dj marc'
D thoṁ Overay	x.s
D Godefr' Pitekot	x.s
D Henr' de Densted	x.s
D Johē Jacob	
mareschail	dj.marc'
D Gilbto Deger'	xx.s
D Ricō bordon	j.marc'
D Robto de Estoñ	x s
D Johē de milsted	xj s vij d
D Johē Tegeler'	xx.s.
D Elya le Webbe	x s
D thoṁ bolherst spic'	dj mrc'
D Luc' Elbryth	dj mrc'
D Henr' de Breggenorth	viij s v d
D Robto Trenchemer	x s
D Johē Otebred	j mrc'
D Ricō de hothfelde	
Tailour	dj mrc'
D Ricō atte Fyspole fil'	
henr' Carpent'	dj mrc'
D Willo de Richard	
Casteil	dj mrc'
... Stephō de hardres	dj mrc'
... Jacobo de Stowtynge	
coco	dj mrc'
... Johē fil' Teobaldi de	
G'meshamme	dj mrc'
D Johē Dyshsher'	dj marc'
D Ricō atte Newcasteil	dj marc'
D Willo baldwyne	dj marc'
D Stepho Blondel coco	dj marc'
D Johe........	
oueyne	x. s

D Carsandra de	
herbaldonne	dj marc'
D henr de mon	dj mrc'
D Nichō de Aras	ij.mrc'
D Robtō Kempe souter'	
de chilham	dj mrc'
D Robtō de	
Wytecherche	
skynner	x.s.
D Marg'ia Garlekes	dj mrc'
D Willō de Tythell	dj mrc'
D Johe mahew pistor'	dj mrc'
D thoṁ de Fav'sham	
flaoner	dj mrc'
D Thoṁ Ryswar'	x..s.
D Barthō le Smyth	dj. mrc'
D Ricō Sheme	dj. mrc'
D Johē Sharp	
hakeneyman	dj mrc'
D marg'ria passour	dj mrc'
D Johe C'stemesse	dj mrc'
D Pet' le Koc	dj mrc'
D Rog'o person	dj mrc'
D Robto Tracy	dj mrc'
D Johē Fairheued	dj mrc'
D henr de bines	
aurifabro	dj mrc'
D Alex'o Gerdler	dj mrc'
D Johē de Ich'm coco	dj mrc'
D Robtō Terry	dj mrc'
D Thoṁ Tork'	dj marc'
D Johē doul	dj marc'
D Ricō heyward de	
Fanth'm	dj marc'
D Johē Skynner fil'	
Juliane la Smale de	
Wytcherch	dj mrc'
D henr' Longe de	
Westgate	x.s.
D Ricō atte Crouche	dj mrc'
D Nichō Brembel	dj marc'
D Willō Skolle	dj marc'
D Willo atte heghelond	
Bocheir	dj mrc'

D Johē Kepwyt		D Andr' Cros	x.
taverner	dj mrc'	D thomas de thetwode	dj
D Johē Rok	dj marc'	D Johe Willde de	
D Willō de Overlonde	dj mrc'	Witham	dj mrc'
D Nicho le Barber de		D Willō Dekne	dj mrc'
Gadesdenn'	dj mrc'	D matild de b(r)chwode	dj mrc'
D		D Henr' de Cokerynge	dj.mrc'
		D Willo fil' Andr'	
	[Column two]	t'nour de Wenchepe	dj mrc'
		D Johē de Orby cl'ico	dj mrc'
D henr de Ewelle	dj mrc'	D Johē baldoc servient	
		Willī de chilleh'm	dj mrc'

Me^d Johēs fleshewer' fec' finē p lib' h'nda p j. mrc'
D qua soluit et no' jur' $-------------------$ ⎤
Et sic no' ingredit^r lib $---------------$ ⎦ dj mrc'

m e^d de nominibus illorum qui admissi sunt et jur ad lib pdcam . . . . . fine facient p consideracon' pdci Simois bertelot . . . . . soc' suor' ad hoc elector' ppt' fidelit' . . . . . sua et be . . . . . fta p'us dce coitati fcta et (inposterū) . . . . . faciend . . . . .

Robtš Peltebem
Willš de Rekolure
Radš Seintdenys
Willš de Toniford
Johs meynard
Johs del ydle
Robtš de Derteford
Wills Besile
Wills hymself
Rads de sco Laur'
Stephš de Delhm
thomas de Estwelle
thomas de Toniford

Me^d de noib' illorum qui admissi st et jur' ad lib pdcam p concens coitatis videl'

Teobaldus de Goldynton
Ricūs de mortone

Willš frere Jur' est ad instanc' Simonis bertelot
Jacobus de Hersing ad instanc' thoм chicche

12

Johs fil Willi Gillemyn ad instanc' dci Willi
Nichs de Fordwych ad instanc' thom de Derham
Johs schot de Ledes ad instanc' Nichi de Dovere
Johs de bourne webbe ad instanc' Willi Frenshe
Johs fil Nichi bost de Gloucestr' ad instanc' Willi de Chilleham
Wills Sangon de maydestan ad instanc' Johs de Wenchep
Alic' de tours de Sonderesshe ad instanc' Elye de morton
Rads de Lenham clericus ad instanc' Anselmi P'trych
Johs Colhoppe ad instanc' Stephi Coupe'
Wills Schot mercer ad instanc' Johis de Standoñ

It' Johs Poukel Jur' et admissus est ad lib' p'dictam instanc' thom Poukel p
eo qd cōitas p'dcā tenebat^r dicto thom pro expensis suis versus versus (sic)
dominam Reginam apud Lond' exist cū coī Litera in .ix. s quos relaxauit

It' Stephs atte Feld carpentar' Jur est et admissus ad lib p'dcaṁ ad instanc'
Ricī de Froskepole qui causa p'dcā relaxauit dōō coiṫati .x. s. j. d. in quibus
eadṁ cōitas dōō Rico tenebat^r.

Verso.

E tercij primo A°

Johs de Watford quia conduxit fil liberi	xj d ob.
Johs De Dorsete quia conduxit fil liberi	xj d ob.
Wills Gordler quia conduxit fil liberi	xj d ob.
Johs de Osprenge quia conduxit fil liberi	xj d ob.
bernardus pouche quia conduxit fil liberi	xj d ob.
Thom Copedok quia fil' lib'i xj d ob.	
Wills Gerveys quia conduxit fil lib'i	xj d ob.
Robŝ Dobyn quia conduxit fil lib'i	xj d ob.
Johs chalker' quia conduxit fil lib'i	xj d ob.
Ad Taverner quia conduxit fil lib'i	xj d ob.
Ric Glesworte de bocton xj d.ob.	
Robs Stodewolde de Crondale xj d.ob.	
Wills de Haghe xj d.ob.	
Robts Kempe xj d ob.	
Johs de Russeby xj d.ob.	
Johs Sir de Scā Margaret' xj d. ob.	
Rads de Cranebrok xj d.ob.	
Robts fil. Pet atte Nelle tanner xj d ob.	
Robts Knokehog xj d.ob.	
Walts de Pondfolde xj d.ob.	
Wills Potter mercer quia conduxit dil libi xj d ob.	
Rads de Sco Laur xj d ob.	

13

Thom de Gravene   xj d ob.
Johs Smyth de Petham   xj d ob.
Johs Austyn   xj d ob.
Johs Page   xj d ob.
Johs de Herford   xj d ob.
Johs Skyph . . . . .   xj d ob.
Johs fil Robti Salmon quia fil lib'i   xj d ob.
thom Auener quia conduxit fil lib'i   xj d ob.
Johs Piteman   xj d. ob.
Johs Skynner de Hardres   xj d ob.
Sim Newman quia fil libi   xj d ob.
Wills Piner de Cherteham   xj d ob.
Wills Enge de Shrouesbery   xj d ob.
Johs Athelard Forbour   xj d ob.
Johs fil thom Pope   xj d ob.
. . . . . le Taverner   xj d ob.
Sim Fairfax   xj d ob.
Johs de trendherst   xj d ob.
Hugo Hadde   xj d ob.
Rog Ploumere   xj d ob.
Johs de Preston   xj d ob.
Simo atte Crouche   xj d ob.
Wills Baynor   xj d ob.
Johs Flaoner   xj d ob.
thom Ploumere   xj d ob.
Hamo Rokke   xj d ob.
Robts de Lyncolne   xj d ob.
Alex Lacy   xj d ob.
Christianus Gules   xj d ob.
Nichs atte Heye   xj d ob.
Alanus le Chaundelar   xj d ob.
Stephs de Danecastr iur' est
Maths le Everard iur' est

Appendix II
Statements of Account from verso *Roll 4*

§ Memorandum quod die sabat' in festo Sancti Vinsenci Anno R R E fil

Reg' E quinto Thom' Chicche recepit xv. s pro expensis parliamentj de argento levato intrancium in presencia Simon' bertelmu et Johannis de bissoppesgate tunc ball' Civitatis Cant'

§ Eodem die et in presencia predictorum eadem causa Johannes Pikeringe recepit . xv.s. Item pro eodem xxv. s

§ Item solutum Johannes de bissoppesgate ball' Civitatis Cant' pro exhennio misso vicecomiti Canc' in festo Natal' domini. xvij. s

§ Item Edmundo le spisier et Joh' de Pikeringge pro expensis parliamenti predict' . xl. s.

Item Robert' le tailour xij d ad emendacionem domus nostre

Item acomodata ij marc' ad solucionem viij li.

Appendix III
Names of Freemen

In the following list first names have been modernised in almost all cases. Other names are unchanged though where "Cantuar" is used simply descriptively of place it has been modernised to "Canterbury". Words used to describe occupations have been modernised where useful modern equivalents exist except where these descriptions were themselves surnames. Abbreviations are used to designate those freemen admitted by redemption (R), marriage (M), patrimony (P), and favour (F). The abbreviation M/P is used to indicate uncertainty as to which of these two kinds of admission was intended.

1297–98 (R/F 1)
William Bailly (R)
Thomas Baldewyne (P)
Walter de Bello, butcher (R)
William Braban (R)
William Cade (R)
Robert de Canterbury le Fisshere (R)

John de Chilleham (R)
John de Chilleham (M)
Simon Cocus de Cranebroke (R)
John de Covyntre (R)
John le Crek (R)
John Cudding (P)
John Digoun (R)
Matthew le Draper (R)

15

Richard Duraunt (R)
John atte Felde (R)
Nicholas le Feliper (R)
Thomas Ferhand (R)
Walter Ganter (R)
Richard de Grove (R)
John de Hakyntone (R)
John de Hamwolde (R)
Ralph Hayne, butcher (R)
John de Kirkeby (R)
John Luterich (R)
William de Mallinge (R)
John Martin (R)
Richard de Oxonia (R)
Adam Parmenter (P)
David le Parmentier de York (R)
Bartholomew Pistor (R)
Brian de Regweye (R)
Richard de Rollingge (R)
Thomas de Schalaria (R)
Robert Sire de Fermerye St
    Augustine (R)
Robert s. Richard de St Edmundo
    (R)
John de Throtyntone (M)
John de Trendherst (R)
Simon le Verrer (R)
John de Weddinge, smith (R)
William de Welles (R)
William de Welles (M)
Laurence de Wy, smith (M)

1302–03 (R / F 2)
Robert Albot (M)
Andrew Algod (R)
Gilbert Aurifaber (R)
Thomas Bene (R)
William Benste (R)
John de Berewyk (R)
John de Bissoppesdenne, cook (R)
Richard le Boghyere (M)
Adam Bolum (R)
Michael Bourgeys (P)
Edmund Boys (R)

Stephen ate Bregge (R)
William de Bregge (M)
Roger de Bregghe (P)
John Brenecour, tiler (R)
William le Bret de Cheleham (R)
John Bryan, tixtor (R)
Richard Calle (R)
Geoffrey Carpentar' (R)
William le Chalkere (R)
William Le Chalouner (R)
William Le Chaundeler (R)
John Cissore de Bourgate (R)
Walter clericus *dictus* Petytwate
    liber ex nacione (P)
William Cocus (R)
Simon Coddyng (P)
Henry Colebrand (R)
Walter Cope (R)
Robert Cornwayle (M)
Roger le Coteler (R)
Henry s. John Le Couper (P)
Hugo Cromphand (R)
John de Croydone (R)
Thomas atte Dane (R)
Stephen le Draper (R)
John de Eastry, taverner (R)
Thomas Edyld (R)
Ralph de Esole (R)
William le Ferrour (R)
Adam le Flanner (R)
Roger le Flanner (R)
William Gobayre, clerk (M)
Robert Godegrom (R)
William Golyf (R)
Simon de Grimeshamme (P)
John Haket (P)
Ralph de Hardres (R)
Walter de Hathewaldenne, baker
    (R)
Stephen de Herst (R)
John de Hertford, clerk (R)
Richard de Ikham (M)
John Keneman (M)
Thomas Kopel (P)

16

William de Kyngestone (M)
William de Lenne (R)
John Lons (M)
John Lord (P)
John le Mareschal de Hegslede (R)
Phillip Moncy (P)
William de Monyggheham (R)
John Mot (M)
John Newman (R)
John Noble (R)
John de Northbourne (R)
Roger de Northampton (R)
John de Offyntone (R)
Adam le Orfreyser de St Salvatore (R)
Nicholas Pagenam (R)
William Parker (R)
Bondino Pas (M)
William Peres, goldsmith *infra portam* (R)
Robert Pellipar' (M)
Thomas Petyt (P)
John Plonte (R)
Henry le Ploumer (R)
John le Ploumere (M)
John Pope (R)
Thomas Pope (R)
Henry Porter (M)
Randolf Prat (R)
Michael de Pysyngh (R)
William Rauf (M)
John de Romenal (R)
William de Romenal (R)
William Russel (R)
Gervase Schereve (M)
John Schereve (R)
Edmund de Schirynghe (R)
Robert Schort, baker (R)
Benedict le Skynner (R)
William Smyth de Sandwich (M)
Richard de Soles (R)
Stephen Sopere, polentar (R)
Thomas de St Salvatore, goldsmith (R)

Henry de Stellynghe, tanner (R)
Robert Storm, taverner (P)
John de Stureye (R)
Walter Styel (R)
Geoffrey Tannatore (R)
Benedict le Taylour (R)
Thomas le Taylour (P)
William s. Geoffrey Tixtor (P)
Robert le Tournour (R)
Stephen Tourte *dictus* Gerold (P)
Richard de Traynges (M)
Robert de Tylebreggh (R)
Edmund Tyxtor de vinar'(R)
Bartholomew le Verrer (R)
John Veysyn (M)
John le Vynch (M)
Thomas de la Waye (M)
Henry de Welles (R)
John de Welles (R)
William de Welles, sutor (R)
John Wolnoth de Romenal (R)
Giles le Wrenne (R)
John de Wroteham (R)

1311–12 (R/F 4)
Simon s. Michael Aurifaber (P)
John Bagard (R)
Robert Baldwyne, butcher (R)
John s. Ralph le Barbour (P)
Stephen Bek (R)
Andrew Bel, cook (R)
William s. John ate Belhouse (M)
Richard de Belle (M)
William de Bereham, tixtor (R)
John Berewyc, chandler (R)
Giles de Beri, goldsmith (R)
Walter Bette, butcher (P)
Robert Biaucol, cook (R)
Adam de Bilsintone, sutor (R)
Robert s. Robert de Bodesham (M)
Richard de Bois, skinner (R)
Roger Boltere (R)
Richard Bolvinch (R)
Richard Bovehecche (M)

Walter Brieuere (M)
John s. Robert ate Brodestrete de
 Wy (R)
John Bronche (R)
William Brul (R)
John Caleward (R)
William de Chaldane, clerk (R)
Reginald servant of Robert de
 Chelesfelde (R)
Robert Chercheward de St
 Augustine (M)
Ralph de Chichestre, skinner (R)
William Child, cordwainer (R)
Edmund Christemesse (P)
Roger de Clam, carpenter (R)
Robert Clerebaud de Bereham (R)
Peter Clerk de Suttone (R)
Ambrose Cocus (M)
John Cocus de Chricherchegate (M)
Roger de Colingeham, limeburner
 (R)
John Cook de Hardres, butcher (R)
Thomas Coting, taverner (R)
John s. Simon Cottevag (P)
William de Dalwode (R)
Simon Daubenay (P)
John de Dittone, goldsmith (M)
Bartholomew de Dunmaue, verier
 (R)
Simon Dunstan de St Paul (M)
Roger de Ebristone (R)
Adam Everard, baker (R)
Walter de Findone (M)
William de Findone (M)
Thomas Fotour, taverner (R)
John Furnier de Sepele (M)
William ate Geiole (P)
John Getis (M)
Gilbert Goring (R)
Nicholas Goring, miller (R)
John de Gravene (R)
Peter Grubbe (M)
Richard de Hadlege (M)
Robert ate Halle, poletier (P)

Hamo de Harnelle, cissor (M)
Richard Hauteyn (M)
Robert de la Haye, draper (R)
Hamo ate Hecche (R)
Bartholomew de Heghhardres,
 cordwainer (R)
Nicholas de Heithorne, smith (R)
John de Helmestede, sutor (R)
James Hering (P)
Bartholomew de Hertford (R)
Henry de Hewelle, tixtor (R)
Phillip de Heye (P)
Stephen de Ho (F)
John Hoppere (R)
Robert ate Horcharde, chandler (M)
Roger de Hortone (P)
John Hosebarne, mercer (R)
Hamo de Hunderkroft (M)
John Justine, baker (R)
Robert Kay, carpenter (R)
Ralph Kete de Natindon (R)
Alan de Kirketone (R)
Stephen Koupere (P)
Thomas Krest de Seldwych,
 cordwainer (R)
John Lamb de Canterbury, mercer
 (R)
John Lamb, jun., miller (M)
Richard Lamb de Kem'tone (M)
John de Leisetre (P)
Thomas de Lenne (M)
John de Lichfield (M)
Robert de Litlebourne, baker (R)
John de Litletege (M)
Robert Lodere (M)
John Maichere (R)
—— Mallingge (M)
Reginald Marscallo (R)
Stephen le Marchal (R)
Luke s. Simon Molendinator (R)
John Monek de Wenchiape (R)
William Mustard, butcher (R)
Thomas Nial, selier de Helam (R)
John s. Maurice de Northewode (R)

Richard Palmere, currier (R)
Thomas Persi (M)
John Peter (R)
John s. Richard de Petham, sissor
   (R)
Thomas Piscatore, baker (P)
Robert Ponchoun, butcher (R)
Peter s. John de Popeshale, chandler
   (R)
Robert Prente (M)
Walter de Prestone (R)
Robert Profete (R)
John s. Thomas ate Reye (P)
Robert ate Reye (?) (M)
Thomas ate Reye (R)
Thomas Ringemere (F)
Thomas de Riple, cordwainer (R)
Robert de Ripple (M)
William de Ripple, sutor (R)
Adam Roggier (P)
Lapin Rogger de Florensia (M)
Robert Salmoun de Hakintone (M)
John de Sayewelle, cook (R)
John de Sellinge, baker (R)
Robert de Sepaie (M)
Roger de Sevenoke (R)
John Sissor s. Thomas Sissor de
   Bisshoppesgate (R)
William Sopman de Limene (R)
John s. Phillip de Stablegate (P)
Roger de Stalesfelde (R)
John Stumbel (M)
—— Suethale (M)
John Sueyn, hackneyman (R)
Roger Thorstein (P)
—— Trendherst (M)
Hamo de Trendherst (M)
Simon Trieuman (R)
William Tropmel (?) (M)
John Turgis *dictus* Hetebriad (R)
Alan Verthing (M)
Robert Verthing (M)
John Vogel (R)
William ate Vorde, carpenter (M)

Hugo Vreinsebakere (P)
John Vreinsebakere (P)
Peter de Walinggeford, butcher (P)
John de Waltham, currier (R)
Roger ate Wexhouse, clerk (R)
John ate Weye (R)
Richard Wigge, baker (R)
Thomas de Witham, chaloner (R)
Adam Wrenne (P)
Roger de Wy (P)
John de Wynchelse, skinner (R)
William Wytikrist (R)
Reginald Wytloc (M)
John de . . . . . ie, tanner (M)
Thomas —— (P)
William ————— (P)

1327–28 (R/F 3)

Nicholas de Aras (R)
John Athelard, furbour (M/P)
Thomas Auener (M)
John Austyn (M/P)
John Baldoc, servant of William de
   Chilleham (R)
William Baldwyne (R)
Nicholas le Barber de Gadesdenn'
   (R)
William Baynor (M/P)
William Besile (F)
Henry de Bines, goldsmith (R)
Stephen Blondel, cook (R)
Thomas Bolherst, spicer (R)
Gervase le Bolter' (R)
Richard Bordon (R)
John s. Nicholas Bost de Gloucestr'
   (F)
John de Bourne, weaver (F)
Matilda de B(r)chwode (R)
Henry Breggenorth (R)
Nicholas Brembel (R)
John Chalker (M)
Alan le Chaundelar (M/P)
Henry de Cokerynge (R)
John Colhoppe (F)

Thomas Copedok (M)
Ralph de Cranebrok (M/P)
—— Criel (R)
John Cristemesse (R)
Andrew Cros (R)
Richard atte Crouche (R)
Simon atte Crouche (M/P)
Stephen de Danecastr (sworn)
Gilbert Deger' (R)
William Dekne (R)
Stephen of Delhm (F)
Henry de Densted (R)
Robert de Derteford (F)
Robert Dobyn (M)
John de Dorsete (M)
John Doul (R)
John Dyshsher' (R)
Luke Elbryth (R)
—— John de Elham (R)
Thomas de Elmested (R)
William Enge de Shrouesbery (M/P)
Robert de Eston (R)
Thomas de Estwelle (F)
Matthew le Everard (sworn)
Henry de Ewelle (R)
Simon Fairfax (M/P)
John Fairheued (R)
William Fankon de Clar' (R)
Thomas de Faversham, flaoner (R)
Stephen atte Feld, carpenter (F)
John Flaoner (M/P)
John Fleshewer (R— not admitted)
Nicholas de Fordwych (F)
William Frere (F)
Richard atte Fyspole s. Henry Carpenter (R)
Margery Garlekes (R)
Alexander Gerdler (R)
William Gerveys (M)
John s. William Gillemyn (F)
Richard Glesworte de Bocton (M/P)
—— John s. Teobald de Godmeshamme (R)

Robert Godwyne, skinner (R)
William Gordler (M)
Teobald de Goldynton (F)
Thomas de Gravene (M/P)
Christian Gules (M/P)
Hugo Hadde (M/P)
William de Haghe (M/P)
—— Stephen de Hardres (R)
William atte Heghelond, butcher (R)
Carsandra de Herbaldonne (R)
John de Herford (M/P)
James de Hersing (F)
Nicholas atte Heye (M/P)
Richard Heyward de Fantham (R)
Richard de Hothfelde, tailor (R)
William Hymself (F)
John de Icham, cook (R)
John Jacob, mareschail (R)
Robert Kempe (M/P)
Robert Kempe, souter' de Chilham (R)
John Kepwyt, taverner (R)
Robert Knokehog (M/P)
Peter le Koc (R)
Alexander Lacy (M/P)
Ralph de Lenham, clerk (F)
Henry Longe de Westgate (R)
Robert de Lyncolne (M/P)
John Mahew, baker (R)
Henry de Maydestan, tailor (R)
John Meynard (F)
John de Milsted (R)
Henry de Mon (R)
Richard de Mortone (F)
Robert s. Peter atte Nelle, tanner (M/P)
—— de Nelme (R)
Richard atte Newcasteil (R)
Simon Newman (P)
John de Orby, clerk (R)
John de Osprenge (M)
John Otebred (R)
Thomas Overay (R)
William de Overlonde (R)

20

John Page (M/P)
Margery Passour (R)
Robert Peltebem (F)
Roger Person (R)
William Piner de Cherteham (M/P)
Godfrey Pitekot (R)
John Piteman (M/P)
Roger Ploumere (M/P)
Thomas Ploumere (M/P)
Walter de Pondfolde (M/P)
John s. Thomas Pope (M/P)
William Potter, mercer (M)
Bernard Pouche (M)
John Poukel (F)
John de Preston (M/P)
Robert de Preston (R)
Robert de Redynge (R)
William de Rekolure (F)
William de Richard Casteil (R)
John Rok (R)
Hamo Rokke (M/P)
John de Russeby (M/P)
Thomas Ryswar (R)
John s. Robert Salmon (P)
William Sangon de Maydestan (F)
John Schot de Ledes (F)
William Schot, mercer (F)
Ralph Seintdenys (F)
John Sharp, hackneyman (R)
Richard Sheme (R)
John Sir de St Margaret' (M/P)
William Skolle (R)
John Skynner de Hardres (M/P)
John Skynner s. Juliana le Smale de
   Wytcherch (R)
John Skyph —— (M/P)
Thomas Slegh (R)
Bartholomew le Smyth (R)
John Smyth de Petham (M/P)
John Sprot (R)
Ralph de St Laur' (F)
Ralph de St Laur' (M/P)
Robert Stodewolde de Crondale
   (M/P)

—— James de Stowtynge, cook (R)
—— le Taverner (M/P)
Adam Taverner (M)
John Tegeler (R)
Henry de Tenham (R)
Robert Terry (R)
Thomas de Thetwode (R)
Richard de Thork lespicer (R)
Thomas de Toniford (F)
William de Toniford (F)
Thomas Tork (R)
Alice de Tours de Sonderesshe (F)
Robert Tracy (R)
Robert Trenchemer (R)
John de Trendherst (M/P)
William s. Andrew Turnour de
   Wenchepe (R)
William de Tythell (R)
John de Watford (M)
Elya le Webbe (R)
Laurence de Westram (R)
John Willde de Witham (R)
—— de Wingeham (R)
Jordan Wolmay (R)
Robert de Wytecherche, skinner (R)
John del Ydle (F)
John —— oueyne (R)

1344–45 (R/F 5 i)
Eustace Baldewene, fuller (F)
Richard s. Richard de Bregge (P)
John Broule (?), sutor (F)
Henry Bruere (F)
John de Cheleham, barber (M)
Robert de Chyltone (M)
John Cok, carpenter (M)
Robert de Coule, butcher (M)
Nicholas le Deghere de Faversham
   (M)
John Dobblerose, weaver (M)
John Duraunte, tailor (M)
John Esly, cook (M)
Richard de Flokkere (M)

21

Andrew Galy s. William Galy de
 Cherteham (F)
William de Haghe, clerk (F)
William de Halkham (F)
Thomas Holstrete (F)
Robert de Hornynggysscherche (M)
William s. William Isak de
 Patrickysbourne (M)
Robert de Kemstone, rector of
 Orlanstone (R)
Thomas Kenyntone, weaver (M)
John Keppe (F)
John de London, shearman, s.
 William Skot de Claverynge
William Melywer, weaver (M)
John Osebarn de Newecherche,
 cook (M)
John Resoun de Broggrove (F)
Thomas Stanford (F)
Gilbert Turnour (F)
Gregory ate Walle (F)

1345–46 (R/F 5 ii)
John Archer, fuller (R)
John Bakere de Westram, corveser
 (R)
William Brabaunt de Wynchepe
 (M)
William Bretoun, corveser (R)
John Brun, saddler (R)
William Champeneys, cooper (R)
Henry Cok, chapman (R)
John Compis, clerk (R)
Robert de Derby, skinner (R)
Henry de Dysburgh (?)(M)
Henry atte Forstalle, miller (M)
John Frapeloun, corveser (R)
John ate Fysspole, cutler (R)
William Gerard (M)
Richard de Herst, fuller (R)
Robert Heved, corveser (R)
John Hwitheved, shearman (R)
Henry Knotte (M)
Thomas Knotte, brewer (R)

William Loffe, corveser (R)
Nicholas de Lyenham, corveser (M)
William ate Med, baker (R)
Henry Moner de Amyas (R)
John Monere (M)
John ate Nesshe, tailor (R)
Robert Nolly, brewer (R)
Thomas Osebarn, weaver (M)
William Oter, tailor (R)
Clement de Oxeneford (R)
John Peche de Cranebroke (R)
William Peleholte, corveser (R)
William Perot, cutler (M)
Laurence Pessoner de la Bateylle
 (M)
Henry Petere (?)(M)
Thomas de Petwode, corveser (M)
Thomas Porteioye de London, clerk
 (M)
Nicholas Poukel de Canterbury (R)
John de Prestone, taverner (R)
John Rande, corveser (R)
John Saghiere (M)
Thomas de Sholdone, polunter (M)
John Short, weaver (R)
Robert Simoun, weaver (M)
Thomas s. Thomas Sprynget de
 Hwytstaple (M)
Hugo de Stanes (M)
Walter de Stoktone (M)
John de Stonpette, barber (M)
Thomas Straumonger (R)
Thomas Taverner s. Nicholas de
 Heure (?)(R)
Richard de Telbregge, chaloner (R)
Henry ate Thorne (M)
Thomas Thorp s. John Roter (R)
John Vrese, cooper (R)
Robert de Westbeche, shearman (R)

1349–50 (R/F 6)
Walter Bard (R)
John Boteler de Wy (R)
Robert atte Brome (M)

22

Thomas s. John Broun (R)
William Burgeys (R)
William de Burghassche (M)
Henry Burnet (M)
Thomas Cap'king (M)
John Carpenter, pollytter (M)
William Carpenter de Lymene (R)
John Cauntelbury (M)
John s. William de Charryng (F)
William de Charryng, mareschal (R)
Roger Chaundeler (M)
John Chichestre (M)
Thomas Chyvalier, jun., tailor (R)
John Clerk de Waltham (F)
Andrew Cocus (M)
John Duk de Sellyng (R)
Giles Dyghere de Gynes (R)
Thomas Eldrych (R)
John Esscheby (M)
Thomas de Frythendenne (M)
William Gerveys de Westgate (M)
John Gyg de Chartham (R)
Robert Gygour (M)
Alex atte Helle (R)
Walter Herlewyne (M)
Elias Joce (M)
Edmund Jolyf (F)
Thomas Knave (R)
John Kyng (M)
John Langnase de Insula de Thanete (R)
Henry de Lincoln (F)
Simon Louetynge, mareschal (R)
Hugo Lymberner (M)
William de Monyngham (R)
Sylvester de Morsston (R)
Richard atte Napelton (M)
William de Nauntewych (M)
George atte Nexe, barber (R)
William de Noramton, saddler (R)
Geoffrey de Notyngham (M)
John Pack(?) de Canterbury (M)
Henry Palmer, spicer (R)
John Ploket (M)

John Pluck (R)
Henry de Preston (M)
Thomas Queynte (F)
Lucas Randolf (R)
Thomas Rook (R)
John de Rysschebourne (R)
Nicholas Samuel (M)
William de Scheldewych, baker (R)
Hamo Schepeye (M)
Richard Scherte (M)
John de Sellyng (M)
Adam Skynnere *dictus* Sprot (R)
John Smyth de Elmestede (R)
William Springet (M)
William de Stourton de Kyngeston (F)
John s. Laurence Strode de Hyerne (F)
Nicholas atte Styghele (R)
Thomas Underwalle (M)
John William de Brabourne (M)
John atte Water (M)
Simon de Wy (F)
Thomas de Wytefelde (R) (crossed out)
William Yssmonger (R)

1350–51 (R/F 7)
Thomas Beamond (R)
John Beregrove (M)
Walter de Berto(), mercennar (R)
John Birch (R)
John Blakebroke (R)
Gwidone Bocher (R)
John Boydene (F)
John Bretoun (M)
Adam Calfard, skinner (R)
Kardo de Celand (R)
Godfrey Chapman (F)
Chaundeler de Cranebroke (R)
John Clerc de Eghethorn (F)
John Cokyn, skinner (R)
Richard Colhod (M)
William Colred (F)

23

Robert Condy de Bekesbourne (R)
John Cook, butcher (R)
Robert Cook (M)
John Crul, fisher (R)
Peter de Essex (R)
Geoffrey de Esshendenne (R)
John Felbergh, jun., de Chileham
  (F)
James Ferour (F)
William Filote, butcher (R)
John atte Forde (M)
John Frensshe de Bromfeld (F)
Roger Gelderode (R)
Richard Grauntcourt (R)
Robert Haldenne de Pensherst (R)
Henry Hamon, cordwainer (R)
Henry s. Thomas Harpour (F)
Thomas Harpour (F)
Thomas Hwytefeld (M)
Richard Isaak (M)
Roger de Kent, baker (R)
Hen Knyght de Cranebroke (R)
John Lalham (M)
John Laurens (R)
Robert Lucas (M)
John Malteby, skinner (R)
John Martyn, brewer (R)
John Martyn (M)
John de Meldone (R)
John atte Nelme, clerk (F)
John de Nodelyng de Norfolk (F)
Thomas Oxenforde (R)
Robert Pipere (R)
John Piriton, cutler (R)
Thomas Polton (R)
William Porchas (R)
William Prat (M)
Phillip Reyner (R)
William de Sherreveslonde (R)
Warin Smyth de Petham (F)
John St'm( ) (R)
Mariota de Sutton (R)
Stephen Taillour (R)
Richard Tynberdenn de Shorham
  (F)

John Watervyle (?) (R)
Jordan Wegheler de Godmersham
  (R)
John Wynnepeny (R)
Thomas Wynner (R)

1354–55 (R/F 8)
William Bocher, baker (R)
Ralph Bolour, fuller (R)
John Breche (M)
Thomas Bryghtwelle (M)
Hamo Coogh (R)
Simon Drew (M)
Roger Eastmer, smith (R)
William Hood (M)
William Hweyte (R)
Ralph Lucas (F)
John de Ottynge (M)
Thomas Petrisfelde (R)
Robert Poltone (R)
William Schoppe (F)
Alexander Scolastre (R)
John Stokeier (M)
John de Wellis (R)
William ate Val (M)

1355–56 (R/F 9)
William Borstalle (M)
John Bregham (R)
William Chapman, marchal (R)
Roger Cornewayle, corveser (R)
Stephen Coumbe (M)
Henry Hendiman (M)
Reginald Leverer, shearman (R)
John Medman (M)
Walter Northfolk, currier (R)
John Rochel (R)
William Toteber(i), taverner (R)
William ate Wode, currier (R)

1356–57 (R/F 10 i)
Edward Bocher (R)
Thomas Bolle, cooper (R)
Bernard Dallynge (R)

24

Robert Gloucestrie (R)
John Godefray (F)
John Guodwyne (R)
John Hicson de Hethe (M)
William Horselake (R)
James s. John Monk (F)
John de Nautone(?) (M)
John Payntur (R)
J. Plokele, clerk (M)
Thomas Prynce (R)
John Talbot de Schepeye (F)
Richard Tylye (R)
John de Wrotham (M)
Robert s. John de Wy (F)

1357–58 (R/F 10 ii)
John Bertelot, fuller (R)
John ate Bertone de Bereham (F)
J. de Bonyngtone (M)
W. s. J. de Bregge de Canterbury
   (M)
John Capele, cook (R)
T. s. T. Clement, jr (M)
William Cole (?) de Stureye (R)
Margaret de Ely (R)
John Freman (R)
William de Hardris, shearman (R)
Robert ate Hecche (R)
Thomas Hemery (R)
John Herward de Stourmowthe (R)
W. Marchaunt (M)
J. Nōhard, carpenter (M)
Adam Noreys, spicer (R)
John Nortone, carpenter (R)
John Philpot, fuller (R)
William Pod (R)
John Pycard de Syberdiswelde (M)
John Rotynge (R)
Thomas Spyle, hatter (R)
James ate Steghle (R)
J. Stud, weaver (M)
Stephen Toddil (F)
Alan Turnour de Ledys (R)
Richard de Tyb'eherst (F)

B. Weldyssche (M)
John Ydeleghe (R)

1360–61 (R/F 11 i)
Robert Bat, turner (R)
Geoffrey Bochier (P)
John C——(M)
Thomas C——(M)
Richard Cook de Hegham (R)
Dounyng de Wyngham (R)
Simon Egerdenne (R)
Walter Haye, *Magister Scolarum
   Cant'* (F)
Simon Maydewell (R)
Newelond, linenweaver (R)
Andrew Offwelle (R)
Nicholas Opmantone (R)
Robert Plot *de parochia de
   Dodynton* (R)
Pollard (R)
Ralph S——(M)
William Salysbery (R)
Andrew Sletaunt, fuller (R)
John ate Sole, currier (R)
Henry Stodewolde (R)
Toneford (R)
John Wardeboys (R)
William Warnyer, skinner (R)
John Werynton, cutler (R)
John de——(M)
Richard——(M)
William——(M)

1361–62 (R/F 11 ii)
Thomas Bakere (R)
Stephen Barbour *de parochia St
   Peter* (R)
Walter Barry, shyvyer (R)
Margaret ate Bregge (R)
John Brystowe (R)
Bartholomew Bussham (R)
Ralph Cappe, fisher (R)
Thomas Coupere de Faversham (R)
Agnes Crabbes (R)

25

Geoffrey Waddene (M)
Richard de Derham (M)
Gilbert Emery (M)
John Farnham (R)
Clement Grenewych, goldsmith (R)
Thomas Hardres, tailor (R)
Geoffrey Hopton Asshtone (R)
Elias Horner (R)
Gwydo de Hwetelee (R)
William Kenynton (M)
Thomas L——— (R)
John Lawe (R)
John Laycestr, bladesmith (R)
Robert ate Melle, plumber (R)
Thomas Michel de Staple (R)
William Mounde, tailor (M)
John Osbarn, weaver (R)
John Page, tailor (R)
Robert Page, fuller (R)
John Payn, fuller (M)
John Paynot, carpenter (R)
Henry Philpot *de parochia St Peter
in Thanet* (R)
Richard Playtere (R)
John Porter, barber (M)
Clement Poteman, fuller (R)
William Preston, taverner (R)
Thomas Roper de Westgate (R)
Richard Rycher (R)
Peter Serles, painter (R)
John Stureye (R)
Robert Wase (R)

John atte Welle de Lose (M)
Alexander Wynter (R)

1362–63 (R/F 11 iii)
Matthew Boghyer (M)
Henry Brygge (?), tanner (R)
Thomas Chaundeler, mason (R)
William Cornewayle (R)
John Cotyng, sutor (R)
John de Dene (R)
Nicholas Doget (R)
John Elys, cook (R)
Henry Garnet (R)
John Gyboun de Haveryng, mercer
(M)
Thomas Goldsmyth (R)
John Hammok, tailor (R)
John Hegham, corveser (R)
John Lad (F)
Richard de Leghe (M)
George Molesshe, goldsmith (R)
Thomas (Mounte) (F)
Henry Newerk (R)
Alexander Porsere (?) (F)
Salmon ate Regge (R)
Richard Ryed (M)
John Selbourne, barber (R)
John de Sholdon (F)
Walter Souththorp, clerk (R)
Ralph Sparewe, tailor (R)
Thomas s. Hugo Stanes (F)
Henry Thornton (R)

A RENTAL OF THE MANOR OF EAST MALLING, A.D. 1410

EDITED BY C. L. SINCLAIR WILLIAMS

ABBREVIATIONS

Arch. Cant.	*Archaeologia Cantiana.*
Brit.	British.
Ekwall.	Eilert Ekwall, *The Concise English Dictionary of English Place-Names*, Oxford, 1936–66.
E.P.N.S.	English Place-Name Society (ed. A. H. Smith), *English Place-Name Elements*, Cambridge, 1956–70.
K.A.O.	Kent Archives Office.
M.E.	Middle English.
O.E.	Old English.
O.Fr.	Old French.
P.C.C.	Prerogative Court of Canterbury.
P.R.O.	Public Record Office.

The earliest known reference to East Malling occurs in the charter of a grant of land at West Malling by King Edmund to the Bishop of Rochester (A.D. 942–946). In defining the bounds the charter mentions *east mealinga gemaera* ("the boundary of East Malling").[1] After this fleeting reference there is silence until 1086 and the Domesday survey.

The Domesday Book entry is telegraphically brief, yet sufficiently informative to illustrate the development of the manor over the three and a quarter centuries to the time of the Rental translated below.[2] It is therefore worth quoting in full. Under the lands of the Archbishop of Canterbury, in the Lathe of Aylesford and the Hundred of Larkfield, is recorded:

"The Archbishop himself holds in demesne Metlinges[3] [East Malling]. It defends itself for 2 sulungs. The land is for 7 ploughs. In demesne are 3 ploughs. And 38 villeins with 12 bordars have 5 ploughs. There is a church. And 5 serfs. And 2 mills at 10 shillings. And 21 acres of meadow. Woodland for 60 swine. In total value, in the time of King Edward it was worth 9 pounds. The same when received. And now as much. And yet it renders 15 pounds."[4]

Here and there throughout the Rental will be found reminiscences of this laconic return.

At what date the manor came into the possession of the Archbishop of Canterbury is now unknown. After the turmoil of the Danish invasions, and a decade in the hands of Odo of Bayeux, the neighbouring manor of West Malling was restored to the Bishop of Rochester in 1076. Gundulph, who was bishop from 1077 to 1108, founded the Benedictine abbey and

27

convent there in the reign of William Rufus.[5] Saint Anselm, Archbishop of Canterbury from 1093 to 1109, granted the manor of East Malling to the Abbess and nuns of West Malling[6] with whom it remained until their dispossession under the Dissolution of Religious Houses in 1538.

The Rental of 1410 is, in effect, a detailed survey of the manor. It throws light on land tenure and the manorial system in late medieval Kent. It provides evidence for further research into the controversial subject of the open fields in Kent. It contributes to knowledge of place-names, family names, genealogy, population and social and economic history. What was conceived simply as a matter of book-keeping, today recreates a rural society in the heart of Kent in the period between the death of Chaucer and the Battle of Agincourt.

The membranes of the document are sewn to form a long continuous roll, and the manuscript continues over to the reverse side. It is written in a neat, cursive Court hand, in heavily abbreviated Latin. It is reasonably legible, except at the end of the roll (a little over half-way through the text, at the end of the obverse and the beginning of the reverse side) where the ink has faded and the parchment is badly rubbed and damaged.

Except for one entry (No. 56) the manuscript appears to be in a single hand. Although the script is, for the most part, well formed, the usual difficulties were encountered in deciphering abbreviations of unfamiliar terms. While *t* and *c* were usually distinguishable, and vigilance was most of the time sufficient to avoid confusion between (in this text) the much more similar *o* and *c*, reading the letters *i*, *n*, *u* and, except initially, *m*, was often dependent upon context or a count of the minims—and, of course, in cases of difficulty, context often gave no help. Just after the beginning of entry No. 77 the script changes, but it is thought to be by the same scribe, writing hurriedly. Not only is there a decline in neatness, but abbreviation is intensified, and the recurrent *idem*, for example, becomes *idm*. The script returns to normal with entry No. 79.

The runic *yogh* appears to have been used only where today we would use *gh*, although there are instances where this phoneme is spelt with the modern two letters.

Modern notions of consistency are not, of course, to be looked for. Variations in the spelling of proper names are so frequent that it was decided to leave most of them without editorial comment; the pages would otherwise have been peppered with the assurance "*sic*".

There is some evidence to suggest that the scribe was not very familiar with the terrain, and that the document was compiled from notes or returns prepared by another, or others, whom the scribe could not readily consult. Errors in place-names are evidently misreadings of carelessly written or hastily read Court hand. For example, *Allemanyskode* (entry No. 47) must be a mistake for *Allemanyswode* (entry No. 11), the second element of cursive Court hand *w* having been read as *k* (which it resembles) and the first element having been overlooked. Again, *Scoheed* (entry No. 46) is certainly an error for *Scolreed* (the same entry and No. 47), the letters *l* and long *r* having been misread as one letter, making what was mistaken for *h*.

The occasional blank spaces can also be explained by difficulties with handwriting rather than absence of information. For example, in entry No. 55 the space is followed by the word *akyr*, and in entry No. 78 the space precedes *felde*. That the word following the space is really the second element of a place-name, suggests that the first element was present but illegible.

Each entry begins with the tenant's name. Christian names are latinised, but surnames are left in English. Place-names, with only one exception, are in English and their Middle English form has been retained in the translation. The exception is New Hythe which is latinised as *Nova Ripa* in the Agreement (see below) and in entry No. 138; but in entry No. 23 it appears as *Newhythe*. The hamlet of New Hythe, which lies in the north of the parish, on the banks of the Medway, is expressly excluded from the Rental, although fields in its vicinity occur in the holdings.

The special interest of the Agreement between the Abbess and her tenants, which precedes the detailed rental, is in the method of assessing annual rents, per acre, according to a grading of the land by quality: best— *optimum solum*, medium—*medium solum*, or "worst" (rendered here as "poor")—*pessimum solum*. It will be seen that the rent for each grade of land was due on a different quarter day, thus: best land, in two instalments each of $1\frac{1}{2}d$. due at Christmas and on Lady Day; medium land at $2d$. on Midsummer Day; and poor land at $1d$. at Michaelmas.

Maitland remarked that "the annual value of an acre in one shot would sometimes be eight times greater than that of an acre in another shot."[7] In East Malling, over three centuries after the period of which Maitland was writing, it will be seen that "best" land was valued at only three times the poorest land. Value also, it seems, was not assessed only by the fertility of the soil; account appears to have been taken of its state of cultivation. A statistical analysis has not been made, but it is apparent that arable, although it is represented in all three grades, tends to be "best" land; meadow is also usually "best" land, but woodland is almost invariably "poor" land. Holdings in the old, open fields are consistently "best" land. Whatever may have been deduced from the records of manors elsewhere, there is certainly no evidence of soil exhaustion in East Malling in the late Middle Ages. On the contrary, the land appears to have been in good heart at the beginning of the fifteenth century, and it speaks well of medieval husbandry here that land which had been under cultivation since the earliest times appears to have remained the most fertile.

A "relief" of one quarter of the annual rent became payable when land changed hands. This "relief" continued at the same rate into the seventeenth century when court rolls show that it was not merely a heriot, or form of "death duty", payable by the heir or heirs of a deceased tenant; it was also due when land changed hands by sale. The new land-holder was then required to "make his fealty" at the next ensuing court, which appears really to have been the acknowledgment of tenancy and its obligations in respect of a specific acquisition of land. Thus, tenants who already held land elsewhere in the manor were still required to observe the formality of homage for newly acquired land.

Much of the demesne land was let out "at farm". Unfortunately, it is not possible to tell whether, in fact, any land in East Malling continued to be directly cultivated by, or for, the demesne. While the rents for farmed-out land were considerably higher than the nominal rents for land held under manorial customary tenure, with due allowance for the money values of the time they were still very moderate. Farm rents took two forms; most were in money, some were in barley. In one instance "palm barley" is stipulated. Latham notes against *hordeum palmatum*—"mainly Kent."[8]

In discussing the distribution of peasants' strips in thirteenth-century manors, Dr. Titow has observed: "It is also a moot point to what extent demesne lands were interspersed with peasant land in the common fields or whether they tended to lie apart altogether. Evidence on this point is usually lacking, though documented instances of either arrangement can be found."[9] In East Malling, in 1410, farmed-out demesne lands appear to have been widely distributed throughout the manor. Although by this time what remained of the earlier manorial system is obscured by the advanced state of the dividing up of the old open fields, and by the large number of small fields presumably assarted during the previous century or two, the pattern at the time of the Rental suggests that demesne land had always been intermingled with villein holdings.

The oddly-named communal rendering of hens provided for in the Agreement continued until at least the second half of the seventeenth century. The survey of the manor under the Act of 1653 for "Abolishing Archbishopps and Bishopps within England and Wailes" has the entry:

"Rent Hennes due to the Lord of the said mannor of East Malling called Smoke hennes payable at Christmas yeerly. Esteemed to be worth per Annum 15s. 0d."[10]

Again, when Charles II granted the manor to Sir John Rayney in 1662, the deed included the passage: "*Ac omnes ill. Gallinas customar. vocat Smoke hennes.*" (and all those customary hens called Smoke hens).[11]

The units of land measurement were the acre, the rood or quarter of an acre, and the daywork at 40 to the acre. Here it is tempting to develop a discussion of field shapes, but it must be sufficient to say that from seventeenth-century estate maps, and from occasional references in the Rental, it is evident that in at least what remained of the open fields the holdings were usually in furlong strips. Obviously, holdings of only several dayworks could not be in furlong strips, and it can only be surmised that some were small plots of land apart from the original open fields, and that perhaps others were short remnants of former furlong strips.

There is a remarkable disparity between the sizes of the holdings, but it would be unsafe to interpret this as an indication of the relative prosperity—or poverty—of individual tenants. Various records reveal that there were some forty discrete means of livelihood, other than husbandry, pursued in East Malling in the seventeenth century. Most were crafts, and some, such as blacksmith, carpenter, miller, were the occupations of more than one head of family in what was still largely a self-supporting community. Most of the craftsmen owned a few acres of land, presumably to supply their domestic needs. Wills, manorial court rolls and other records, and the testimony of houses of the period still standing and identified to tenants of those times, make it clear that craftsmen had the social status and standard of living, if not of the wealthiest, then at least of the general run of yeomen whose prosperity in Kent had become proverbial. While the projection of seventeenth-century evidence back to the later Middle Ages must be treated with caution, it is a reasonable inference that in 1410 a number of tenants would have been craftsmen, and that these craftsmen are likely to have been among the smaller land-holders.

Holdings are occasionally described as in the "1st furlong" or the "2nd furlong". In most instances the holdings so described are in *Estfelde*. These are clearly references to "shots", which Maitland explained as follows: "A natural limit to the length of the furrow is set by the endurance of oxen. From this it follows that even if the surface that lies open is perfectly level and practically limitless, it would none the less be broken up into what our Latin documents call *culturae*. The *cultura* is a set of contiguous and parallel acre-strips; it tends to be a rude parallelogram; two of its sides will be each a furlong ('furrowlong') in length, while the length of the other sides will vary from case to case. We commonly find that every great field (*campus*) is divided into divers *culturae*, each of which has its own name. The commonest English equivalent for the word *cultura* seems to have been *furlong*, and this use of *furlong* was very natural; but as we require that term for another purpose, we will call the *cultura* a *shot*."[12] An immaculate example appears in an estate map of Ringwould, Kent, dated 1709. Here an open field is marked "Furlongs" and is divided into sets of parallel strips, each set lying end-on to the strips of the neighbouring set. The sets of strips, or *culturae*, are named from (roughly) north to south: "Teen-End-Shott", "Cholk-Pitt-Shot", "Second Shott" and "Drove-Shott". To the west of this field, from which it is divided by a narrow strip of land marked "The Linch", lie "Rogers Close Shott", "Shott heading to Rogers Close", "Meeds Close Shott" and "Glebe Shott".[13]

It is significant that while the term "Common" does not occur in any field-names in 1410, several fields became so named within the next two centuries. *Wetefelde* became the "Common Fielde" with "Common Field

Lane" (now Stickens Lane) forming its eastern boundary. Maps from a survey made over the period 1681–84[14] show part of what must have once been *Estfelde* as "Common Field", and part of "Hammille Meadowe" (*Hammellemede* of the Rental) as "the 5 Divisions of Common Mead", and "Part of the Common Mead" in the same locality. An estate survey made in 1699[15] of an area not included in the 1681–84 survey, gives what is clearly another part of the former *Estfelde* as "Footway Cant in Com'on Field", "Middle Cant in Com'on Field", and "Upper Cant in Com'on Field". (For the benefit of extra-Kentish readers, a "cant" is a piece of land divided off from a larger whole, a meaning slightly, but significantly, different from the more general meaning quoted by E.P.N.S. It was known to Pegge,[16] and it is used in the Kentish sense today by East Malling woodmen for a part of a wood marked off for felling. Kentish "cant" appears to derive from O.Fr. *cantel*—"portion", as used by Chaucer, rather than from Brit. *canto-*, *canti-*, Welsh *cant*, postulated for place-names elsewhere.)

The concentration of meadow land in the northern, riverside district of the manor is, of course, consistent with the ancient practice of exploiting well-watered, riverside land for the cropping of hay. Numerous field-names in "mead" and "meadow" show that the sites of *Hammellemede*, Elyndene and *Cobbemede* were still predominantly meadow land at the time of the Tithe Awards of 1839–42.

It is noteworthy that the Rental contains only one certain reference to pasture, and this was "at *Le Hoo* on land of the Lady" for which John Taylour paid "3 shillings at the four principal terms". In this isolated instance it is not clear whether the reference is to pasture land or to rights of pasture. A glance at the map (Appendix I) will show that, even with the relatively small number of named fields which have been plotted, it is evident that arable, meadow-land and woodland account for virtually the entire extent of the manor except for East Malling Heath and Larkfield Heath. Even if their area was sufficient, the heaths are unlikely to have provided suitable grazing for herds and flocks of a size which could have sustained the community. Despite what has been written about the agrarian system in medieval Kent, the inference must be that, in East Malling at least, the cattle grazed the fallow land.[17]

Maitland identified the *fertinus* or farthing as a quarter of a virgate in Somersetshire, while Round recognised the "Ferndel or Ferdingel" as the fourth part of the virgate in Devon and Cornwall. R. Welldon Finn mentions the "ferding or ferling or ferting" in these three south-western counties "and occasionally elsewhere".[18] H. L. Gray, however, found the ferthing as a quarter of the Kentish yoke, or *iugum*, in a survey of Gillingham in 26 Henry VI. The East Malling field-name *Le Ferthyng* must therefore mean a quarter of a yoke. Entry No. 80 below shows that Nicholas Stevens held six parcels of land in *Le Ferthyng*, totalling 8¾ acres. No other tenant of land in *Le Ferthyng* is mentioned, so that Nicholas

Stevens' $8\frac{1}{4}$ acres accounted for the entire field. When this acreage is multiplied by four the result of 35 acres is remarkably close to what Maitland maintained to have been the fiscal, and originally actual, virgate of 30 acres. Maitland also observed: "We may suspect that the Exchequer was reckoning 120 (fiscal) acres to the sulung but can not say that this is proved."[19] Too much should not be argued from an isolated instance, but whatever variations of area of the yoke may have been noted in late-medieval Kent, the acreage of the field named *Le Ferthyng* in East Malling is at least consistent with the belief that, in early times, the Kentish sulung, like the hide, was physically in the region of 120 acres, and that the area of the yoke, or *iugum*, like the virgate, was around 30 acres.

This is not the place for a detailed discussion of place-names, but it is perhaps worth remarking that, while a number of the names occurring in the Rental survived, though often modified or distorted, to the time of the Tithe Awards, some even to today, the greater number have disappeared. The form of many of these place-names is a reminder that the time of the Rental was closer to Old-English Kent than to our own day. There is the usual common occurrence of eponymous tenants, a number of whom can be recognised among the Rental land-holders. Among those family names which no longer figure in the manor in 1410, a number can be found under Larkfield Hundred, and neighbouring hundreds, in the Kent Lay Subsidy of 1334–35.[20] The map at Appendix I gives only the more readily identifiable fields. Further study of abutments, and the often descriptive nature of the names, might enable a more detailed, topographical, map of the medieval manor to be drawn.

It is a little surprising that there is no mention of Well Street, an ancient hamlet rather less than a mile south-west of the village centre. Several of the tenants can be identified as having holdings or their messuages there (entries Nos. 43 to 46). Well Street is mentioned in the will, dated 1490, of a successor to the house of John Derby (entry No. 45), by then called "Derbies" and described as "sett in Well Street".[21] The Rental has, however, two references to *Goderysstrete*, or *Goderistrete*, one of which is in entry No. 45. This suggests the very tentative explanation that until some time between 1410 and 1490 Well Street may have been known as *Goderysstrete* (Goder's Street). It also postulates an early association with someone bearing the good Saxon name *Godhere*.[22] (Wallenberg's thirteenth-century attributions to Well Street are considered to be confusions with Ewell,[23] once a precinct of the manor of West Malling, lying to the west in the direction of Offham).

The Chapel of *Saint Thomas Martyr* by the gate of the Abbey, mentioned in entry No. 67, survived the spoliation following the Dissolution, and it was spared the rough treatment of the Abbey main buildings by various owners during subsequent centuries. It still adjoins the medieval gatehouse, which was also spared. It has been cleared of nineteenth-century accretions and in recent years has been sensitively restored. No other record of the early dedication of the chapel to St. Thomas à Becket is known, and, until it was revealed by this entry in the Rental, was not otherwise remembered. Yet a guest-room over the western end of the chapel had been felicitously named "Thomas à Becket", partly to commemorate charter associations, and partly because there is a legend that the fleeing assassins of the saint came to the Abbey for food, which the nuns supplied, but it was removed by angel hands.[24]

The method underlying the order in which the Rental was compiled remains obscure. Although individual holdings tend to be distributed over a wide area, there is occasional evidence of a sequence of neighbouring tenants; but the order does not seem to follow an itinerary. The method certainly appears to be geographical, and sequences which emerge from the index of place-names (Appendix III) strongly suggest that the order is based on the locations of the fields rather than the tenants.

The spellings of place-names in the original text have been retained in the translation, that is, apart from extensions of abbreviations. In a number of cases the extensions have been confirmed in documents of a later date (in a few cases they are also known from an earlier period.) These other occurrences of place-names, with their dates, are given in Appendix III.

Every endeavour has been made to keep the translation as close as possible to the original. The only conscious liberty taken with the text has been the omission of the repetitive *idem* ("the same"), except where its retention is essential to the sense. Where the translation, or transcription of the Latin, is in doubt, the English rendering, and, when appropriate the doubtful transcription, is enclosed in round brackets. Square brackets have been reserved for editorial interpolations and direct quotations of the Latin. An illegible word is indicated thus (...), and a phrase thus (..........). Punctuation has been added, or modified, in the course of translation to assist reading. Each entry has been numbered to facilitate reference. In the indexes the numbers refer to entries, not to pages.

The translations of several recurring terms perhaps require some explanation as there may well be differing opinions about the choices made.

Although "garden" is probably the more usual translation of *ortus* (the form of *hortus* used throughout this document) its less usual meaning "orchard" has been chosen as the scribe uses *gardinum*, presumably for garden. But, of course, the two meanings could be reversed, and it is by no means unlikely that one of these terms is used here for the Kentish "back-side" commonly occurring in later documents.

The abbreviation *latand.* has been translated "alongside" on the assumption that it is the gerund of the verb *laterare*—"to lie sideways (normally used of land)".

For "abut(s)" and "abutting" the scribe used *capitat ad*, *capitand. ad* and

34

capitant. ad. After some hesitation it has been translated without a preposition.

When intended as a capital letter *ff* has been transcribed as F. There seems to be no justification for perpetuating this late- and post-medieval eccentricity, particularly as it confounds indexing. Moreover, it could cause confusion if it were necessary to quote from the Welsh in the discussion of place-names origins.

Arabic numerals replace the Roman numerals of the original text. Where numbers are spelt out in the original they are spelt in the translation. Some untidiness results, but, as has been said, the scribe had little regard for petty consistency.

Thanks are due to the Kent Archaeological Society, the owners of the manuscript, and the Kent County Council (Archives Office), its custodians, for permission to publish this translation. Special thanks are owed to the County Archivist for his encouragement and advice, and to his staff for their always helpful services.

THE RENTAL*

Rental of Estmallyng, except New Hythe [*Nova Ripa*], made and renewed in full Court held there on the day of Saint Katherine the Virgin in the twelfth year of the reign of Henry the fourth since the Conquest of England. It is agreed between the Lady Isabel Ruton, Abbess of Westmallyng and the Convent of the same place, and all the tenants there, that any acre written below as best land pays on the day of the Nativity of the Lord 1d. halfpenny, and on the day of the Annunciation of the Blessed Virgin Mary 1d. halfpenny. And any acre written below as medium land [pays] on the day of the Nativity of St. John the Baptist 2d. And any acre written below as poor ["worst"] land pays on the day of St. Michael the Archangel 1d., Fealty Suit of Court. And any acre [which] has been relieved pays a fourth part of the sum of the annual rent. And it is finally agreed that the aforesaid tenants elect among themselves two tenants in the court held there next after the Feast of St. Michael the Archangel, of whom one, at the choice of the aforesaid Lady Abbess, will do the duties of reeve for one whole year, the which reeve will carry out all the orders of the Courts and the procurement for them [as?] demands require. And also [that] all [and] singular the customary hens called Smoke-hens, for the entire tenancy or vill of Estmallyng, have been assembled and handed over and rendered to the aforesaid Abbey. And on whatever day the Court is held there he shall have a meal with the Steward, or two pence, at the choice of the Lady Abbess or her deputy. And that all other customary rents and the sum total are annulled for ever.

[1] [Christian name lacking]²⁵ Dank senior holds where his granary stands 1 rood. In *Estfelde* in the first furlong, formerly Alexander Bedyll, 3 roods. In the same place, in the 2nd furlong, half an acre. In *Brantoncrofte* 2 acres and a half. In *Tenacre* [sic.] 1 acre. In *Gosecrofte* next to *Lompette* 3 roods. In his upper [supior.] messuage 1 rood and a half. In *Suthfelde* in 2 equal parcels, 1 acre. In *Blakemanys* 3 acres. In *Thomelyns* 2 acres 1 rood. Best land. Sum: 12 acres 1 rood and a half. The same holds in *Brownecrofte* 2 acres. Poor land. Sum: 3s. 3d. half a farthing. For one acre in *Pregelys*, at the term of St. Michael 4d. and 3 bushels of barley as he holds of the Lady. For half an acre and 3 dayworks in *Smythelonde*, at the term of St. Michael 10d. Sum: 3s. 3d. half a farthing, except farm.

[2] Walter Colte with John Danck [sic.] in their messuage 5 dayworks of land. Best land. Sum: a farthing and a half.

[3] John Hore holds in his messuage 1 rood. In *Estfelde* in the first furlong 1 rood. In *Suthfelde* 2 acres 3 roods. In the messuage *de Hore* 1 rood. In farm of William Cheyne in *Welfelde* 1 acre and a half. Best land. The same holds in *Estyrlane* 1 acre. Medium land. The same holds in *Gorsrede*, with woodland there, 1 acre. At *Taylys* 1 acre and a half. Poor land. Sum: 22d. The same holds of the Lady in farm in *Estyrlane* 1 acre, and in *Gorsreed* aforesaid 1 acre of land, whence at the term of St. Michael 18d. For 5 roods by *Pregelys* whence at the 4 principal terms 2s. Sum: 22d. except farm.

[4] John Parys holds in messuage 1 rood. In messuage next to Nicholas Terry 2 acres. Best land. At *Brochole* 3 acres and 1 rood. Medium land. Sum: 13d. farthing. The same holds of the Lady in farm half an acre within a messuage next to the aforesaid Nicholas, and at *Brochole* 3 roods, whence at the term of St. Michael 3 bushels of barley. Sum: 13d. farthing, except farm.

[5] William Lyle holds in messuage with outhouse [or workshop] and garden 1 rood. In *Estfelde* in *Blakemanyschot* 5 roods. In the same place next to *Brodelond* half an acre and half a rood. In the same place 3 roods and a half. By *Bramtongate* half an acre. Sum: 3 acres and a half. Best land. 10d. halfpenny. The same holds of the Lady in farm a (...—*pnn*?) messuage next to his [own] messuage, whence at the 4 principal terms 28d. The same, for 3 acres called *Samuelyslond* at the aforesaid terms 5s. Sum: 10d. halfpenny, except farm.

[6] Thomas Wolford holds in *Cotmanfelde* 3 roods. The same, in the same place half an acre, and in the same place 1 rood. In the same place half an acre and 3 dayworks. In *Melfelde* 5 roods. In *Tenaker* next to *Torel* 1 acre 3 roods. Best land. Sum: 15d. farthing.

[7] Thomas Kayle holds in messuage and garden half an acre. In croft adjacent 5 roods. in *Rabattyshawe* half an acre. By *Poteberghe* 1 acre, enclosed. In *Belkhawe* 1 rood, enclosed. In *Cotmanfelde* 1 rood and a half. Best land. At *Warynys* half an acre. Poor land. Sum: 12d. half a farthing.

[8] John Cowherde holds next to the messuage of the said Thomas 1 rood. In *Estfelde*, in the first furlong, 1 rood and a half. By *Crudehale* half an acre. Best land. Sum: 3d. farthing and a half. In the messuage where he lives, that he holds of the Lady in farm, 1 rood. The same in *Estfelde*, in the first furlong, 1 rood and a half, and at *Crudehale* 5 roods, whence at the four principal terms 3s. 6d. Sum: 3d. farthing and a half, except farm.

[9] Henry Brow holds in his messuage half an acre. Best land. Sum: 1d. halfpenny.

[10] The heir of Richard Catewerthe holds in messuage half a rood. In *Cornerdyscrofte* 3 acres. At *Crudehale* 1 rood. In *Northfelde* 1 acre 3 roods. In *Perysfelde*, enclosed, 4 acres. Best land. Sum: 2s. 3d. farthing and a half.

[11] William Lynche holds in the messuage where he lives 1 rood. Next to the messuage of Roger Fythyon half a rood. In messuage by the spring with land in *Estfelde* adjacent [*coiacent.*] there, and with a little orchard in the same place, 6 acres 1 rood. In *Bornebeye* half an acre. In the same place, in *Le Helde*, 1 acre. In *Morisfelde* 1 acre. In *Denysgardyne* 1 acre 1 rood. In *Lanefelde* 1 acre. In *Estfelde*, at *Le Wronge*, 3 roods and a half. Best land. Sum: 12 acres and 1 rood. The same holds in *Moltecrofte* 1 acre. In *Preestysfelde* 3 roods. Medium land. At *Moltelonde*, woodland, 3 roods. In the same place, in *Allemanyswode* 3 acres and 3 roods. At *Royserede* 1 acre. In *Hencoterede* 2 acres. Poor land. Sum: 3s. 11d. halfpenny farthing.

[12] John Dank Junior holds in his messuage 3 dayworks. Best land. Sum: A farthing. For half an acre in *Forcheld* [or *Fortheld*] 2 bushels of barley.

[13] Agnes Smythe holds in the messuage where she lives half a rood. The same, opposite that place half a rood [and] in croft there 1 rood. In *Cotmanfelde* 5 roods abutting the King's highway. In the same place 3 roods abutting the land of the Lady. In the same place, in *Le Gore* half an acre. In *Le Readehawe* half a rood. In *Estfelde* in the first furlong, half an acre. In *Suthfelde* 3 roods. In the same place half an acre. In the same place half an acre [*sic*.]. In *Westreede* 3 acres. Best land. Sum: 8 acres 1 rood and a half. By *Horelane*, woodland, half an acre. At *Warynys* 3 acres. The same, on the other side of the highway, in two conjoined parcels called *Vpper Warynys* 5 acres 1 rood. In *Paynyscrofte* and *Heghecrofte* 3 acres. In *Estreed*, enclosed, 1 acre and a half. Below *Estreed* 3 roods. Poor land.

Sum: 14 acres. The same holds of the Lady in farm, in the same place, 3 roods for 8d. Sum: 3s. 3d. half a farthing, except farm.

[14]   The heir(s) of William Rang in messuage half a rood, and in the same place, in *Cotmanfelde* half an acre, and in the same place half an acre and 1 rood. In *Readehawe* half a rood. In *Suthfelde*, in two parcels, 3 roods 3 dayworks and the third part of one daywork. [Space.] The heir(s) of Ronge for a fourth part in the same place. In *Southfelde* [sic.], with Isabel jointly, 2 acres. Best land. In *Sorewode* 1 rood and a half. Poor land. Sum: 13d. a farthing and a half.

[15]   John Heyward holds in his messuage 1 rood and a half. In *Cotmanfelde* 1 rood and a half. In *Estfelde* 3 roods and a half. In *Terryishulle* 3 roods. Best land. At *Periereed* 1 rood. Poor land. Sum: 7d. farthing and a half.

[16]   John Parker in (*dncl? ducl?* or *dmcl?*) messuage, formerly Nicholas Fylle, 7 dayworks. Best land. Sum: a halfpenny and 3 quarters of a farthing.

[17]   Richard Elwyne holds in messuage with croft 5 roods. In *Estfelde*, in the first furlong, 3 roods. In the same place half an acre. In the same place, in the 2nd furlong, 1 rood and a half. By *Bramtongate* half an acre and half a rood. Next to *Brodelonde* 1 rood 3 dayworks. At *Crudehale* half an acre and half a rood. Best land. Sum: 4 acres 1 rood and 8 dayworks. Sum: 13d. farthing and a half.

[18]   Roger Adeth holds in messuage with a field adjacent 6 acres and a half. At *Lynche* in the 2nd furlong 1 acre. At *Branette*, in the same place, 2 acres. In *Northfelde* 3 acres and 1 rood. In *Smythlonde*, enclosed, 2 acres. [In] *Preggel* 2 acres 1 rood. In the same place, called *Preggelishawe*, 1 rood. Best land, 17 acres 1 rood, whence 3s. 9d. halfpenny farthing. Next to *Thomyscrowche* 3 acres. In *Brochole*, enclosed, 2 acres. Medium land, whence 10d. At *Le Hoo* 14 acres. Poor land, whence 14d. The same holds of the Lady in farm 5 roods in *Blakemanyschote*, whence at the 4 principal terms 2s. Sum: 6s. 3d. halfpenny farthing, except farm.

[19]   John Adeth holds in his messuage half a rood. In *Estfelde*, in the 2nd furlong, 18 dayworks. In *Preggle* 1 acre. In *Crowdehale* 1 acre and a half. Best land. Sum: 9d. farthing.

[20]   Constance Solman holds in her messuage half a rood. In the 2nd furlong next to *Brodelonde* 1 acre. At *Terryishulle* next to *Lompette* 1 acre. In *Ordwynys* 2 acres 1 rood. Best land. In *Taylys*, by (*Ranautys* or *Rauantys* etc.) 2 acres. Medium land. Sum: 17d. half a farthing.

38

[21] John Ruffyn holds near *Abbesse Hoo* 5 roods of woodland, poor land. Sum: 1d. farthing.

[22] Simon ate Nassche holds in messuage, with croft adjacent, 4 acres and a half. In *Estfelde*, abutting the same place, half an acre. In the same place, at *Lynche*, 5 roods. In the 2nd furlong in the same place half an acre, and 1 acre in the same place called *Scoyerisakyr*. In the same place, next to *Smythlonde*, 1 acre. In *Northfelde* half an acre. In *Blakemanys*, enclosed, 5 roods. In *Chapmanys*, enclosed, 1 acre and a half. Best land. Sum: 12 acres. In *Wrongereed* 6 acres. Poor land. Sum: 3s. 6d. half a farthing. The same held [*tenebat*] of the Lady 2 acres by the footway in *Estfelde* for 6 bushels of barley. The same holds in the 2nd furlong of *Estfelde* 1 rood and a half. Best land, lately Nicholas Fille.

[23] Daniel Man holds in messuage, and within the same place, 1 acre and a half. In *Estfelde*, in the 2nd furlong, half an acre and half a rood. In the same place one rood and half. Upon *Terryishulle*, the perquisite of John Smythe of *Newhythe*[26] 3 roods. In *Swechecrofte*, on the north side, 1 rood. Best land. Sum: 3 acres and a half, whence 10d. halfpenny. For 3 roods in the 2nd furlong and 1 rood and a half at *Crudehale*, which he holds of the Lady in farm, at the term of St. Michael 4 bushels of barley. Sum: 10d. halfpenny, except farm.

[24] Rosa Scharnale holds in messuage, garden and croft, lying together [*coniacent*], 2 acres and a half. In *Estfelde*, alongside her garden, 3 acres. In the same place, *de Wronge*, one acre and half a rood. In the same place, abutting *Pregell*, 3 roods. In *Seerselonde*, 3 roods. At *Northfelde* 5 roods. In *Northscarnale* 5 acres. In *Wynys* 3 acres and 3 roods. The same holds in *Great Eldelonde* 5 acres and 1 rood. Upon *Terryishulle*, abutting the King's highway, 1 acre. In *Stombylmede*, 2 acres. Sum: 26 acres 3 roods and a half best land, whence 6s. 8d. halfpenny half a farthing. In *Suthssarnale* 10 acres. Medium land. The same holds in *Clagge*, with woodland and garden, 3 acres and a half. Poor land. The same holds of the Lady in farm 2 acres in *Northssarnale* [sic.] aforesaid, whence 18d. at the 4 principal terms. In Little [*puo.*] *Eldelonde* 2 acres for 3s. at the aforesaid terms. In *Great* [*Magno*] *Eldelonde* 3 roods for 12d. at the aforesaid principal terms. 3 roods in *Suthssarnale* aforesaid, on the east side, for 5d. halfpenny at the term of St. Michael. Sum: rent [*redd.*] 8s. 8d. half a farthing, except farm.

[25] William and Richard Scharnale hold in messuage and an old garden in the same place 3 acres. The same hold with land which they hold in farm of John Suthwyk in *Horefelde* 10 acres, one third part the said John's. The same hold in *Haryhore Crofte* 1 acre and half a rood. In *Pypewys*, in the same place adjacent, one acre and a half, enclosed. In *Ordwynys*, on the

southern side of the highway, 3 acres and a half; a part which the Vicar of Estmallyng holds there is half an acre. In *Longfelde* 3 acres, enclosed. In *Swechecrofte* 3 roods. In *Franceys* 1 acre and half a rood in the middle of the field. On the southern side of the same field 3 acres 1 rood. Best land. Sum: 27 acres 1 rood, whence 6s. 9d. halfpenny farthing. In *Sparwecrofte* 5 roods. In the same place, in *Ethelerys* 2 acres. In *Pryckefelde*, enclosed, 5 acres. In *Sorewestreed* 10 acres. In the same place, in *Westreed*, 3 acres. Medium land. Sum: 21 acres 1 rood, whence 3s. 6d. halfpenny. In *Ethelerys* aforesaid 2 acres of woodland. In *Sorewode* 3 acres. Poor land. Sum: 5 acres, whence 5d. The same hold of the Lady in farm 3 roods on the south side of *Napylton* aforesaid [sic.] for 12d. at the term of St. Michael. Sum: 10s. 9d. farthing, except farm.

[26] John Taylour holds in messuage, and within the same place, 3 roods. In *Estfelde* at *Preggelys* 1 acre and a half. In *Blakemanys* 1 acre and half a rood. In *Smythelonde* half an acre. In the same place, in *Le Wronge* 1 acre and half a rood. In *Suthfelde* 1 acre and a half. At *Jacobbys*, next to *Thomlynyscrowche*, half an acre. Best land. Sum: 7 acres, whence 21d. The same holds in *Taylys*, enclosed, half an acre, and in the same place 1 acre of woodland. The same, above [supius.] *Brodescarnale* 3 acres. Poor land. Sum: 2s. 1d. halfpenny. The same holds of the Lady in farm at *Jacobbys* aforesaid, 3 roods for 14d. at the terms of St. Michael and Easter. For pasture at *Le Hoo*, upon land of the Lady, at the 4 principal terms 3s.

[27] John Rocher of *Aylysforde* holds in messuage, and within the same place, 7 acres. Best land, whence 21d. The same holds of the Lady in farm 3 acres called *Abbessecrofte* for 4s. at the four principal terms. Sum: 21d., except farm.

[28] The heir(s) of William Yonge in messuage and garden 1 rood. In the same place, adjacent, in *Southfelde* 5 roods. In the same place 11 dayworks and a fourth part of 1 daywork. In *Estfelde de Wronge* half an acre. In *Wynys*, alongside the southern hedge, 2 acres. Best land. The same holds in *Alhertys* 2 acres, enclosed. Medium land. In *Hothree* [sic.] 2 acres of woodland. In *Hoolane* half an acre. Poor land. Sum: 9d. farthing and a half.

[29] Geoffrey Brapson holds in messuage 2 dayworks and a half. In *Suthfelde*, abutting *Alhertys*, 5 roods. In the same place, half an acre. In the croft before his messuage 3 roods and a half. In *Ordwynys* 1 acre and a half. In *Schepherdys Crofte* 3 roods. In *Francysys* 1 acre half a rood. Best land, 6 acres 2 dayworks and a half. At *Brochole* one acre. The same holds in three conjoined parcels (there?) called *Boyredys* 3 acres. Medium land. Of the Lady in farm one acre for 12d. at the term of St. Michael. Sum: 2s. 2d. 3 quarters of a farthing.

[30]   John Salmon holds in messuage with adjacent croft 1 acre. Best land. Sum: 3d.

[31]   Thomas Brapson holds in messuage and gardens (on both sides of the lane—*ex. vtraq. pte. venelle*) there, 1 acre. The same in *Crudecrofte*, in the same place, 1 acre and a half. In *Le Helle*, enclosed, half an acre. With his messuage in *Westfelde* 8 acres. In *Suthfelde*, next to the footway, 3 roods. In the same place 3 roods, and he holds of the Lady in farm there, lying by the hedge, half an acre for 2 bushels of barley. The same holds in *Cotmanfelde*, next to *Hegedale*, half a rood. Best land. Sum: 13 acres 1 rood and a half. The same holds in *Le Herne* 1 acre and a half. At *Brochole* 1 acre. Medium land. And he holds of the Lady in farm 1 acre for 12d. at the term of St. Michael. The same holds in *Woderede*, enclosed, 4 acres. By *Forewode* 1 rood and a half. Poor land. The same holds of the Lady in farm a piece of land called *Jacobreed* [for] 5s. at the 4 principal terms. Sum: 4s. 1d. halfpenny, except farm.

[32]   Nicholas Terry holds in messuage, with croft adjacent, 3 acres. In *Reycrofte* 2 acres 3 roods. In *Westfelde* 2 acres and half a rood. Best land. In *Pryckerede* 1 acre and a half. Medium land. In *Ealderede*, enclosed, 3 acres. In *Le Dele*, with woodland there, 3 acres. At *Cripsyshoo* 2 acres 1 rood and a half. The same holds of the Lady in farm, in the same place, 3 roods for 3d. at the term of St. Michael. The same holds at *Swynden*, woodlands, 1 acre and a half. In the same place, 1 rood. At *Heygate* half a rood. At *Heendysdyche* 1 rood. Poor land. Sum: 10 acres and a half. Sum: 3s. 1d. half a farthing, except farm.

[33]   William Cood holds at *Boltysstole* 3 acres. Poor land. Sum: 3d.

[34]   The heirs of William Webbe hold in messuage with garden 1 rood and a half. In *Dodelysdale*, enclosed, 1 acre and a half. Best land. In *Sorewode* half a rood. In *Payiscrofte* 1 rood. Poor land. Sum: 6d.

[35]   William Elde holds in messuage, garden, and in a piece of land adjacent called *Pryckehulle*, 9 acres. In *Lyttelewyn* 4 acres. In *Cryckele* 8 acres. In *Dodelysdale* 1 acre and a half. In *Cotmanfelde* 2 acres and a half and half a rood. In *Koockowcrofte* 4 acres and a half. In *Elynden* half an acre of meadow. Best land. Sum: 30 acres and half a rood. Sum: 7s. 6d. farthing and a half.

[36]   The heir of William Smythe holds in messuage with garden 6 dayworks and a half. Sum: a halfpenny.

[37]   The heirs of Joan ate Forde hold in messuage, with garden and crofte

41

adjacent, 2 acres. In two old gardens half an acre. In the same place, called *Le Hetter*, half an acre. In the same place, in *Cotmanfelde*, 3 roods. In the same place, next to *Hegedele*, half a rood. In *Suthfelde* 2 acres. Also in the same place 2 acres 1 rood. In the same place, by *Horehegge*, 3 roods. In *Pryckeheth* half an acre. Best land. Sum: 9 acres 1 rood and a half. In *Esttyrlane* 2 acres. Medium land. In *Estreed*, enclosed, 1 acre and a half. At *Brochole* 1 acre and a half. In *Preestyslonde* 1 acre and a half. In *Jacobbysreed* 3 roods. By the heath called *Falkehook* 1 acre. Poor land. Sum: 3s. 2d. farthing and a half.

[38]   Richard Hoyton holds in his messuage half a rood. Best land. Sum: A farthing and a half.

[39]   Thomas Reygate holds in his messuage, and within the same place, 1 acre. In *Cotmanfelde*, in the same place, 2 acres and a half. In the same place 2 acres. In *Dodelisdele* 3 acres. Best land. In *Baselyreed* 7 acres. Medium land. At *Swynden* 2 acres. Poor land. Sum: 3s. 3d. halfpenny.

[40]   Alice Adam(s) holds in her messuage 1 rood. In *Cotmanfelde* 5 roods. Next to *Dodelisdele* half an acre. In *Northhelde* 1 acre. In *Falke Hawe* 1 rood 2 dayworks and a half. Best land. Sum: 9d. halfpenny and three quarters of a farthing.

[41]   Alan Kat(er)yne[27] holds of the Lady in farm one messuage with croft adjacent as included for 3s. 6d. at the four principal terms.

[42]   Joan Stonhard holds in messuage, with 2 crofts (lying together— *coniacent*), 2 acres 3 roods. Best land. Sum: 8d. farthing.

[43]   The heirs of William Chalner hold in *Gulgishawe*, by the spring, 1 acre and half a rood. Best land. Sum: 3d. farthing and a half.

[44]   John at Helle holds in messuage, by the spring, 1 rood. Best land. Sum: A halfpenny farthing.

[45]   John Derby holds in messuage, and within the same place, 1 acre and 3 roods. Best land. The same in croft at *Goderysstrete* 2 acres. Medium land. Sum: 9d. farthing.

[46]   Robert Deen holds in *Pacfelde* 3 acres. In *Estfelde* 2 acres and a half. In *Delefelde* 5 acres. In *Bernhawe* 2 acres. In *Bromfelde* 1 acre. In *Denysgardyne* half an acre. Sum: 14 acres. Best land. The same holds in *Scoheed* [*sic.*—error for *Scolreed*?] 2 acres and 1 rood. In *Brodecrofte* 4 acres. In *Reycrofte*, with woodlands there, 1 acre. In *Pyghtele* 12 acres.

Medium land. Sum: 19 acres and 1 rood. In *Readecroftis* 3 acres. In *Le Beer*, with woodland there, 5 acres. In *Westreed* 4 acres. Next to *Scolreed* half an acre of woodland. Poor land. Sum: 12 acres and a half. Sum: 7s. 9d.

[47] Thomas Sextayn holds in messuage and garden half an acre. In *Cotmanfelde*, beside the footway there, 1 acre and a half. The same holds of the Lady in farm 1 rood for 1 bushel of barley. Sum: 2 acres. Best land. The same in *Scolreed*, next to *Le Helme*, with woodlands there, 2 acres and 1 rood. In *Ynyhesele* 3 roods. Medium land. In *Roysereed* 2 acres and a half. In *Allemanyskode* [error for *Allemanyswode*?] 2 acres and a half. Poor land. Sum: 17d. except farm.

[48] Nicholas Allyn holds in messuage, garden and 2 conjoined crofts, 5 acres and 1 rood. In *Cocardiscrofte* 1 acre. Best land. The Lady and Master [*Dns.*] Nicholas hold equally in 2 crofts called *Ynyhesyl* 2 acres. The Lady holds in the same place, enclosed, 3 roods. Sum: 1 acre, [*sic.*] [Interlineation unreadable.] Medium land. In *Roysereed* half an acre. In *Payiscrofte*, with land lately the heirs of Range [*cf.* No. 14] 3 roods. Poor land. Sum: 22d. farthing, except farm.

[49] Thomas Reve holds in messuage, and within the same place, 8 acres. In *Estfelde* 2 acres and a half. In *Holcrofte* 5 roods, enclosed, with 1 rood for his way [*p. via sua*] there. In *Estfelde*, called *Brodelond*, 3 acres and 3 roods. In *Lompettes* 3 acres. In *Tyckele*, separately, half an acre. In *Lanefelde* half an acre. Best land. Sum: 9 acres and a half, whence 4s. 10d. halfpenny. The same holds in *Wolnenelond*, in 2 parcels, 14 acres. Poor land. Sum: 6d. halfpenny.

[50] Thomas ate Melle holds in *Estfelde*, in the middle of the field, 2 acres 1 rood. Best land. Sum: 6d. halfpenny farthing.

[51] The heirs of John Longe hold in messuage with garden 1 rood and a half. In *Scolyshulle* 2 acres and a half. In *Tyckele*, separately, half an acre. Best land. The same hold in *Le Helde* at *Jonegate* 2 acres and 1 rood. At *Wodeprestislonde* 1 acre and 1 rood. Poor land. Sum: 13d. halfpenny half a farthing.

[52] John Loder, son of William, holds in messuage, and in a garden formerly William Heyward, 3 roods. The same, in croft in the same place 5 roods and 6 dayworks. The Lady [interlineation: (...) Robert Gryggs] holds there 1 acre. The same John holds in *Myddylfelde* 3 acres. Best land. The same holds in *Roysereed* 1 rood. Poor land. Sum: 15d. halfpenny farthing.

[53] Agnes Fythyan holds in messuage, garden and *Lanefelde*, adjacent, 1 acre. Best land. Sum: 3d.

43

[54] Joan Paidman holds in messuage 1 rood. In *Morysfelde* 1 acre. In *Moriscrofte* 3 roods. The same in messuage at *Melstrete* 1 rood. The same in *Melstrete*, in the same place, 5 roods. Best land. The same at *Jonegate* 2 acres and a half. Poor land. Sum: 13d.

[55] Roger Fythyan holds in messuage 1 rood. In *Lanefelde* 1 acre and 2 dayworks. In *Cotmanfelde* 1 rood called [space] *akyr*. Best land. The same holds in *Tayloriscrofte* 5 roods. Medium land. Next to *Westrede* 3 roods. Poor land. Sum: [space].

[56] John [surname lacking] holds in messuage with garden and croft in the same place, on the east side, 4 acres. The same holds there 1 rood. In the same place half an acre. In *Bromefelde* 1 acre. In *Northyld* half a rood. In the same place 1 rood and a half. The same holds of the Lady in farm three acres called *Bolttiscroft* [marginal note in a different hand: *Bolstcroft*] for 4 shillings at the 4 principal terms. The same holds in messuage *de Frenys* with adjacent land there, enclosed, 4 acres. In *Wetefeld* 1 acre. In *Tenaker* 3 roods and a half. In *Welfeld*, on the north side, half an acre and half a rood. In the same place, 1 rood and a half. In *Belkefeld*, abutting the way towards the East, 1 acre. Best land. Sum: 26 acres 1 rood and a half, whence 6s. 7d. half a farthing. The same, alongside *Goderistrete*, enclosed, 3 roods. In messuage near to *Larkfeld*, and within the same place, 4 acres and a half. Medium land. Sum: 5 acres and 1 rood, whence 10d. halfpenny. The same holds in *Constablesdene* 2 acres. At *Swyndene* 2 acres. At *Hencoterede* 1 rood 6 dayworks and a half. At *Swynden* half an acre. Poor land. Sum: 4 acres 3 roods 6 dayworks and a half, whence 4d. halfpenny and 3 quarters of a farthing. Sum: 7s. 10d. halfpenny and 3 parts of a farthing. [This entry is in a hand different from the rest.]

[57] The heir of Robert Clerk holds in messuage and garden 1 rood. In *Perysfelde* 3 acres. In *Lambardys* 1 acre. Best land. The same at *Skotlonde* 2 acres. Medium land. Sum: 16d. halfpenny farthing.

[58] Henry Goodborgh holds in messuage with garden 3 roods. The same holds of the Lady in farm, in the same place, 2 [space] for 18d. (per annum?). The same holds in a messuage on the other side of the highway there, with croft, 2 acres. In *Bromfelde* 1 acre and 3 roods. In messuage at *Le Helle* 3 roods and a half. At *Le Steyle* 5 roods. In *Westdene* 3 roods. Best land. Sum: 7 acres 1 rood and a half. In *Nether Reed* 3 acres. The Lady holds there (in respect of rent [of] the said Henry?—*in mail. dc. Henricus*) half an acre alongside the King's highway for 2 bushels of barley. The same, in *Huppyr Reed*, in the same place, 3 acres. Medium land. Sum: 6 acres. And the Lady in the same place 3 roods on the east side, (which?) the same Henry holds in farm there, with one acre and a half in the same place called

Abbesse Crofte, whence at the 4 principal terms 2s. 6d. The same holds at *Skotlond* 3 roods. Poor land. Sum: 2s. 10d. halfpenny, a farthing and a half, except farm.

[59] William Goodborgh holds in *Perysfelde*, about in the middle of the field, 3 roods. Best land. Sum: 2d. farthing.

[60] The heirs of Nicholas ate Helle hold in messuage and garden 1 rood and a half. In *Le Dene*, on the east side, 1 rood. In *Perysfelde* 3 roods. In *Stocwelle* 3 roods, and in the same place 13 dayworks and a half. The same holds of the Lady in farm, in the same place, 6 dayworks and a half for 4d. The same holds in *Le Dene* 1 acre. The same [holds] of Roger Pympe in farm in *Belkefelde* 1 acre. In *Little Pyghtele*, next to the land of Martin Heler, half a rood. Best land: Sum: 14 acres and a half, 3 dayworks and a half whence 13d. halfpenny farthing. The same holds in *Bresottyscrofte* 5 roods. In *Rock Reed* 2 acres. Medium land. The same holds in *Wardyscrofte*, next to *Lewstanys*, 1 acre and a half. Sum: 21d. halfpenny farthing, except farm.

[61] Martin Helere holds in messuage, with croft adjacent, 3 roods. At *Stoksteyle* 3 roods, enclosed. In *Cokkystofte*, enclosed, 1 acre. In *Le Dene* 1 acre. In *Tenakyr*, abutting *Belkefelde*, half an acre. Best land. Sum: 4 acres, whence 12d. By *Rokysreed*, enclosed, 3 roods. The same holds in *Rogem'reed* [abbreviation of *Rogemanreed* or *Rogemanysreed*?] 4 acres. Poor land. The same holds of the Lady in farm 1 acre in *Belkefeld* for 2s. Sum: 17d. halfpenny, except farm.

[62] Joan Glaswreghte holds in messuage [and] garden, with a field to the east, 8 acres. In *Morysysfelde* 2 acres and 1 rood. In *Lanefelde* 1 rood and half. In the same place 2 acres and a half. In *Tyckele* 4 acres and a half. In *Perisfelde* 1 acre and a half. Sum: 19 acres and half a rood, whence 4s. 9d. farthing and a half. The same holds in *Rokyreed* 2 acres. Medium land. The same holds in *Kenreed*, on the east side of the highway, 2 acres. In *Pyrereed*, with woodland there, 3 acres and half a rood. At *Le Beer*, enclosed, 5 roods. In *Le Swer* 2 acres. Adjacent, in the same place, enclosed, 1 acre (...) on the east side of the highway there. In *Enotereed* 4 acres. Next to the highway and the heath on the other side 3 acres. Poor land. Sum: 16 acres 1 rood and a half, whence 16d. farthing and a half. The same holds of the Lady in farm 3 acres in *Lovelockyscrofte* for 3s. at the 4 principal terms. Sum: 6s. 6d. halfpenny farthing, except farm.

[63] William Menewar holds 15 acres, enclosed, called *Downhonelond*. Best land. And he holds of the Lady in farm 2 acres, enclosed, for 2s. at the 4 principal terms. The same holds in *Walfordyslond* by *Conegherhelle* 3 acres. At *Skotlond* 5 acres. Medium land. In his messuage at *Larkefelde* 3

dayworks. Best land. At *Wythotys* 1 acre and a half. Poor land. Sum: 5s. 2d. halfpenny farthing, except farm.

[64]   The heirs of Nicholas Kook in *Conegher Crofte* 4 acres. Best land. In the same place, alongside the King's highway, 5 acres. Poor land. Sum: 17d.

[65]   Roger Breggys holds in *Cruchecrofte*, enclosed, 2 acres. At *Lundesford* in *Hammelmede* 5 dayworks. In 2 neighbouring crofts, in the same place, 3 roods and a half. Best land. Sum: 9d.

[66]   Robert Sextayn holds by *Le Berghe* 4 acres and 1 rood. Best land. Sum: 12d. halfpenny farthing.

[67]   John Goos senior holds in *Herfelde*, on the south side, 5 roods. In *Middylfelde* 4 acres and a half. The same holds, in the same place, on an old lease [*ex Antiqua Dimissione*] half an acre for 8 pence annual rent, payable at the Chapel of St. Thomas, Martyr, the building by the gate of the Abbey of Westmallyng, at the term of the Nativity of the Lord, for all services. The same holds in *Congher Crofte* 1 acre. The same 1 acre in *Hammelmede*, next to the land of John Smythe, towards the south. Best land. Sum: 7 acres 3 roods, whence 23d. farthing, except 8d.

[68]   Richard Byyn holds 2 acres in *Herfelde*. At *Reysshessteyle* half an acre. Best land. The same holds of the Lady in farm, in the same place, 1 acre and a half for 16d. at the 4 principal terms. Sum: 7d. halfpenny, except farm.

[69]   John Rokysle holds in *Cruchefelde* 1 acre and 1 rood. The same holds of William Cheyne in farm, in the same place, 2 acres and a half. The same holds of the said William in farm near *Poteburgh* 2 acres and 1 rood. Best land. Sum: 6 acres, whence 18d.

[70]   John Heeckstaple holds of the Lady in farm next to the King's highway and the footway towards *Mallyng* for 2s. at the 4 principal terms [acreage not given]. The same holds of the Lady in farm 2 acres at *Vnder Nelys* for 1 quarter of barley at the term of St. Michael. Sum: None, because farm.

[71]   John de Hoo holds at *Potebergh* called *Fayrefeld*, abutting the King's highway, 3 acres. The same holds in the same place, lately John Corbe, 3 acres. Best land. Sum: 18d.

[72]   John Owynham holds 5 roods at *Potebergh*. Best land. Sum: 3d. halfpenny farthing.

[73]   Nicholas Stefene junior holds in messuage at the *Heghestrete* 1 acre. Best land. The same holds of the Lady in farm half an acre at *Mellonde* for 12d. at the 4 principal terms. Sum: 3d., except farm.

[74]   Henry Goos holds in *Tenakyr* 1 acre 3 roods. Best land. The same holds of the Lady in farm 5 dayworks in half a garden by the *Heghestrete* there for 8d. at the term of St. Michael. Sum: 5d. farthing, except farm.

[75]   John Loder junior holds in messuage in the same place half an acre. The same, on the other side of the highway there, enclosed, half an acre. Next to the land of the Lady half an acre. In *Northhelde* 1 acre. In *Tenakyr* 1 rood and a half. In *Lanefelde* half an acre. In *Tyckele* half an acre. Next to *Torel* 1 acre. In *Hammellemede* 1 acre. The same in half a garden next to · *Goodborghis* 5 dayworks. [The other half of the garden in 74 above?] Best land. Sum: 16d. halfpenny.

[76]   Daniel Hamkyn holds in messuage, and within the same place, 1 acre. Best land. The same holds of the Lady in farm in *Northawe* 1 rood, whence at the term of St. Michael 6d. The same, below [*sub*] his messuage 1 acre. Medium land. Sum: 5d., except farm.

[77]   John ate Cruche holds in his messuage 1 rood. In *Le Berghe* 1 acre and a half. By *Coppedehalle* 1 acre. In *Grenysfelde* 3 roods. In *Eldehawe* 2 acres. In *Holcroft* 3 roods. At *Wynterswell*, on the west side of the highway, 1 acre and a half. Next to the land of Daniel Hamkyn aforesaid half an acre. Beside the same place 1 acre. Medium land. Sum: 9 acres and 1 rood. 18d. halfpenny. In *Gerrard(s)*, next to *Gremmysfeld* [*sic.*—error for *Grenysfeld?*] 2 acres 3 roods. Next to *Hodon*, on the southern side, 1 acre. In *Hammelmede*, next to the land of the Lord of Paddelisworth, 1 acre and 5 dayworks, and in the same place between the (...—*pte.*) of the Lady Abbess and the Lord of Cobham, half an acre and half a rood. Next to the (...—*pt.*) of the Lord of Cobham, half a rood. In the said (...—*pte.*) of *Hemphawe* half a rood. Best land. Sum: 5 acres and 3 roods. Sum: 17d. farthing. The same holds at *Le Hole*, abutting *Everardislane*, 1 acre. In *Lanecroft*, next to the garden of Robert Fris., in 3 parcels, 1 acre. Poor land. Sum: 3s. 1d. halfpenny farthing.

[78]   Robert at [*sic.*] Cruche holds in (messuage), and within, 1 rood. In *Tenaker* 1 acre. In [space] *Felde* 3 acres. In *Eldehawe* 2 acres. In *Litilheld* 3 roods. In [space] 1 acre. In *Le Helde* 3 acres. In *Hammelmede*, next to the meadows of the Lord of Padlesworth, 3 roods and a half. Next to the meadows of the Lord of Cobham 1 rood and a half. In the same place, next [space], half a rood. In *Hemphawe* half a rood. Best land. Sum: 12 acres and a half, whence 3s. 1d. halfpenny. Next to the land of Daniel Hamkyn half

an acre. In *Hoolecrofte* 3 roods. By *Wynterswell* 1 acre and a half. Medium land. Sum: 2 acres 3 roods, whence 5d. halfpenny. In *Lanecrofte* 1 acre. At *Le Noke* 1 acre. In *Huphawe* half a rood. Poor land. Sum: 3s. 8d. halfpenny farthing.

[79] The heir(s) of Joan Gervays in messuage, and in the same place, 13 dayworks. Best land. Sum: 1d.

[80] Nicholas Stevens holds in messuage and in *Greenisfelde* 5 acres and half a rood. The same, on the otherside of the lane there, in a little messuage, half a rood. In *Bregfelde* 2 acres. In *Huphelde* 5 roods. On the northern side of *Everardyslane* 2 acres and half. In *Le Ferthyng* half an acre. In the same place, alongside *Blakelond* 2 acres. In the same place 2 acres. In the same place 2 acres and 1 rood. In the same place, abutting *Northbynne* 1 acre, and in the same place *Sowcher* [or *Sowther*] 1 acre. In *Cornerdiscrofte*, alongside *Mellestrete* 1 acre and 3 roods. The same [in] *Vnder Nelys*, next to *Tenaker*, 1 acre. In *Melfelde* 1 acre, and in the same place, where his grange stands and in his other messuage there, 6 dayworks. In *Tenakyr* 1 rood and a half. In *Wetefelde* 2 acres and 3 roods. In the same place half an acre and half a rood. In the same place, next to *Gonnorecrofte* 1 acre. On the southern side of *Torelys* half an acre. In *Gonnorecrofte*, enclosed, 4 acres. In *Belkefelde* 1 acre. In the same place, on the northern side, 1 acre and a half. And he holds of the Lady in farm, on the southern side of the same place, half a rood for 3d. at the term of St. Michael. In *Welfelde* 4 acres and a half and half a rood. In the same place 3 roods and a half. In *Le Dene* 4 acres. In the same place, adjacent, in *Lanefelde* 1 acre and a half. In *Tyckele* 5 roods. In croft and in a garden next to *Le Elme* 3 roods and a half. In *Elyndene* half an acre of meadow. In *Stomubylmede* [or *Stoumbylmede*] with *Le Pyghtele* there, 2 acres. In *Blachildecrofte*, on the west side, 3 roods. In *Welfelde* alongside the King's highway, half an acre. In a little garden next to the messuage of Thomas Brapson 1 rood. In an orchard at *Melstrete* 1 daywork and a half. In a messuage, lately William Mymys, next to his own messuage, 2 acres and 3 roods. Best land. Sum: 53 acres 1 rood 2 dayworks and a half, whence 23s. 3d. halfpenny farthing and 3 quarters of a farthing. In *Cornerdyscrofte*, next to *Le Brome*, 2 acres. At *Bryddockysakyr*, by the heath, 8 acres. Medium land. Sum: 10 acres, whence 20d. The same holds in *Le Reed*, next to *Wellone*, 3 acres. At *Warynys*, with woodland there, 3 acres and a half. Poor land. Sum: 6 acres and a half, whence 6d. halfpenny. Sum: 15s. 6d. farthing 3-quarters of a farthing, except 3d. farm as shown.

[81] John Tornor, in his messuage and within the same place, 5 roods. In *Northfelde*, by the western hedge, 3 roods. In *Pykyshawe* half a rood. Best

land. The same holds of the Lady in farm half an acre in *Northehelde* for 2 bushels of barley. Sum: 6d. farthing and a half, except farm.

[82] Nicholas at Melle holds in messuage with garden 1 rood. Alongside *Blakelond* 1 acre. In the same place, in *Northebynne*, 1 acre and 3 roods and 2 dayworks. In the same place, next to his messuage, 3 roods. In *Northehelde* 1 acre. In *Northebynne*, next to his garden, half an acre. Best land. Sum: 5 acres 1 rood and 2 dayworks, whence 15d. halfpenny farthing and a half. At *Le Beer* 4 acres and a half. In the same place, on the highway side, woodlands, 2 acres and a half. Poor land. Sum: 7 acres, whence 7d. The same holds of the Lady in farm in *Tenaker* 2 acres and a half, in 2 parcels, for 4s. at the four principal terms. For 2 acres 1 rood in *Stapylfelde*, whence 4s. at the aforesaid terms. The same (*de*—at?) *Scollysgardyn*, at the term of St. Michael [acreage not given], farm 3d. Sum: 22d. halfpenny farthing 3-quarters of a farthing, except farm.

[83] Christine Balton holds in her messuage 3 dayworks. Best land. Sum: A farthing.

[84] John Frost holds in his little orchard, in the same place, 2 dayworks and a half. Sum: 3-quarters of a farthing.

[85] Joan Garvays holds in messuage and garden 7 dayworks and a half. Best land. Sum: Halfpenny half a farthing.

[86] John Detlyng holds in his messuage 1 rood. Best land. Sum: Halfpenny farthing.

[87] John Loder holds in his messuage and in *Northbynne* 2 acres and 1 rood. In *Solaghcrofte* 3 roods. In *Churchfelde* 5 roods. In *Le Helde*, next to *Torelys*, half an acre. Best land. Sum: 4 acres 3 roods, whence 14d. farthing. The same, half an acre at *Swynden*. At *Hencotereed* 1 rood 6 dayworks and a half. Poor land. Sum: 15d. 3-quarters of a farthing.

[88] Benedicta Lodere holds in messuage with garden 1 rood. In the field adjacent 1 acre. The same, by the eastern hedge, 1 acre half a rood. In the same place, on the hill, 5 roods. In *Wetefelde* 1 acre. In *Belkefelde* 1 acre. And she holds of the Lady in farm, in the same place, half a rood for 3d. at the term of St. Michael. The same holds at *Le Helme*, in 2 conjoined crofts, 4 acres. Next to *Kenred(e)*, enclosed, 3 roods. In *Belkefelde* 1 rood. Best land. Sum: 11 acres and half a rood. The same, next to *Kenreed*, woodlands, 3 roods. Poor land. Sum: 2s. 2d. halfpenny half a farthing, except farm.

[89]   Gregory Loder holds at *Swynden* half an acre. At *Hencotered(e)* 1 rood. Poor land. Sum: Halfpenny farthing.

[90]   John Stretend holds in his messuage half a rood. Best land. Next to *Sorewode*, woodland, 3 roods. Poor land. Sum: 1d. half a farthing.

[91]   William Loder holds in his messuage, with garden there, 1 acre. In a garden in the same place, on the other side of the highway, 5 roods. In *Vndernelys*, below his messuage, 1 acre and 3 roods. In *Tenaker*, at his gate to the field, 3 roods. In the same place, 5 roods. In *Wetefelde*, alongside the way there, 1 acre. In *Beeldewynys* 1 acre. In *Hammelmede* half an acre. Best land. Sum: 8 acres and a half, whence 2s. 1d. halfpenny. The same, lying next to *Jonegate*, conjoined, 14 acres. At *Roysherne* 1 rood. Poor land, whence 4d. farthing. Sum: 3s. 3d. halfpenny farthing.

[92]   Alexander Bedyll holds in a little orchard beside *Mellestrete* 5 dayworks. Best land. Sum: A farthing and a half.

[93]   Peter Stephene holds in messuage 3 dayworks. In *Bonefacyshawe* 5 dayworks. In *Tenaker* 1 acre. In *Northhelde* 3 roods. In *Lyttelehelde*, on the other side of the highway there, 5 roods. Best land. Sum: 3 acres 8 dayworks. The same holds in *Le Brome*, beside *Everardyslane*, 2 acres. At *Hencoterede* 1 acre and a half. Poor land. Sum: 13d. half a farthing.

[94]   John Zarnaway holds in messuage, by right of [his] wife, half a rood. The same in *Melfelde* 1 rood. Best land. Sum: 1d. half a farthing.

[95]   John Stephene holds in messuage and in *Mellefelde*, adjacent, half an acre and half a rood. In *Wetefelde* 1 acre and a half. In *Le Helde*, by *Bornebeye*, 3 roods. Best land. In *Hothreede*, next to *Brodescarnale*, 2 acres. Poor land. Sum: 10d. halfpenny half a farthing.

[96]   Henry Lorkyn holds in messuage and within the same place 7 dayworks. In *Welfelde*, beside *Chercheweye*, 3 roods and a half. In *Mellefelde*, next to the way, 1 rood. In *Estfelde*, in the first furlong, 2 acres and a half. Best land. At *Brodefelde* 5 roods. Poor land. The same holds of the Lady in farm 1 acre in *Wetefelde*, 1 acre in *Belkfeld* and half an acre in *Tenaker* for 5s. at the 4 principal terms. Sum: 12d. farthing and (4 − 3?) parts of a farthing, except farm.

[97]   Robert Gryg holds in messuage and within the same place 1 acre. In *Mellefelde* 1 acre 3 roods and 7 dayworks. In the same place, by *Bornebeye*, 1 acre. In *Teenakir* 3 roods and a half. Best land. Sum: 4 acres 1 rood 2 dayworks. The same holds in *Longcrofte*, above *Northhelde*, half an acre.

Medium land. The same holds in *Sparwegrove* 3 roods. Poor land. The same holds of the Lady in farm 3 roods in *Mellefelde* [and] 1 rood, next to the messuage of John Loder, for 20d. at the 4 principal terms. The same for 5 roods and 1 rood lying separately in *Tyckele* 2s. at the aforesaid terms. Sum: 14d. halfpenny 3 quarters of a farthing, except farm. The same for 1 acre, enclosed, next to *Tyckele* at the aforesaid terms 2s.

[98] John Glaswreghte holds in messuage by the mill 3 roods. By *Bornebeye* 1 acre. In Messuage late of John Chapman 1 rood. In *Welfelde* 3 roods. The same, below the same place, 1 rood and a half. At *Stocstyle* 1 acre, enclosed. In *Le Dene* 3 roods and a half. Best land. Sum: 5 acres. At *Estwodegate* 1 rood. Poor land. The same holds of the Lady in farm in *Northhawe* 3 roods, enclosed. In *Coppedehalle* 8 dayworks. At *Melstyle* half an acre. In *Belkefelde* 2 acres and in *Hawkynscrofte* 3 acres, for 8 shillings at the 4 principal terms and 2 bushels of barley at the term of St. Michael. Sum: 15d. farthing, except farm.

[99] Nicholas Kat(er)yne[28] holds in messuage with crofte adjacent 1 acre. In *Estbynne*, on the other side of the highway there, 2 acres 3 roods. In *Tayloryshawe* 12 dayworks. The same holds of the Lady in farm, in the southern corner of the same place, a parcel of land for 2 pence at the term of St. Michael. The same holds in *Melfelde* 1 acre and half a rood. The same, between the land of William Kat(er)yne called *Le Helde*, 3 roods and 2 dayworks. Best land. Sum: 5 acres 3 roods 9 dayworks. The same holds in *Wrongereed* 1 acre and a half. In the same place 1 rood. At *Vyelysreed* half an acre. In the same place 1 acre. Poor land. Sum: 21d. halfpenny, except farm.

[100] The heirs of William Kat(er)yne[28] hold in messuage with garden, and in *Bornebeye* 2 acres and a half. In *Smythecrofte*, before their gate, 3 roods. At *Bornebeye*, called *Nethirhelde*, 3 roods. Also, in the same place, on the other side of the runnel, 5 roods. On the upper side of *Cotmanfelde* 5 acres. Best land. [Sum:] 10 acres 1 rood, whence 2s. 6d. halfpenny farthing. The same hold in *Stokkyshalle* 3 acres. At *Eastwodegate* 1 acre, and at *Vyelysreed* 1 acre. Medium land. Sum: 5 acres, whence 10d. The same, next to [space] 1 acre. The same [space] 1 rood and a half.

[From this place in the text to entry No. 112 the manuscript is badly faded, damaged and rubbed. The transcript here was made with difficulty and it is not claimed to be entirely reliable.]

The same, next to *Jacobreed*, called *Sparwegrove*, 3 roods. Poor land. Sum: 3s. 6d. halfpenny farthing and a half.

[101] John Everard holds in messuage and in *Bregcrofte* 1 acre and a half. In *Northfelde* 3 acres and 1 rood. In *Steylefelde* 2 acres and a half. Sum: 7

acres 3 roods. Best land, whence 23d. farthing. The same holds in *Cruchehelle* 4 acres. Medium land. The same holds of the Lady in farm 1 acre in *Steylefelde*. The same, 1 acre and a half in *Longefeld*, in about the middle of the field, for 3s. at the 4 principal terms. The same holds of the Lady in farm 3 acres called *Frostishulle* for 4 shillings at the aforesaid terms. The same holds 2 acres [in] *Swynstycrofte* for 4 shillings at the aforesaid terms. [Space] Sum: 2s. 7d. except farm.

[102]   John Spryngett holds in messuage and in the same place, half an acre. In the same place, in croft alongside the [*lana*.][29] 2 acres and 1 rood. Best land. The same holds of the Lady in farm 5 roods on the northern side of *Hupfeld* for 16d. at the 4 principal terms. Sum: 8d. farthing, except farm.

[103]   Walter Fylle holds in messuage, and within the same place, 5 roods. The same on the other side of the highway, in the same place in a little orchard, half a rood. Best land. The same holds of the Lady in farm a piece of land called *Sowtyscrofte* for 5s. at the 4 principal terms. Sum: 4d. half a farthing, except farm.

[104]   William Pyk. holds in messuage with croft adjacent 5 roods and a half. In a garden with croft next to the messuage of Walter Fylle aforesaid, 5 roods. In *Halefelde* 2 acres and a half. In *Welfelde* 1 rood and a half. Best land. Sum: 5 acres and a half, whence sum 16d. halfpenny.

[105]   The heirs of Nicholas in le Hale hold in messuage with garden 1 acre. [In?] *Heybussoke* 2 acres and a half. In the same place, in *Halefelde*, 4 acres and a half. In the same place, in *Soortelonde*, 1 acre and a half. In the same place, in *Estlonge*, 1 acre and a half. In the same place, in *Le G'nette*, 4 acres. Best land. Sum: 15 acres, whence 3s. 9d. The same hold by *Brochole* half an acre. Poor land. The same hold of the Lady in farm 4 acres at *Crudehale* for 6s. at the 4 principal terms. Sum: 3s. 9d. halfpenny, except farm.

[106]   The heirs of Thomas Perys hold in messuage and garden, on both sides of the water rising there, 5 roods. In the same place, abutting the said water, 1 acre and 3 roods. In the same place, abutting the said water (with?) *Le Hedland* 5 acres. The same abutting (......). Medium land. Sum: 2s. 11d.

[107]   Robert (Eldebel?) for land (.........)
[This is the last entry on the obverse of the roll. Wear and fading have rendered it illegible. The entries at the beginning of the reverse side which follow are barely legible.]

[108]   William Lylye holds in farm (......) before (...) The same (......) on

the east side, lands (...) there, 1 acre and 1 rood (...) in *Elynden* 1 acre (...). Best land. Sum: 9 acres 1 rood, whence 2s. 3d. The same (......) next to (.........). The same in *Suth(b?)enys* otherwise called *Samuelyslond* 6 acres. In *Castelfelde* 5 acres. At *Poteberghe*, on the east side, 5 roods. Medium land. Sum: 36 acres 1 rood, whence 6(s.) (.........) halfpenny. The same holds in *Bromefelde* 2 acres. Poor land, whence 2d. Sum: 8s. 6d. farthing.

[109] John Breggys holds in messuage with croft to the east of the same place, extending towards *E(din)ylane* 3 acres. In *Bradb'eysfelde*, abutting the (runnel) there, 1 acre 3 roods. At *Notetre*, enclosed, 3 acres and 1 rood. In *Toselynys* 3 acres and a half. The same holds of the Lady in farm, in the same place, 1 acre and a half for 3s. 4d. at the 4 principal terms. By *Ca(c)helebregge* [or *Ca(t)helebregge*] 2 acres and a half. In *Le D(e)nys* 5 acres. In meadow at *Lonsforde*, enclosed, 4 acres. In *Cleochecrofte* 5 roods. Best land. Sum: 24 acres 1 rood, whence 6s. halfpenny farthing. The same holds in *Melleryshulle* 5 acres. In *Hobbyscrofte*, abutting *Helleslane*, 2 acres and a half. The same, abutting the King's highway at *Poteberghe*, next to (the land otherwise known as) *Eldyrbel*, 2 acres. In the same place, enclosed, 4 acres. Medium land. Sum: 13 acres and a half, whence 2s. 3d. [Sum total lacking.]

[110] The heirs of Walter Polynteer hold in messuage 1 rood. In *Albynyscrofte* 4 acres and 3 roods. In *Menefelde*, enclosed, 1 acre and a half. In upper *Menefelde* 3 roods. In *None(ma)ysfelde* [*Nonemanysfelde*?] 2 acres and 1 rood. In croft next to (...) at *Le Helle* 1 acre and a half. In *Longfelde* 4 acres and a half and 7 (dayworks?). In *Gulchys*, in the same place, enclosed, 1 acre and a half. In *S.y.crofte* 2 acres. In *Elendene* (meadow) 1 acre and half a rood. Best land. Sum: 20 acres 1 rood, whence 5s. 1d. At *Le Nessche* [or *Nassche*], abutting the King's highway, 2 acres 3 roods and a half. In the same place, on the other (......) in *Fyllehoodon*, 3 acres. In *Bromecrofte*, enclosed, 1 acre and a half. In *Wetefelde* 1 acre. In *Denys*, enclosed, 5 acres. Medium land. Sum: 13 acres 1 rood and a half, whence 2s. 2d. halfpenny farthing. The same hold at *Le Wyche* 3 acres and 3 roods, and in the same place by *C..ryssteyle* (......). Sum: 13 acres 1 rood and a half. Poor land, whence 2s. 2d. halfpenny farthing. Sum: 7s. 9d. halfpenny.

[111] Thomas Claygate holds in his messuage 2 dayworks. In *Froggeshawe* 1 rood and 8 dayworks (......). At *Chaplaynis*, by *Lonsforde*, 3 acres and 1 rood. In *Northcrofte*, with a little garden there, 2 acres. In a messuage, late of John at Helle, with garden and croft there, enclosed, 2 acres and 1 rood. Medium land. Sum: 13d. halfpenny.

[112] John Polayn holds in messuage, and within the same place, half an acre. The same in land called *Larkefelde*, enclosed, 3 acres. In *Bromedyche* 1 acre. In *Elynden* (meadow) 2 acres. Best land. Sum: 6 acres and a half,

whence 9d. halfpenny. The same holds in *Le Bregge* 1 acre and a half. In the same place, half an acre abutting the King's highway. In *Wychottys*, on the eastern side, 1 acre and a half. Medium land. Sum: 3 acres and a half, whence 7d. Sum: 26d.

[From this point the text is reasonably legible.]

[113] William Prover holds in messuage, late of John Pastron, 1 rood. Best land. Sum: Halfpenny farthing.

[114] John Bette holds in messuage, late of Richard Hancon, with croft adjacent, 3 roods. Best land. Sum: 2d. farthing.

[115] Richard Knyght holds in messuage, late of Thomas Tanner, with croft adjacent, 7 acres 1 rood. The same, by *Cachelebregge* 2 acres. In *Mysehoden* 2 acres and a half. In *Stomubylmede*, on the eastern side, 1 acre and 1 rood. Best land. Sum: 13 acres, whence 3s. 3d. Sum: 3s. 3d.

[116] The heirs of John Everard hold in messuage at *Larkefelde* 3 dayworks. In *Froggyshawe* 5 dayworks. Best land. The same, abutting *Hellane*, enclosed, half an acre. Medium land. Sum: 1d. halfpenny half a farthing.

[117] Robert Benayt junior holds in messuage, and within the same place, 1 rood. By *Browndyche* 1 acre 3 roods and a half. Best land. Sum: 6d. farthing and a half.

[118] John Henden holds in his messuage 6 dayworks and a half. Sum: A halfpenny.

[119] John Maryote holds in a corner messuage, with croft adjacent, 3 roods. In *Froggyshawe* half a rood. In *Stonecrofte*, enclosed, 3 acres and 1 rood. In croft next to *Toselynys*, enclosed, half an acre. Best land, 4 acres and half and half a rood, whence 13d. halfpenny farthing. The same holds in an old garden, with croft adjacent, 3 acres 1 rood. In *Westmede*, by *Lonsforde*, 5 acres. Medium land. Sum: 8 acres 1 rood, whence 16d. halfpenny. Sum: 2s. 6d. farthing and a half.

[120] Robert Benaytt holds in messuage with 2 conjoined crofts 4 acres and a half. In *Colardys*, enclosed, 2 acres, 3 roods. In *Stomubylmede* 1 acre and half a rood. In the same place, enclosed, half an acre. At *Le Helle*, next to *Belkefelde* 4 acres and 1 rood. The same holds of the Lady in farm, in the same place, 3 roods for 9d. at the term of St. Michael. The same holds in *Pryckreed* 1 acre and a half. By *Bradborne*, in a messuage late of Joan Hoo, 2 acres. In a little messuage next to the messuage of John Detlyng 1 rood. In

Newelond 1 acre. Best land. Sum: 17 acres 1 rood and a half, whence 4s. 4d. half a farthing. The same holds in 3 parcels called *Le Peche* 8 acres and a half. In *Frenefeld*, on the western side, 2 acres; and in a little croft there 1 acre. At *Lonsforde* in *Watpettyscrofte* 2 acres. In croft next to *Baselyreed* 2 acres and 1 rood. In *Constabelysdene* 1 acre. In the same place, enclosed, called *Cherchecrofte*, 1 acre and a half. Medium land. Sum: 18 acres 1 rood, whence 3s. and a halfpenny. The same holds in *Snorhelle* (or *Suorhelle*) 2 acres and 1 rood. Of the Lady in farm 3 roods for 6d. at the term of St. Michael. Next to *Hodon* 1 acre and a half. At *Estwodegate*, woodland, half an acre. At *Hencotereed* 1 acre. At *Brochole* 1 rood. In *Estfelde*, next to *Dytton*, half an acre. In the same place, 2 acres abutting the land of the parish of *Dytton*. In the same place in *Estfelde* 1 rood. Poor land. Sum: 8 acres 1 rood. Sum: 8d. farthing. Sum: 8s. and a halfpenny a farthing and a half, except farm.

[121] John Hyckeys holds in his messuage and within the same place 1 acre. Best land. Sum: 3d.

[122] William Newman holds in messuage and within the same place 1 acre and a half. Best land. In the same place, abutting the next field, half an acre. Medium land. Sum: 5d. halfpenny.

[123] Joan at Stone holds in messuage next to *Le Stone* 3 roods. Best land, whence 2d. farthing. Next to *Cherchecrofte* 1 acre. In *Hendyiscrofte* 3 roods. By *Le Nasshe* 3 roods and a half. In Little *Menefelde* half an acre and half a rood. In *Nonemanyshale* 5 roods. In *Wetefelde* 1 acre. In *Castelfelde* 1 rood. Medium land. Sum: 5 acres 3 roods. Sum: 9d. halfpenny. In *Le Dene*, abutting *Cherchecrofte*, 5 roods. In *Estfelde* half an acre. Poor land, whence 1d. halfpenny farthing. Sum: 15d. halfpenny.

[124] John Knyght holds in messuage with croft adjacent 1 acre and 3 roods. In *Westfelde*, abutting the King's highway, 2 acres and 3 roods. In a messuage late of William Knyght 1 rood. Best land. Sum: 4 acres 3 roods, whence 14d. farthing. In Little *Swollonde* 2 acres 3 roods. In a messuage before his gate half an acre. In *Swolonde* by *Lonsforde* 6 acres. Medium land. Sum: 9 acres 1 rood. Sum: 2s. 8d. farthing.

[125] John Detlyng senior holds in messuage half an acre. Best land. In *Hendyscrofte* 3 roods. In *Estfelde* 3 roods, and in the same place, between the land of John Suthwyk and John Maystyr [*cf.* entries Nos. 129 and 131 below] 1 rood. In the same place, on the northern side, 2 acres. In *Constabelysdene* 3 roods. Medium land. Sum: 4 acres and a half. Sum: 10d. halfpenny.

[126]   William Detlyng holds in messuage and within the same place 2 acres and a half. The same and John Austyn in *Heghefelde*, late of Sybil Riperose, 1 acre 3 roods. Medium land. The same, 1 rood in *Huettyshawe*. Best land. Sum: 9d. farthing.

[127]   William Knyght holds in messuage with croft adjacent 3 roods. In *Negheneker* 2 acres. In *Constabelysdene* half an acre. In *Estfelde* 3 roods. In a messuage late of Sybil Riperose 1 acre and a half. The same holds of the Lady in farm, in the same place, 1 acre for 4 bushels of barley at the term of St. Michael. The same holds of the Lady in farm, in the same place, 5 dayworks of land abutting the King's highway on the north side of the said messuage, for 4 pence at the term of St. Michael. In *Estfelde*, abutting the land of William Newman, 1 rood. Medium land. Sum: 5 acres 3 roods. Sum: 11d. halfpenny, except farm.

[128]   William Frenshe holds in messuage with croft adjacent 5 acres. Medium land. Sum: 10d.

[129]   John Maystyr holds in messuage and within the same place 1 acre. In *Hammellemede* meadow half an acre and 8 dayworks. In the same place 1 rood. Best land. Sum: 1 acre and 3 roods 8 dayworks, whence 5d. halfpenny a farthing and a half. The same holds in the field below his messuage 6 acres. In *Horsecrofte* 2 acres. In *Negheneker* 2 acres. In the same place 2 acres 1 rood. In a little enclosure [*hagha*] there 1 rood. In *Estfelde* 2 acres 3 roods. In *Swollonde* 2 acres. Medium land. Sum: 17 acres 1 rood, whence 10d. halfpenny. Sum: 3s. 4d. farthing and a half.

[130]   John Ropere holds in messuage with crofte adjacent there, 1 acre and a half. The same, in the adjacent field below *Wyndmellehelle* 1 acre and a half. The same holds of the Lady in farm, in the same place, half an acre for 1 bushel and a half of barley at the term of St. Michael. The same holds in his messuage half an acre. In *Heghefeld*, enclosed, 2 acres. In *Huettyslane* 1 rood. Medium land. Sum: 5 acres 3 roods, whence 11d. halfpenny. The same 1 acre and a half in *Negheneker*. Poor land. Sum: 13(d.), except farm.

[131]   John Sw.hwyk [Suthwyk? *vide* 125 above] holds midst [*inter*] the land of the heirs of Nisholas in the [*sic.*] Hale 1 acre and a half. In *Gonnorfelde* 1 acre. In *Brodewatercrofte* with *gore* and *laghton* there 3 acres. In *Newlond*, abutting *Schepladecrofte* 4 acres. The same, half an acre in the same place. In the same place, extending as far as the eastern hedge, half an acre. In *Bromham* 1 acre and 1 rood. In *Elyden*, enclosed, 5 roods. In *Seneakyr*, the perquisite of Robert Twynde [or Twynge], 4 acres and a half. In the same place, formerly of John ate Lee, 3 roods. Best land. Sum: 18 acres 1 rood, whence 4s. 6d. halfpenny farthing. The same holds in

Pyperyscrofte 1 acre. On the southern side of the same place 1 acre and 3 roods. On the other side of the highway 1 acre. In *Negheneker*, by *Lonsforde*, 3 acres. In the same place, the same holds of the Lady in farm 1 acre for 5d. halfpenny at the term of St. Michael. The same holds in the same place 3 roods. In *Estfelde* 1 rood and a half. In *Constabelysdene* 2 acres. Medium land. Sum: 9 acres 3 roods and a half, whence 19d. halfpenny farthing. Sum: 6s. 2d. halfpenny, except farm.

[132]   John Matter holds in messuage 1 rood. Best land. Sum: Halfpenny farthing.

[133]   John Benayt holds in *Yfelde* in messuage, and within the same place, 4 acres. Medium land. Sum: 8d.

[134]   John Codland holds in messuage 1 rood. In *Gonnorfelde* 3 roods and 3 dayworks. In the same place, beside the King's highway, 1 rood. In another messuage 5 dayworks. In *Bromham* 1 acre and a half. In *Newlond* 1 acre. Best land. [Interlineation: (*q. sup. Robtus. Benayt vt. p. sutea.*).] Sum: 2 acres 3 roods 8 dayworks. Sum: 8d. halfpenny and three quarters of a farthing.

[135]   Richard Fuller, next to (...) messuage of John Codland, 5 dayworks. Best land. Sum: A farthing and a half.

[136]   Thomas Halle holds in messuage where Henry Olyver lives, 1 rood. In the same place, in *Gonnorefeld*, 1 acre. In the same place, 2 acres and a half which Robert Edword(s) holds in farm. In the same place, alongside *Newlond* 3 roods. In the same field 2 acres and a half which John Ropere holds in farm. The same holds in the middle of *Newlond* 1 acre 3 roods. In *Ryssette*, enclosed, 1 acre and a half. Next to *Colmanislese*, meadow, 2 acres and a half, formerly Robert Drake, enclosed. In *Lyttele Elynden*, enclosed, 1 acre and a half [which?] John Blythehayt holds in farm. In *Hormogeryscrofte*, next to the messuage of Riperose, 1 acre. Best land. Sum: 15 acres 1 rood, whence 3s. 9d. halfpenny farthing. On *Wyndmellehelle*, next to the Field of *Lonsford* 3 acres. In *Colmanyslese*, with meadow there, 7 acres. In *Chylderynwode* half an acre. In *Northwode* 1 rood. In *Bromham* half an acre. Medium land. Sum: 11 acres 1 rood, whence 22d. halfpenny. Sum: 5s. 8d. farthing.

[137]   John Harberegge holds in *Gonnorefeld* 2 acres and a half. Best land. On *Wyndmellehelle* 3 acres. In *Northwood* [sic.], woodlands, 2 acres. Medium land. Sum: 17d. halfpenny.

[138]   John Smythe of New Hythe [*Nova Ripa*] holds half an acre in

57

Elyndene. In *Goldislese* 11 acres. Best land, whence 2s. 10d. halfpenny. In *Constabelysdene* 5 roods. In the same place, abutting the land of William Newman, half an acre. Poor land, whence 1d. halfpenny farthing. Sum: 3s. 0d. farthing.

[139] Daniell atte Broke (...) heirs hold in messuage next to *Gonnorfelde* 3 dayworks. In the same field 2 acres and a half. In *Bromhame* half an acre. Best land. In *Steylefelde* 3 roods. Medium land. Sum: 10d. halfpenny farthing.

[140] Geoffrey Westman holds in *Elynden* half an acre. In the same place, 1 acre formerly William Mymys. The same holds in *Cattyscrofte* 2 acres. Best land. Sum: 3 acres and a half, whence 10d. halfpenny. The same holds in *Herefeld* 4 acres. Medium land, whence 8d. Sum: 18d. halfpenny.

[141] The heir of Thomas Hosmonge(r) holds in *Newlond* 1 acre and 1 rood. In *Bromham* 3 acres. Best land. The same holds in *Plesotecrofte* 3 roods and a half. In *Heghefelde*, on the other side of the highway, 5 roods. In *Preestyscrofte*, next to *Elyndene*, 1 rood. Medium land. The same holds, in the same place, half an acre. Poor land. Sum: 18d.

[142] The heir of Thomas Kough holds half an acre in *Gonnorfelde*. Sum: 1d. halfpenny.

[143] Robert Drake holds on *Wyndmellehell.* half an acre. Medium land. Sum: 1d.

[144] Adam Palmer holds by *Wyndmellehulle* 3 acres. Medium land. Sum: 6d.

[145] The Lord of Dytton holds in *Elynden* 2 acres, meadow. Best land. In *Badenautys* [or *Badeuantys* etc.] 5 acres. Medium land. At *Taylys*, woodlands, 2 acres and a half. Poor land. Sum: 18d. halfpenny.

[146] Richard Hamon(d) holds in the messuage where he lives 1 rood. In the same place, on the other side of the way, 1 rood. In the same place, by the water bridge, [*iux. pntem. aquaticu.*], enclosed, 1 acre. In messuage by *Morcokkys* half an acre. In the garden of Goldherst 1 rood. The same, adjacent there in *Suthfelde*, 1 rood. The same holds of the Lady in farm in the same place, 1 rood for 6d. at the term of St. Michael. Next to the land of John Rasyll there, on the northern side of the same field, 3 roods. In the same place 3 roods. In the same place 1 rood. The same, 8 dayworks there called *Le Skache*. The same holds next to the messuage of John Bette at *Larkefelde* 1 rood. Best land. Sum: 4 acres 3 roods 8 dayworks, whence

14d. halfpenny a farthing and a half. The same holds in *Clapfelde*, on the southern side, 1 acre 3 roods. In *Le Broke* half an acre. By *Hoodon*, enclosed, 3 acres. In [the?] *Broka*, next to *Suthfelde*, half an acre. Medium land. Sum: 4 acres 3 roods, whence 9d. halfpenny farthing. Sum: 2s. 0d. farthing and a half, except farm.

[147] Henry Mabbe holds in messuage with a parcel of land in the adjacent field 5 roods. Best land. Sum: 3d. halfpenny farthing.

[148] The heirs of John Swayn hold in messuage by *Le Nassche* [interlineation: *alio*] 1 rood. In *Le Gor* in *Estfelde* half an acre. The same, a meadow at *Parrocke*, enclosed, half an acre. In messuage at *Morcokkys*, in 2 parcels, 6 dayworks. In the same place, adjacent to the southern hedge, 1 rood. And the Lady holds there half an acre for valuation *post mortem* William Cothorn. The same Lady holds there in a little garden between the messuage garden and the garden of the said heirs, for the same valuation, 1 daywork and a half where (a little?) (*n...*) stands. The same Lady holds in the same place 5 dayworks of land next to the messuage of the aforesaid Henry Mabbe, called *Boonfasishawe*. Sum: best land 1 acre and a half 3 dayworks, whence 5d. The same, by a messuage in *Suthfelde* 1 acre. In *Clerkys Hawe*, in the same place, 5 roods. In *Le Broke* half an acre. In *Pyrlond* half an acre. In *Estfelde*, abutting *Clerkyshawe* aforesaid, half an acre. Medium land. Sum: 3 acres and 3 roods, whence 7d. halfpenny. Sum: 12d. halfpenny, except farm.

[149] The heir of William Smythe holds in messuage and within the same place 2 acres and half a rood. Best land. In *Estfelde* 1 acre. Medium land. Sum: 8d. farthing and a half.

[150] The heirs of Ralph de la Hay hold in messuage, with a water-meadow [or brook][30] there, 1 acre. In *Risschette*, meadow, 3 roods. In croft next to the messuage of the said Henry Mabbe, enclosed, half an acre. On the other side of the lane there, 1 acre and a half. Best land. Sum: 3 acres and 3 roods, whence 11d. farthing. The same in a messuage (*vsto.*—lying waste?) half an acre. In croft, by *Lonsford* 3 roods, enclosed. In an adjacent croft in the same place, 1 acre 3 roods. Medium land. Sum: 17d. farthing.

[151] Stephen Richenyle holds in messuage with garden half an acre. The same, adjacent in *Estfelde*, half an acre. In *Le Brocpece* half [*sic*.] 6 dayworks and 2 parts of 1 daywork. In *Le Gore* 3 roods, and in the same place half an acre. In the same place 1 rood 3 dayworks and a 3rd part of 1 daywork of [*de*] *Rownde Akyr*. In *Welfelde* 1 acre 3 roods and a half. In *Eldecrofte*, with an adjacent parcel, 3 roods, meadow. Best land. Sum: 5 acres 3 roods and a half, whence 17d. halfpenny half a farthing. At *Estlond*,

59

abutting the land of the Lady, 3 roods. In *Perylond* 3 roods, and abutting the same place, half an acre. Medium land. Sum: 2 acres, whence 4d. In *Estfelde*, in 2 parcels, 3 roods. In *Caldecotecrofte* 2 acres. Poor land, whence 2d. halfpenny farthing. The same holds in farm by *Lonforde* [*sic.*], enclosed, 3 acres of the lands of the Lady Abbess for 3s. at the 4 principal terms. Sum: 2s. a farthing and a half, except farm.

[152]   Joan Goosseye holds in messuage and garden 1 rood and a half. In the same place, in a field called *Blachildecrofte* 1 acre. In the same place 3 roods. In *Welfelde*, on the eastern side, 1 acre and 3 roods. In the same place 5 roods 3 dayworks and the third part of 1 daywork. In *Rysschette*, with a little water-meadow [or brook][31] there, 1 acre. On the north side of her messuage, called *Meedcroftys*, 2 acres. In *Brocpece* 1 rood 3 dayworks and one third part of 1 daywork. The same holds in *Estfelde*, called *Marchountislond*, alongside the highway, 1 acre and a half. In *Le Gore* 1 acre. At *Suthbynne* 1 rood and a half. Best land. Sum: 11 acres 1 rood 6 dayworks 2 parts of 1 daywork. The same holds in *Pyrylond* half an acre. At *Rowndeaker* 1 acre and a half and 6 dayworks and 2 parts of one daywork. In *Lucylond* 1 acre and a half. In messuage in the same place 5 roods. Next to *Morcokkys*, enclosed, 2 acres. Medium land. Sum: 6 acres 3 roods 6 dayworks 2 parts of 1 daywork. In *Estlonde* 1 rood 3 dayworks and a 3rd part of 1 daywork. In the same place, next to *Caldecote*, 3 roods. Poor land. Sum: 4s. 1d. farthing.

[153]   Joan Hende holds in messuage half an acre. In a meadow with a little orchard, on the other side of the highway, 3 roods. In *Brocpece*, next to *Wetefelde*, 1 acre. In the same place, with a little garden, 3 roods and in the same place 1 rood. In *Welfelde* 2 acres. Best land. Sum: 5 acres 1 rood. In *Buttislonde* 1 acre. At *Rowndeaker* 1 acre. In *Perylond* half an acre. In *Estlonde* 3 roods. In the same place half an acre. Next to the messuage of the heirs of Ralph de la Hay 1 acre. Medium land. Sum: 4 acres 3 roods. Sum: 2s. 1d. farthing.

[154]   Stephen Hende holds in messuage [and] garden, with a little orchard adjacent, 1 acre. In *Estfelde* half an acre and 7 dayworks. The same, a meadow at *Rysschette* half an acre. In *Blachildecrofte* 1 acre and 3 roods. In *Hammellemede* and [*sic.*] 8 dayworks. Best land. Sum: 4 acres 1 rood and a half. In *Pyrylond* half an acre. At *Rowndeakyr* 1 acre. At *Herlond*, enclosed, 2 acres. Medium land. Sum: 3 acres and a half. The same holds next to *Rowndeaker* half an acre. By *Caldecote* 3 roods. In *Bromfelde*, alongside the highway, 1 acre and a half. In the same place, in the middle of the field, 3 roods. Poor land. Sum: 3 acres and a half. Sum: 23d. halfpenny half a farthing.

[155] Thomas Chapman holds in messuage and garden half an acre. In *Brocpece* half an acre. In *Stombylmede* 1 rood. In *Hammellemede* half an acre and half a rood. 1 rood in the same place. The same holds in *Elyndene* with his (*pre.*—meadow?) half an acre and half a rood. Best land. Sum: 2 acres 3 roods. The same holds in *Estlonde* 3 roods. Medium land. The same holds of the Lady in farm 1 rood in *Blachildecrofte* 1 acre in *Churchecrofte*. In *Northbynne* 4 acres, enclosed, whence at the term of St. Michael (three) bushels of palm barley. The same holds 1 acre in *Hammellemede*, best land, lately Nicholas Stevens. Sum: 12d. halfpenny farthing, except farm.

[156] William Sclynere [or Sclyuere] holds in *Suthfelde*, next to the land of the heirs of John Swayn, half an acre. In *Ympton* 3 roods, and he holds of the Lady in farm there 1 rood for 6d. at the term of St. Michael. The same holds next to the garden of Goldherst [*de Goldherst*] 1 rood and 3 dayworks. Best land. In *Chaplaynys* half an acre and half a rood. Medium land. Sum: 6d., except farm.

[157] John Rasyll holds in *Suthfelde*, at *Lonsforde*,[32] next to *Le Sokache*, 1 acre. In the same place half an acre. Next to the land of William Sclynere [or Sclyuere], in the same place, 3 roods. In the same place, next to the messuage of Richard Hamon, which is of [*de*] John Loder, 2 acres. In *Estfelde*, by *Le Goore*, 3 roods. In *Meneherne* 1 rood, enclosed, meadow. In *Bromham*, enclosed, 2 acres. In *Prettyscrofte* 1 acre. Next to *Bromham* 5 roods. In *Gonnorfelde*, alongside the land of John Codlond, 3 roods and 3 dayworks. In the same place half an acre and half a rood. Best land. Sum: 10 acres 3 roods 8 dayworks. The same holds in *Nelyscrofte* 3 roods. Medium land. In *Estfelde*, by *Chaldecote*, 1 acre. Poor land. Sum: 2s. 11d. farthing and a half.

[158] Robert Swayn holds in messuage next to *Forstall*, with croft adjacent, 5 roods. In *Phylpottyshawe* 1 rood, garden. In *P'rokmede* 1 acre, enclosed. In *Le Gore* half an acre. Best land. Sum: 3 acres. In *Northbynne*, next to *Cherchwaye*, half an acre. In the same place, 1 acre called *Buttysaker*. In *Perylonde* half an acre. In *Chaplaynys* half an acre and half a rood. In *Clep'felde* 3 acres 1 rood. Medium land. [Sum:] 5 acres 3 roods and a half. On the upper side of *Estfelde* 3 roods. Poor land. Sum: 21d. halfpenny.

[159] Sir John Oldcastell,[33] knight, holds in *Hammellemede*, called *Le Watlel*, 2 acres. The same, by the walls there, half an acre, and in the same place 1 rood. The same, 1 acre called *Longakyr*. In the same place, abutting *Frythbrooke*, half an acre. In the same place, in *Le Swer*, 2 acres, and the same, half an acre the perquisite of Nicholas Terry. The same, 1 acre and a half the perquisite of William Mynys, abutting the walls.[34] Half an acre

alongside the same place and belonging to the Lord Bishop of Rochester. In the same place 3 roods, the perquisite of the said William. Best land, 9 acres and a half. Sum: 2s. 4d. halfpenny.

[160] The Master of the College of Cobham holds in the same place 1 acre called *Bakerysakyr*. Best land. Sum: 3d.

[161] The Lord of Pedelesworth, namely Robert Clyfforde, holds 1 acre in *Cobbemede*. In *Hammellemede*, abutting *Frythe Broke*, 5 roods. In the same place 1 rood. Best land. Sum: 7d. halfpenny.

[162] The Lord of Leyborne, namely the Abbot of Towrhull, holds in *Cobmede* 5 acres. In *Erlyslese* 3 roods. Best land. Sum: 17d. farthing.

[163] The heirs of William Snethe hold in *Bromfelde*, late of John Cote, 2 acres and a half. Poor land. Sum: 2d. halfpenny.

[164] William Marchountt holds in *Hammelle*, abutting *Reynoldyscroftys*, 1 acre and a half. Best land. Sum: 1d. half a farthing.

[165] Robert Hende of Beerlyng holds in the same place 1 rood and a half. Best land. Sum: 1d. half a farthing.

[166] The heirs of Thomas Roote, namely John Rolfe, John Brown, by right of their wives, and Agnes late wife of John Large, hold equally 1 acre and a half abutting *Frythbroke*. The same, in 2 conjoined parcels of (meadow) called *Rotyselyndenne*, next to *Blakebroke*, 4 acres. Best land. Sum: 16d. halfpenny.

[167] William Bedyll holds in *Hammellemede*, next to *Frythbroke*, 3 roods. Best land. Sum: 2d. farthing.

[168] Robert Rowe holds of the Lord of Ponyg. in farm one acre called *Acre de Petynton*. Best land. Sum: 3d.

[169] John Dawe holds by right of his wife, the daughter of John Thomelyn, 1 rood and a half in a garden next to *Forestalle*. Best land. Sum: 1d. half a farthing. The tenants or occupants of the same place of *Forstall*, term of St. Michael, 2d. Sum: obvious.

[170] Tenement Robert at Hend. The water course as far as the land of the Lady Abbess of Westmallyng at *Stomubylmede*, at the term of the Nativity of the Blessed Virgin Mary, annual farm as the custom has been time out of mind, pays at the said term 2s. 4d. Sum: obvious.

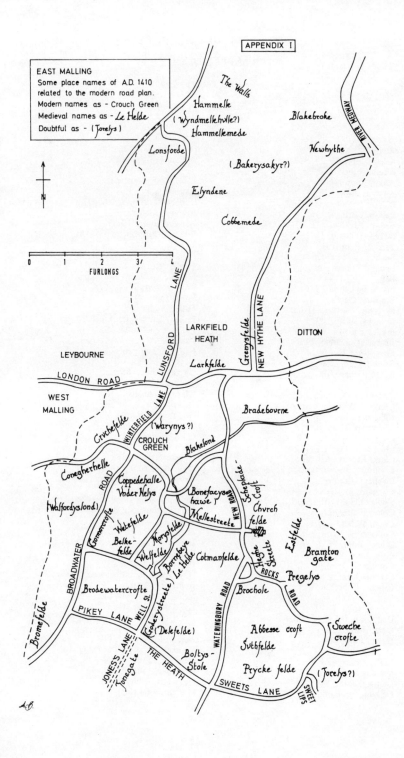

APPENDIX I

EAST MALLING
Some place names of A.D. 1410
related to the modern road plan.
Modern names as - Crouch Green
Medieval names as - *Le Helde*
Doubtful as - (*Jorelys*)

APPENDIX II

INDEX OF PERSONS

Adams(s), Alice, 40
Adeth, John, 19
Adeth, Roger, 18
Allyn, Nicholas, 48
Austyn, John, 126

Balton, Christine, 83
Bedyll, Alexander, 1, 92
Bedyll, William, 167
Benayt, John, 133
Benaytt, Robert, sen. 120, 134
Benayt, Robert, jun. 117
Bette, John, 114, 146
Blythehayt, John, 136
Brapson, Geoffrey, 29
Brapson, Thomas, 31, 80
Breggys, John, 109
Breggys, Roger, 65
Broke, Daniell ate. 139
Brow (sic.), Henry, 9
Brown, John, 166
Byyn, Richard, 68

Cateworth, Richard, heir of, 10
Chalner, William, heirs of, 43
Chapman, John, 98
Chapman, Thomas, 155
Cheyne, William, 3, 69
Claygate, Thomas, 111
Clerk, Robert, heir of, 57
Clyfforde, Robert, Lord of Pedelesworth, 161
Cobham, Lord of, 77, 78
Cobham, Master of the College of, 160
Codland, John, 134, 135, 157
Colte, Walter, 2
Cood, William, 33
Cothorn, William, 148
Corbe, John, 71
Cote, John, 163
Cowherde, John, 8
Cruche, John, ate, 77
Cruche, Robert at (sic.), 78

Danck, John, 2
Dank, sen. (no first name) 1
Dank, John, jun. 12
Dawe, John, 169
Deen, Robert, 46
Derby, John, 45
Detlyng, John, sen. 125
Detlyng, John, 86, 120
Detlyng, William, 126

Drake, Robert, 136, 143
Dytton, Lord of, 145

Edword(s), Robert, 136
Elde, William, 35
(Eldebel?), Robert, 107
Elwyne, Richard, 17
Everard, John, 101
Everard, John, heirs of, 116

Fille, Nicholas, (cf. Fylle), 22
Forde, Joan ate, heirs of, 37
Frenshe, William, 128
Fris., Robert, 77
Frost, John, 84
Fuller, Richard, 135
Fylle, Nicholas, (cf. Fille), 16
Fylle, Walter, 103, 104
Fythyan, Agnes, 53
Fythyan/Fythyon, Roger, 11, 55

Garvays, Joan, 85
Gervays, Joan, heir(s) of, 79
Glaswreghte, Joan, 62
Glaswreghte, John, 98
Goodbergh, Henry, 58
Goodborgh, William, 59
Goos, Henry, 74
Goos, John, 67
Goosseye, Joan, 152
Gryg, Robert, (cf. Gryggs), 97
Gryggs, Robert, (cf. Gryg), 52

Hale, Nicholas in le, heirs of, 105
Hale, Nicholas, in the (sic.), heirs of, 131
Halle, Thomas, 136
Hamkyn, Daniel, 76, 77, 78
Hamond/Hamon, Richard, 146, 157
Hancon, Richard, 114
Harberegge, John, 137
Hay, Ralph de la, heirs of, 150, 153
Heeckstapele, John, 70
Helere, Martin, 60, 61
Helle, John ate, 44, 111
Helle, Nicholas ate, heirs of, 60
Hende, Joan, 153
Hende, Robert (at), 170
Hend(e), Robert of Beerlyng, 165
Hendon, John, 118
Heyward, John, 15
Heyward, William, 52
Hoe, John de, 71

Hoo, Joan, 120
Hore, John, 3
Hosmonge(r), Thomas, heir of 141
Hoyton, Richard, 38
Hyckeys, John, 121

Kat(er)yne, Alan, 41
Kat(er)yne, Nicholas, 99
Kat(er)yne, William, 99
Kat(er)yne, William, heirs of, 100
Kayle, Thomas, 7, 8
Knyght, John, 124
Knyght, Richard, 115
Knyght, William, 124, 127
Kook, Nicholas, heirs of, 64
Kough, Thomas, heir of, 142

Large, Agnes, 166
Large John, 166
Lee, John ate, 131
Leyborne, The Lord of, 162
Loder, Gregory, 89
Loder, John, 87, 97, 157
Loder, John, jun. 75
Loder, John, son of William, 52
Loder, William, 91
Lodere, Benedicta, 88
Lorkyn, Henry, 96
Longe, John, heirs of, 51
Lyle, William, 5
Lylye, William, 108
Lynche, William, 11

Mabbe, Henry, 147, 148, 150
Man, Daniel, 23
Marchountt, William, 164
Maryote, John, 119
Matter, John, 132
Maystyr, John, 125, 129
Melle, Nicholas ate, 82
Melle, Thomas ate, 50
Menewar, William, 63
Mymys, William, 80, 140
Mynys, William, 159

Nassche, Simon ate, 22
Newman, William, 122, 127, 138

Oldcastell, Sir John, 159
Olyver, Henry, 136
Owynham, John, 72

Paddelisworth/Padlesworth, The Lord of, 77, 78, 161
Palmer, Adam, 144
Paidman, Joan, 54
Palmer, Adam, 144
Parker, John, 16
Parys, John, 4
Pastron, John, 113

Pedelesworth, see Paddelisworth
Perys, Thomas, 106
Polayn, John, 112
Polynteer, Walter, heirs of, 110
Ponyng, Lord of, 168
Prover, William, 113
Pyk, William, 104
Pympe, Roger, 60

Rang, William, heirs of, 14
Range (no first name) heirs of 48
Rasyll, John, 146, 157
Reve, Thomas, 49
Reygate, Thomas, 39
Richenyle, Stephen, 151
Riperose, Sibil, 126, 127
Rocher, John, of Aylysforde, 27
Rochester, Bishop of, 159
Rolfe, John, 166
Rokysle, John, 69
Ronge (or Rouge) (corr. Rang?) 5
Roote, Thomas, heirs of, 166
Ropere, John, 130, 136
Rowe, Robert, 168
Ruffyn, John, 21
Ruton, Isabel, Abbess, Intro

Salmon, John, 30
Scharnale, Richard, 25
Scharnale, Rosa, 24
Scharnale, William, 25
Sclynere (or Sclyuere), William, 156, 157
Sextayn, Robert, 66
Sextayn, Thomas, 47
Smyth, John, of New Hythe, 23, 138
Smyth, William, heir of, 149
Smythe, Agnes, 13
Smythe, John, 67
Snethe, William, heirs of, 163
Solman, Constance, 20
Spryngett, John, 102
Stefene, Nicholas, jun. 73
Stephene, John, 95
Stephene, Peter, 93
Stevens, Nicholas, 80, 155
Stone, Joan at, 123
Stonhard, Joan, 42
Stretende, John, 90
Suthwick, John, 25, 125
Swayn, John, heirs of, 148, 156
Swayn, Robert, 158
Sw. hwyk (Suthwyk?) John, 131

Tanner, Thomas, 115
Taylour, John, 26
Terry, Nicholas, 4, 32, 159
Thomelyn, John, 169
Tornor, John, 81
Towrhull, Abbot of, 162
Twynde (or Twynge), Robert, 131

Vicar of East Malling, 25

Webbe, William, heirs of, 34
Westman, Geoffrey, 140
Wolford, Thomas, 6

Yonge, William, heirs of, 28

Zarnaway, John, 94

(Surname lacking), John, 56

APPENDIX III

INDEX OF PLACE-NAMES

'Comonfeilde *als.* Wheatfeild' 1649;
    Common Field 1839.
Wodeprestislonde, 51
Woderede, 31
Wolnenelond, 49
Wronge, Le, (*cf.* Estfelde de Wronge), 11, 24, 26
Wrongereed, 22, 99
Wyche, Le, 110
Wychottys, (*cf.* Wythottys), 112

Wyndmellehelle, Wyndmellehulle, 130, 136, 137, 143, 144
    (Winmon Hill 1787?).
Wynterswell, 77, 78
Wynys, 24, 28
Wythottys, (*cf.* Wychottys), 63

Yfelde, 133
Ympton, 156
Ynyhesele, Ynyhesyl, 47, 48

APPENDIX IV

NOTES ON SOME OF THE PLACE-NAMES

The origins of most of the place-names which occur in the Rental are given, or can be readily traced, in such standard works of reference as The English Place-Name Society (ed. A. H. Smith): *English Place-Name Elements*, Cambridge, 1970, or E. Ekwall: *Oxford Dictionary of English Place-Names*, Oxford, 1936–66. Among the possibly more obscure are some which topography or local records help to explain. A few others are of particular interest in the local context. Notes on some of these place-names, with suggestions of their derivations, are given below. In the absence of earlier spellings (which in many instances may well never have existed) some of the derivations are necessarily speculative.

Belkefelde, Belkehaw: The first element may derive from O.E. *belucan*—"to enclose", which would give "enclosed field", "enclosed haugh". The location suggests that *Belkefelde* may originally have been part of the open field *Wetefelde*, from which it was separated and enclosed.

Blakebroke: The Black Brooks of later years (e.g. an estate map of 1706) were meadows in the north of the parish in the well-watered land by the Medway. *Broke* or *brook* is evidently used here in the Kentish sense "water meadow", rather than with the more general meaning "small stream".

Bornebeye: "Bay" is a "pond-head, or a pond, formed by a dam, for the purpose of driving mill-wheels" (Ogilvie's Dictionary, London, 1864). Immediately above the remains of what is still known as "Old Upper Mill" near Mill Street, the stream that rises in Well Street is widened to form something like a mill-pond. Adjacent field names in the Rental (*Mellefelde, Le Helde, Nethirhelde*) are consistent with the identification of this widened

71

stretch of the stream as the *Bornebeye*, and in entry No. 98 *Bornebeye* and a reference to "the mill" occur in juxtaposition.

Bradeborne: "Broad stream". The present Bradbourne House, which can be traced only to Tudor times and was rebuilt in the early eighteenth century, stands on the stream mentioned above. This stream is indeed broad in many places, but no direct reference to it as the Bradbourn has been found— unless this is one.

Brochole: This seems to be "Gilletts Hole", primly renamed "Gilletts Lane" during the past decade. It is a hollow, and a stream rises there. In this instance, O.E., M.E., *broc*—"brook" appears to be used in the sense "small stream", though O.E. *broc*—"badger" cannot be ignored. (The Gillet family lived nearby in Tudor and Stuart times. Their home, the present Ivy House Farm, was known as "Gillets" in 1693, "Gilletts" in 1694.)[35]

Brodewaterecrofte: Wallenberg's earliest reference is "de ·Bradwat.— 1240".[36] The name survives in Broadwater Farm and Broadwater Road. Today there is only a small, spring-fed pond nearby in what was known as Waterdown Bottom in the seventeenth century. There is charter evidence of a spring here in the tenth century.[37]

Caldecote, Chaldecote: The alternative spelling suggests an interesting persistence of O.E. *ceald*, the palatilised Kentish and West Saxon form which gave way to the Anglian *cald* to become the modern English "cold", (*vide* E.P.N.S. XXV, 77).

Castelfelde: No castle, or site of a castle, is known in East Malling and, unfortunately, the location of this field remains untraced. Three possible candidates are: Pine Toll (*Conegherhelle?*) upon which there are traces of what may have been earthworks; the site of the earlier Bradbourne House which, in Tudor times, is said to have been a moated house; and "Rats Castle", the Kentish "mocking name" for the land in the angle between Wateringbury Road and Sweets Lane. It was of somewhere in this locality that Ireland wrote: "The ground then rises up to East Malling heath, on the entrance to which is the appearance of a Roman tumulous."[38]

Clapfelde: Possibly derived from M.E. "clapper", dialect for a rough bridge or stream crossing. (E.P.N.S.). Unlocated.

Conegherhelle, Conegher Crofte: There is a reference in 1627 to the "causeway between West Malling and Conigar Hill",[39] which leaves little doubt that this is the hillock now known as Pine Toll, by Crouch Green. M.E. *coningere*—"rabbit burrow or warren" would seem to fit, but so perhaps would Latin *coniger*—"bearing fruit of a conical form". The hillock is surmounted by conifers.

Coppedehalle: An example of a snare for the unwary, and an interesting evolution of a place-name. Having become "Copthall" by the seventeenth century, when the surviving house was built, it has been known as "Cobbs Hall" since at least the early nineteenth century. Cobb was, in fact, a local family name, and there was a "Cobbs Acre" at the other, northern end of the parish, in 1681–2; but the Cobb family had nothing to do with Cobbs Hall, at least, as far as is known. Under O.E. *copp*—"top, summit", Ekwall cites: "Copped Hall, Ess. La Coppedehall 1272 Ch." with the meaning "hall with a high roof". "High", when applied to a roof can only mean "steep". Surviving medieval houses in East Malling show that steeply pitched roofs were not unusual, and were probably commonplace, in the locality in the Middle Ages. It seems more likely, then, that in this instance the adjective *"coppede"* is used in the M.E. sense "having a crest". The hipped roof typical of the district had gablets which are believed to have had the function of providing an outlet for the smoke from the central hearth in the open hall. It is suggested that the medieval Cobbs Hall may have had a louvred vent on the ridge of the roof, more characteristic of other regions. Such a roof may have been sufficiently unusual in mid-Kent to have prompted the epithet *"coppede"*, giving "crested hall" as the origin of the name Cobbs Hall.

Cornerdyscrofte: No doubt named after an earlier tenant. The Kent Lay Subsidy of 1334–5 has Robert, Walter and Simon Cornerde in the Vill of Mallyng (West Malling). Great Cornard and Little Cornard are villages in Suffolk and it is a reasonable assumption that the Malling Cornerdes were so named because they came from one of the Suffolk parishes. The Abbess and nuns of West Malling held the manor of Cornard in Suffolk, and the *Inspeximus* of 21 Edward III records that it was the gift of Robert son of Haimon confirmed in 1106 by King Henry I.[40]

Cotmanfelde: The form of this field-name appears to exclude the possibility that it derives from a personal name; such field-names occurring in the Rental invariably have the first element with the genitive ending *-ys* or *-is*. Furthermore, *Cotmanfelde* was considerably larger than any field named after a tenant, and in 1653 it was referred to as "Comon Feild *als*. Cotman Feild".[41] R. Welldon Finn has observed: "Cottars and bordars suggest those who dwell, not in the villages, but in cottages some little distance away."[42] *Domesday Book* records 12 bordars in East Malling. *Cotmanfelde* lay south of Mill Street and west of the High Street, just outside the original village nucleus. It may be, then, that it was here that the bordars, or *cotmanni*, had their cottages and small-holdings.

Cruchecroft, Cruchefelde: "Crouchfield" is mentioned in an estate survey of 1787,[43] and it is shown on the map of the Tithe Awards of 1839 as lying north-west of the road junction at Crouch Green, near the border with West Malling. It is a likely place for a roadside cross (M.E. *crouche, cruche* etc.—"cross"). It might be left at that, but for the fact that also adjoining Crouch Green, but to the south-west, is the small hill (vide *Conegherhelle*) surmounted by what may be earthworks. It may be improbable, but the alternative cannot be ignored that this name possibly derives from British *cruc*—"heap, barrow, hill, esp. a round hill". (Ekwall, E.P.N.S.)

Cryckele: Possibly cognate with Crichel, Dorset, and the first two elements of Cricklewood, Middlesex, for both of which Ekwall suggests Brit. *cruc*—"hill" with "explanatory" O.E. "hyll". Ekwall gives Brit. *cruc* for all places mentioned with first elements "Crich-", "Crick-", "Cruch-" and "Cruck-". (It is not difficult to imagine how a Saxon settler came to adopt such a tautological name by mistaking a British common noun for a proper name. The best known example is, of course, River Avon. Perhaps the story of the African place-name which translates: "You'll have to ask the chief" is not, after all, apocryphal.) The corruption of M.E. *Le Beer* (*q.v.*) into "Beeres Wood" shows the process at work through the forgetting of an old word (O.E. *bearu*—"grove, copse, wood" etc.)

Elyndene: This meadow-land lay towards the northern boundary of the manor. O.E. *ellende* was "foreign, strange, exiled". Bearing in mind that people dwelling just over the West Malling borders were "foreigners" in eighteenth century East Malling rate books, it is perhaps not too fanciful to suggest *ellende-denu*. (Clark Hall gives *denu*—"plain, valley". The first meaning is not given by Ekwall or E.P.N.S.)

Estyrlane: Today Easterfields is a lane leading to the boundary of the parish in the south-east. The location and etymology are against a geographical ("east") derivation. It would be gratifying to be able to claim it as the sole English place-name commemorating the Saxon Spring goddess *Eostre*. The most likely origin, however, is from O.E. *eowestre*—"sheep fold" (*cf.* Ekwall on High Easter, Essex.)

Falke Hawe: Possibly from M.E. *falghe*—"fallow", from O.E. *fealg, fealh, felh*—"ploughed land".

Ferthyng, Le: See Introduction, above.

Gore, Le: Goore, Le: "Gore" appears to be used with both its meanings. The occurrence in entry No. 131, it will be seen, is: "In *Brodewaterecrofte* with gore and *laghton* there 3 acres." In this instance it appears to be not a proper name, but merely descriptive; and its association with "*Brodewaterecrofte*" and "*laghton*" (from M.E. *laghe*—"pool"?) suggests that it is used in the sense "muddy land", from O.E. *gor*—"dung, filth, dirt" (*cf.* Kensington Gore, the old muddy, western approach to London). There is some evidence that in this vicinity there was a contracting pool.[44] In other entries, "gore" probably has its more usual meaning "triangular piece of land", from O.E. *gara*—"corner, cape" etc., as for example Nos. 151 and 157.[45]

Helde, Le; Nethirhelde: *Helde* is O.E. "slope, declivity" (E.P.N.S.). Between Old Upper Mill, just south of Mill Street, and the spring-head near Well Street, the land slopes down sharply to the stream and the *Bornebey* (*q.v.*).

Hupfelde, Huphawe, Huphelde, Huppyr Reed: "*H* is not a letter", said Hengham, Chief Justice of the Common Pleas, 1304.[46]

Lovelockyscrofte: This romantic field-name derives, alas, only from the name of a past tenant, for the Kent Lay Subsidy of 1334–5 shows Ellis Lovelok' under Rochester.

Mellestrete: It is perhaps worth remarking of this self-evident name that all its known mills were water-mills. The remains of Old Upper (Paper) Mill are a hundred yards or so to the south; Weir Mill, now derelict, though the buildings and mill-wheel are intact, where the stream crosses under the modern Mill Street; and Middle Mill where Mill Street merges into Clare Lane.[47]

Menefelde, Meneherne: E.P.N.S. gives *mesne*—"demesne land." *Maene* was M.E. "mean, common", but both fields are too small ever to have been common fields. M.E. *mene*—"middle" seems the most likely derivation, though "demesne" cannot be ruled out.

Moorcokkys: Moor-cock today is another name for red grouse. It is suggested that in medieval East Malling it was another name for moor-hen, a water bird still plentiful along its streams. But Morecock occurs locally as a family name in 1658.

Northebynne, Suthbynne: O.E. *byn*—"cultivated, inhabited".

Parrocke: Ekwall, under "Paddock Wood" gives "*pearroc*—M.E. paddock, enclosure", and Stratmann gives "*parroken*—M.E. impark, enclose, shut in." Somner, however, under "Swine-gavel" says that, in the Weald, a Paroc was "a Court-like kind of meeting" between lord, or his bailiff, and tenants where accounts were settled for swine-pannage, and he suggested that this was the derivation of the name "Paddock" by Blean Wood, near Canterbury.

Rock Reed, Rokysreed etc.: Rocks Road, with "The Rocks", is a lane leading south-eastwards from the High Street, along which there are outcrops of rock (Kentish rag-stone). East Malling is on the lower greensand ridge. (Recent re-naming extended Rocks Road into a considerable length of what was previously Sweets Lane—to confuse future research).

Schepladecrofte: O.E. *lad* was "path" etc., thus "the croft by the sheep path, or sheep walk". A shrubbery within Bradbourne Park bore the name "Sheep Walk" at the time of the Tithe Awards, 1839.

Sorewode: *Sore* was M.E.—"a buck of the fourth year". The wood may therefore have taken its name from bucks or stags there.

(Sharnale), Brodsharnall, Northscarnale, Suthssarnale: E.P.N.S. gives *scearn, scarn*—O.E. "dung, muck, frequent with words for 'stream' etc." and quotes "Sharnal, Kent, *wella*". So we should have "mucky stream" (though today the streams of East Malling, before they reach the industrialised area, are remarkably clear). The Rental shows the Sharnhales to have been prosperous tenants in East Malling. The family was here in the previous century: John 1332, and William fl. 1368–84 who was a mason of some distinction.[48] This William, or his son, was involved in a dispute with the Abbess of West Malling in 1408. The question remains whether the field name was descriptive, with possibly the family taking its name from it, or whether the field name derived from the family name? Was the family so named because it came from Sharnal Street, near Gravesend?

Steyle, Le: O.E. *stigel*—"stile", M.E. *steil*—"step". The name survives in a curiously tautological form in modern housing development, in what was until recent years part of Clare Park—"Stepstile Estate".

Torel, Torelys: The *Calendar of Charter Rolls* notes that the *Inspeximus* of 21 Edward III (*vide* note 41) confirmed "the gift of Henry Torel of Malling to Isabel de Kailli abbess of Malling and the convent of all his lands in the town of Eastm.", and "the gift of the same Henry of all his tenement in the town of Malling and all his messuage in Eastmalling and of a yearly rent of 5s. ½d. and two hens in the *tenura* of East Malling and Malling." Dates of these gifts are not given; but as Isabel de Kailli is not among the abbesses listed in the Victoria County History, they must be earlier than 1321.

Wronge, Le; Wrongreed: A derivation from M.E. *wrang*—"crooked, twisted" seems likely, but C.S. and C.S. Orwin give "*wong, woung*—a piece of meadow land. A portion of uninclosed land under the open-field system."[49]

Yfelde: By analogy with Ifield, Kent (Yfelde 1198) and Ifield, Sussex (Yfelde 1212), from O.E. *iw*—"yew", the meaning is "yew field" (*vide* Ekwall. See also E.P.N.S. under *iw*).

Ympton: O.E., M.E. *impe*—"young tree" and O.E. *tun*—"enclosure, hedge", perhaps?

Notes

1. P. H. Sawyer, *Anglo-Saxon Charters*, London, 1968, 514, and W. G. de G. Birch, *Cartularium Saxonicum*, London, 1885–93, 779.
2. K.A.O., U49 M6.
3. It is suggested that the intrusive *t* is a scribal error, possibly resulting from the misreading of the crossed *l* used in medieval abbreviations. This spelling is ignored by Ekwall who uses only the West Malling and South Malling (Sussex) *Domesday* references. It is quoted by Wallenberg without comment.
4. Translated from the facsimile in L. B. Larking (*ed.*), *The Domesday Book of Kent*, 1869.
5. F. H. Fairweather, "The Abbey of St. Mary, Malling," *Arch. Journ.*, lxxviii (1932), 176.
6. J. Thorpe, *Registrum Roffense*, London, 1769, 481.
7. F. W. Maitland, *Domesday Book and Beyond*, (Fontana edn. 1960), 441.
8. R. E. Latham, *Revised Medieval Latin Word List*, London, 1965, 228.
9. J. Z. Titow, *English Rural Society 1200–1350*, London, 1969, 21.
10. Lambeth Palace Library, *Comm.* XIIa/23/127, 179.
11. K.A.O., U49 T1.
12. F. W. Maitland, *op. cit.*, 441.
13. F. Hull (*ed.*), *Catalogue of Estate Maps 1590–1840 in the Kent County Archives Office*, 1973, Plate 8.
14. K.A.O., U49 P4.
15. "An Exact Map of a Capitall Messuage ... called Paris ..." 1699. In the possession of East Malling Research Station.
16. Samuel Pegge, *An Alphabet of Kenticisms*, 1735–6, *Arch. Cant.*, ix (1874), 55.
17. A study of field systems in Kent, including evidence from East Malling records, is in progress.
18. F. W. Maitland, *op. cit.* 551; J. H. Round, *Feudal England*, London, 1909, 62–3; R. Welldon Finn, *An Introduction to Domesday Book*, London, 1963 103; H. L. Gray, *English Field Systems*, Cambridge, Mass., 1915, 284.
19. F. W. Maitland, *op. cit.* 557.
20. Kent Archaeological Society, *Kent Records*, vol. xviii, Ashford, 1964, 58–172.
21. P.R.O., P.C.C., Milles 206 (amended from 26).
22. *cf.* Ekwall, where Godrington, Dorset, (Godrintone, *D.B.*) is given as "The *tun* of Godhere's people."
23. J. K. Wallenberg, *The Place-Names of Kent*, Uppsala, 1934.
24. The Abbey is not open to the public. Access to the chapel was by the kindness of the present Steward, Dr. Nosworthy. Information about the chapel, and the legend, were related by Sister Perpetua, O.S.B., of the Abbey.
25. Probably John; see entries 2 and 12.
26. *Newhythe* is not latinised in this instance.
27. Abbreviated as *Kat'yne*. The surname Katerine occurs in the Kent Lay Subsidy of 1334/5 under Larkfield Hundred. (Kent Archaeological Society, *op. cit.* in note 20).
28. As note 27 above.
29. Possibly an abbreviation of *domus lanarius*—"wool shed". (The scribe uses *venella* for "lane").
30. *Broka*—"brook" is Kentish for "water-meadow", although it is also used in the common sense "small stream". (See Appendix IV under *Blakebroke* and *Brochole*).
31. As note 3, above.
32. A surprising location for *Suthfelde* since *Lunsford* (*Lonsforde*) is in the north-west of the parish. Possibly a scribal error.
33. The ill-fated knight who became by marriage Lord Cobham. For his adherence to

Wyckliffe he forfeited his life in 1417. Traditionally the prototype of Shakespeare's Falstaff.

34. Edmund Flatchere, Vicar of East Malling, who died in 1541, bequeathed 6s. 8d. for "mending the Blakwall in this parishe". (P.R.O., P.C.C. 28 Allenger). An estate map dated 1706 (in Maidstone Museum, a tracing in K.A.O.) shows "The Wall Way" as a footpath traversing the "Black Brooks" in the extreme north of the parish.
35. K.A.O. U38 T212.
36. J. K. Wallenberg, op. cit.
37. Arch. Cant., lxxxix (1974), 135.
38. W. H. Ireland, "England's Topographer, or a New and Complete History of Kent", 1828–30, Vol. III, 602.
39. K.A.O., U49 M1.
40. P.R.O., Calendar of Charter Rolls, Vol. V, 56 et seq.
41. Lambeth Palace Library, Comm. XIIa/23/127, 179.
42. R. Welldon Finn, Domesday Book, Chichester, 1973, 36.
43. K.A.O., U49 E4.
44. Arch. Cant., lxxxix (1974), 135.
45. Explained C.S. and C.S. Orwin, The Open Fields, London, 1951–65, 124.
46. Quoted by L. C. Hector, The Handwriting of English Documents, 1958–66, 24.
47. The mills are described by M. J. Fuller, The Watermills of East Malling Stream, privately published, 1973.
48. Arch. Cant., ii (1859), 98–9, and John Harvey, English Medieval Architects, London, 1954, 242.
49. C.S. and C.S. Orwin, op. cit., 191.

MEMORANDA FROM THE QUEENBOROUGH STATUTE BOOK

FELIX HULL

INTRODUCTION

i

The first formal record of the little town of Queenborough, excluding the charters, may be justly regarded as a minute book for the View of Frankpledge, starting in 1496[1]; for from that time the history of the town's administration is reasonably complete and there is no evidence that any earlier attempt was made to create a methodical series of records. It is for this reason that the apparently haphazard memoranda found in a medieval statute book take on a greater significance.

The Queenborough statute book[2] is itself a beautiful volume and presents something of an enigma. Basically, it consists of a copy of those Statutes at Large current in 1325, a date which must be the latest possible for the early part of the book. There are then some late-fourteenth century additions, but the volume must have been substantially as we now find it by the time that Queenborough was incorporated in 1368. How the book reached Queenborough is unknown for it antedates the town by nearly half a century and it may well have belonged to an early town clerk or possibly to a distinguished burgess, so that in the fifteenth century it became a revered and precious possession of the corporation.

It seems reasonable to suppose that in the middle of that disturbed century a town clerk of some distinction felt that it would be well to record the names of the burgesses and also the by-laws of the town and that for this purpose blank leaves in the statute book might be used. Thus, from about 1452, the fly-leaves and vacant spaces of this volume were used, apparently in no particular order, to record any special decision of the corporation and this usage, common till about 1490, continued on occasions for over a hundred years.

The purpose of this paper therefore is to present the series of some eighty ordinances and memoranda and to draw attention to this important earlier record in Queenborough's history.

ii

In order to understand better the nature and reason of this usage it is necessary to examine briefly the early history of Queenborough. The peace of Brétigny, which ended the first episode of the Hundred Years War in 1360, provided Edward III with an opportunity to examine his defences, especially those covering London. The Cinque Ports, already in decline, had suffered from French raids and were no longer the scourge of the Channel as they had been in the days of the King's great-grandfather, and it seems that he spent little time or money on them but instead concentrated on the defence of the Thames. Hadleigh Castle in Essex was rehabilitated at this time, and in 1361 no less a man than Henry Yevele was responsible for designing a fortress for the Isle of Sheppey.[3] This remarkably advanced construction was situated near the south-west corner of the island where a small navigable creek entered the Medway, just north of the mouth of the Swale. In 1366, the King visited his new castle and, as the preamble to Queenborough's first charter reads, "having well considered a certain place in the Island of Sheppey being a situation very commodious and safe and an arm of the sea of great breadth and depth and a convenient harbour for shipping" he decided to build a town which should be an ornament to the realm and should be called Queenborough in honour of his queen, Philippa.[4]

The charter is explicit: the new town is to be a free borough controlled by a mayor and two bailiffs, and to have two weekly markets and two annual fairs; the burgesses shall be quit of tolls, have infangenthef and outfangenthef and be exempt from all assizes and other courts of justice, free from jury service, and free from tallage, tenths and fifteenths and other quotas, quit of right-prise on the tonnage of wine, and completely free from interference or control by the Lord Warden of the Cinque Ports. It is difficult now to assess the full implication of all these privileges, but it would appear that Edward set the men of Queenborough on a par with the Portsmen, without the corresponding obligations.

As if to underline the peculiar status of the new town every effort was made to ensure economic independence even to the extent of granting Queenborough a place amongst the wool staples of the nation.[5]

This royal support lasted a mere decade. After the death of Edward in 1377, the government of his grandson knew nothing and cared less about the wishes of the old monarch. Just what happened subsequently is impossible to determine, but it seems that the town very quickly reverted to its original state as an oyster fishing community and despite a succession of noble constables of the castle the town ceased to be a significant factor in government policy. Doubtless, its burgesses met and dispensed justice or made orders within the terms of their charter; on the accession of a new monarch a confirmatory charter was petitioned and received, but no record was kept of day-to-day affairs and indeed the very meaning and purpose of the original grant became overlaid with a web of conjecture and tradition not always in keeping with the facts.[6]

It may be significant that the awakening came not long after Jack Cade unsuccessfully sought refuge in the castle of Sheppey and one can only postulate that by 1452 Queenborough found it desirable to employ a town clerk who was both literate and aware of his responsibilities. It was this unknown but credible personage who decided that year to record the names of the burgesses and to set down, probably for the first time, the ordinances or by-laws of the corporation. The almost superstitious solemnity of the occasion is indicated by the use of the old statute book, rather than a new volume.

iii

The result, however, may not have been quite what the learned clerk wished, for from this time in no order, in a wild variety of hands, in Latin, in English and once in French, entries were added, written over and between other entries and sometimes a page was scrubbed to allow a new entry to be made. Lists of names were likewise amended from time to time so that the result is confusion most confused. Finally, someone, probably before the end of the fifteenth century added ribald verses about a friar to the front fly-leaf of the volume.[7]

The editor, therefore, is faced with a number of problems. There is a series of entries beginning in 1452/3 which are formal in character, always in Latin and written in a number of good hands of the period. These are mainly dated entries and are in the main in some order and may represent the clerk's and his successors' attempts to keep a formal book of records. Interspersed with these, however, and also scattered on fly-leaves and on any small area of space throughout the whole volume are a number of other entries, usually in English and not always dated, which relate in particular to admissions to freedom of the borough. The language of these entries needs to be read to be believed; it is a very debased English probably the dialect of Sheppey at the time.

The editor therefore must decide whether to leave the entries in the original order and in the language as written or whether to attempt to discover the order, if any, and to make the result more intelligible to the reader. After much thought, it has seemed best to translate the formal Latin entries, but to leave the English ones untouched, and to attempt to place the whole in chronological order, though giving reference to the folio on which the original occurs. A word is required however about the nature of the specific entries.

iv

In the first place there are lists of burgesses for 1452/3, 1459/60, and 1471, but the first is so altered and amended that it is difficult to determine the original list and impossible to say when the alterations were made. Related to these lists are two other shorter lists, undated, which record the custody of the charters and other treasured possessions of the corporation at that time. The first of these appears as a palimpsest and is partially illegible, but it seems that it dates from about 1455 while the latter is probably about 1475 in date.

Second, there are the series of ordinances. Considering the high hopes centring round the founding of Queenborough these indicate clearly enough the actual poverty of the town. The majority relate to rights of common on Queenborough Green which lay to the north of the town, one relates to the holding of "schelpas" (? oyster beds) on the shores of the Swale, three to the oyster fishery and one to the admissions of freemen. Of by-laws of the usual public health nature regarding butchers and offal or dung-heaps, or of rules for holding meetings, there is nothing.

The third category is somewhat miscellaneous in character but consists principally of licences to build or dwell in the town, paying a customary annual rent of 4*d*. at the church on the feast of Trinity.

Finally, there are the admissions of which there are more than twenty. Some are formal and are straightforward acceptances of freemen but others raise a number of problems. Instead of a simple request to be admitted these usually take the form of a petition to receive the franchises of Queenborough for safeguard of body and goods, sometimes adding a reference to the privileges ordained by King Edward. As time goes on, especially with the anglicized version of these entries there is an increasing tendency to read a form of sanctuary into the plea. These are not sons of freemen or apprentices, but strangers from near and far seeking a special privilege: one refers to the dangers he is in and for breaking out of Dover Castle and the impression gained is that the newcomers to Queenborough were seldom men of substance, rather a trickle of refugees from justice seeking asylum. Although the word never appears in this volume the concept of sanctuary remains and actually in the first minute book the following entry appears:

"Md. that I Robert Cambrecht maryner hathe here Taken senttory for the safegarde of my body and my godes the xxxti day off June and Thomas Robynson meer The xix yere off the Rayne of Kyng Hari the viijti wettenes that Robert Bowton, Robert Brette, John Swond, Richarde Skynner"[8]

It is to be noted that such admissions cease after the abolition of sanctuaries in 1536.

v

The question still arises, however, as to how this concept arose. There is no question of sanctuary in the religious sense, although one entry refers erroneously to papal ratification of the privileges and a papal bull concerning the free chapel of Holy Trinity was amongst the town's treasures.[9] On the other hand, it would appear that the men of Sheppey, isolated from the mainland and with privileges only dimly understood regarded themselves as free from all interference by the royal and county officers and free from the Cinque Ports jurisdiction, so that if a person once held property within the town he claimed to be a free burgess and the quite usual privileges granted by the 1368 charter were built up into a much greater franchise than even Edward III had intended. Tradition once established dies hard and if indeed no records were kept for nearly a century the implementation of the original grant would have developed in strange and unexpected ways. This it seems is what happened and the evidence suggests that by 1450 the burgesses of Queenborough neither understood what the King's great-great-grandfather had determined nor what was the true import of the grant of a "free chapel" by Pope Nicholas V.

vi

The entries are translated or transcribed in full with modern dating added in square brackets and footnotes are kept to a minimum. Where they occur it is usually for the purpose of explaining the dating of a particular item, or to comment on some special aspect of the text.

THE MEMORANDA FROM QUEENBOROUGH STATUTE BOOK, 1452–1556

1. [f. 228] These are the 12 burgesses of Queenborough, *anno* 31 Henry VI [1452–3]

Thomas Cokerel [*struck through*]   John Bret, sen.

Geoffrey Benet [*struck through*]   John Northwode, esq.

Alan Jacob

Laurence Thomas [*struck through*]   John [Grean *struck through* Lowge *added*]

William Brette sen.

William Canon [*struck through*]   William Cokerell

John Bret [*struck through*]

William Baker

John Grean [*struck through*]

[*Interlineated and added in a different hand*]

John Swalman

John Willes

William Brette, jun.

Nicholas Poore [*struck through*]

John Ledes

It is ordered by the twelve above-written that the mayor and bailiffs shall not receive any foreigner to sojourn within or without the liberties but with the deliberation or assent and agreement of the mayor and the aforesaid twelve burgesses.

Item it is ordered that the twenty-six sheep pastures shall continue for future time according to the ancient view and custom.

Item it is ordered that everyone of the burgesses may have and hold one boar and four pigs on the common pasture at their will.

Item every commoner[10] may have one pig for fattening[11] and if they shall hold or have more pigs on the pasture than is here ordained the whole number of the innocent commoners shall pay to the common purse 40*d.*

Item it is ordered that if anyone who holds any of the pigs permits any without a ring in its nose to make an encroachment on the pasture, forsooth by the turning over of the soil to the destruction of the pasture, for two days before report to the bailiff, he shall pay 4*d.* to the common purse and 1*d.* to the bailiff who distrains him.

Item it is ordered that everyone of the burgesses may hold and have 2 ganders and 4 geese for a whole year and they may keep them until the feast of St. Michael and no longer on pain of 2*d.* for each gander, viz. 1*d.* to the common purse and 1*d.* to the bailiff of the town, besides the four geese which each of the burgesses may hold and have, in his pasture for the said time until hay harvest.

[f. 228v.] And each commoner may hold 1 gander and 2 geese in his pasture for the same time and extension as far as the feast of St. Michael upon the foresaid pain and two geese for the same time for his (?) own use until hay harvest and no further upon the said pain.

And if any may hold a horse on his pasture allocated to him, then for each horse there shall be pasture for 9 sheep and for every cow pasture for 5 sheep.

Item it is ordered that no-one shall have sheep upon his pasture within the liberty from the feast of St. Peter in Chains until the feast of All Saints, except that each may have 4 sheep upon his pasture for the use of his household who may have and hold the 26 pastures there as is the custom, upon pain of 4*d.* to the common purse and 1*d.* to the bailiff for each sheep.

Item it is ordered that if anyone shall not occupy his pasture in the winter then it is permitted for him to dispasture on his pasture for 20 sheep, 40 lambs from the feast of the Annunciation of the Blessed Virgin Mary until the feast of St. Peter in Chains.

And he who occupies his pasture with sheep in the winter time shall drive 20 sheep out of the pasture at the same feast of the Blessed Mary and for that he may dispasture 30 lambs upon the said pasture for the same time. And he who holds and has more of the same shall pay to the common purse 2*d.* for each lamb and ½*d.* to the town bailiff.

Item it is ordered by the 12 before written that Robert de Walesby shall pay to the common purse 10*s.* as his entrance fine for Munkeplace and he shall pay this on the 20th of the month of September next coming. Item it is ordered that all men shall have their "schelpas"[12] upon the shore of the Swale just as if the mayor with his council had ordained and assigned them, viz. John Brettes, next to the north John Marchall sen., William Norman, William Aldham, Thomas Man, Mathew Bulstrod, John Bernard, John Walysby, Robert Howlot, Richard Sygor, John Sygor, John Skalsfyn, John Spaldyng, Richard Marchall, Robert de Walesby, Ralph Howlet, William Baker, Henry Cusakes,[13] Thomas (?) Nete jun. [struck through], Robert Daye, William Schyrbourne, William Cordewaner, John Clyfforde, John Legyly, John Brette, John Thedham, sen., Roger Jude, John Benet sen.

[The above entry is much altered and in nearly every case fresh names are written above the original entries. The following is a list of these alterations in the order in which they occur.]

John Ha[?] written above William Barbour [written above John Brettes as the original name], John Warde written above Henry Style, John Benet, William Child, John Chayne, Robert Paynot, Richard Hokeday, William B[?], William Sumptor, William Cannon, Henry Passhele, Geoffrey Benet, John Grene, William Howlot, John Willes south, Henry Jacob, John Gold (?) south, Robert Sumner (?) south, Laurence Thomas, south, William at Bathe,[14] Richard Walesby, south, Walter (?) Brasier.

William Aldham and John Nete are elected by the said twelve sworn men[15] to the office of Treasurers for the keeping of all goods and profits pertaining to the common [f. 229] purse and from thence to return their account annually to the corporation of the town, viz. on the eve of St. Michael.

It is ordered that all men who have goods and chattels pertaining to the common purse shall return and pay to the treasurers before the feast of Pentecost on pain of 6s. 8d.

It is ordered that in the future no one shall have freedom to tend the oyster fisheries within a cock-boat, which grow in the said waters on pain of 20s. paying his fee [?] to the common purse and paying [?] to the mayor and bailiffs. [All struck through] Item it is ordered that the mayor has a fourth part of all forfeitures, escheats and wrecks and the rest goes to the common purse.

Item it is ordered by the mayor, burgesses and commons of the same town that it is not allowed to dredge any oysters from William Chaynes Fleet to ward in Holflet[16] except only at their own charges, on pain of paying 6s. 8d. to the common purse.

2. [f. 229v. N.D., c. 1455.] It is ordered by the mayor, 12 burgesses and the whole community of the town of Quenburgh that no man or

woman no matter of what status, grade or condition he was or they were nor any Balengerman[17] coming to the same town with any goods or chattels or any kind of merchandize to lend or to sell may do so without licence of the mayor on pain of forfeiture to the mayor of the whole of that which he would lend or sell. And moreover that he shall make a fine to the mayor for the time being, at the will and in the name of the mayor.

3. [f. 229. 1455.] On the tenth day of January in the 33rd year of the reign of Henry VI came a certain gentlewoman by the name of Cristina daughter of Ralph Blakelowe before the mayor of Quenborgh the bailiffs and 12 burgesses of the said "burge Regine" and humbly sought to be admitted to the francpledge[18] with those goods she might have properly then in her possession and for all other future happenings, to which supplication we, the aforesaid mayor and bailiffs together with our said 12 burgesses,[19] the said Cristina being humbly disposed was admitted to our said francpledge with all her goods in the name and on account of the most excellent King Edward II[20] and his successors, Kings of England and thus the aforesaid Cristina was entered for a record into our liberties in accordance with all our privileges in all our charters. And that [all and singular *written above*] those privileges we have granted her which were graciously ratified by our Christian father and lord, the lord Pope Nicholas IV,[21] all which writings are witnessed by the mayor, bailiffs and 12 burgesses as appears in the Statute Book.[22]

4. [f. 230. 1455] On the first day of March in the year of the reign of King Henry VI, after the conquest, 33rd [1454/5] a foreigner came before the mayor, bailiffs and other burgesses of the town of Burgi Regine and humbly prayed to be admitted to the said town and frankpledge on account of divers and legitimate causes which he feared might happen to him in the future. Who, this stranger by name John Sammesby, the mayor aforesaid, one of the bailiffs together with other said burgesses, unanimously and with one accord freely admitted to the said liberties according to the liberties and form of the charters of the most excellent King Edward II[23] and of Kings Henry, Richard, Henry and Henry the successors of the said King Edward, for which grant the said John shall give to the defence of the said town whatever the mayor, bailiffs and burgesses shall determine to be given.

5. [f. 230. 1455] On the twenty-sixth day of November[24] in the 34th year of the reign of King Henry VI there came two strangers before the mayor, bailiffs and other burgesses of the Queen's town of Queneburgh and humbly sought to be admitted to the frankpledge of the same town on account of the fear of death which they dreaded might happen to them in the future. On their supplication, we the mayor, bailiffs with the burgesses of the said town admitted them to the foresaid frankpledge according to the liberties and tenor of our charters, etc. The

names by which the aforesaid were called are Henry Rogger, Adam Petyr.

6. [f. 230. N.D., ? 1455] Memorandum that Richard Rand has built a new house with appurtenances in the same borough, and he accepts for himself and his heirs for all time to pay annually at the chapel of Quenburgh on the feast of Holy Trinity ... 4*d*.[25]

7. [f. 230. N.D. ? 1455] Item John Swalman pays for his newly built messuage annually at the said feast of Holy Trinity at the said chapel ... 4*d*.

8. [f. 230. N.D. ? 1455] Richard Rande has bought a tenement with appurtenances from Henry Smyth, paying at the chapel on the feast of Holy Trinity ... 4*d*.[26]

9. [f. 227. N.D., *c*. 1455. *List of charter holders, a palimpsest partly illegible and in a variety of hands.*]

>William Baker has a charter of Henry VI
>John Norman
>Henry Jacob has a [? *word missing*] and the common seal
>Mathhew Bulstrode has one
>John Bret has a charter of [-]
>Thomas Cokerell mayor of Quensburgh has one
>Burgis. Robert Sumpter   John Wellys
>Richard HokedayThomas Mane
>[*written above* John ? Glyn]
>John Bret   William of Hoo William Bret
>Henry Jacob   John Gren   Geoffrey Benet
>William Sumter   John Benet

10. [f. 233. N.D., *c*. 1458] A accion of a playnt in the law for 6 li. of debt that William Clark owyth to John Jacob the mayr of Quenbo' [Qweborow quowgh *added*].

11. [f. 232. N.D., ? 1458-9] Memorandum that Rechartt Mondfford axit Frangys of the mayer of Quynborgh in the kynges name for the saffgard of his body and his godes for axeyns as Furre as the strenthe as ower Fre Franges strecheth. Wittenys John Jacob, Raff Ran[?], John Gossan, Rechertt Besy and mony other.

12–21.[f. 231] The v day of June the yer of the Kyng Herry the six after the conquest xxxvij [1459].

12. Be hyt knowen to all maner of menn that y Franco de Fornarey syde *queq alyo cumque alyo nomyni seuscatur.*[27]

13. Item and anneys is veyff askyt and requeryt the mayre and[28] all the borges of the seyd towne of Quenburgh at the reverens of God and kyng Hedward to hafe the franches[29] of this towne of Quenborough for hymm and ys wfe [*sic*] and all ys Godys.

14. Also as for a childe that ys callyd Jermyne Rede perayth to have the seyd franches in the same casse.[30].

15. (?)Testes John Warderope pays for a messuage (?) newly built and pays annually at the Chapel of Holy Trinity, 4*d*.

16. (?) Item Levied between John Jacob, Wylyam Brett [and Thomas Pelhocke written above], John Brett, John Ledys, Welyam Butt.

17. Memorandum that y Robert Hayward askyt perayyt Requeryth the mre at the Revenss of Gode and for hys soulle that hordeynyd the fransches for devers dangerrys that he ys in and in esspessyall for Brekyng of peresson of the Castell of Dover.

18. Memorandum that y Ummfryd Lythefott jettylman latt of Esex *et* John Byschop latte of Kentt 3eman askyth at the Reverens of God and kyng Heduard['s] [soulle *written above*] to hafe the franches of thys [towne *written above*] of Quenburnah for hus and hour Godys.

19. Memorandum that Tomam Henry askyt and prayeth the mayre att the reverens o Godre and for kyng Heduardys soulle to haff the franches of the toune of Quenburrugh.

20. Memorandum that Edmunde Werner askyd and p[r]ayd the mayr of Qwenbroght at the reverans of gode and for kynge Ewerde sake (?) welle to have the franches of the town of Qwenbroht a for[saide *written below*].

21. Memorandum that Robert Kegewyn late dwellyng in Myddilton besyde Sedyngborne askyth at the Reverens of Gode and Kyng Edward to have the Franches of this towne of Quenbrowe ffor me and my godys.

22. [f. 231v.] Memorandum that Herry Smeth ath purchessyd the grond be twex John Reginald and yeng Wylliam Brette as far toward the north as the hege of the said Wylliam and a both sydes fro[m] hege to hege.

23. [f. 230v.] The names of the burgesses of the town of Quenburgh in the time of John Swalman mayor of Quenburgh Anno 38 Henry VI [1459–60][31]

> [-] Northwode, esq. [*inserted above next name*]
> John Swalman, mayor
> William Bret, sen. ['mort' *added in another hand*]
> William Bret, jun.
> John Bret [*struck through*]
> Geoffrey Benet [*struck through*, 'mortuus est' *added in another hand*]
> Alan Jacob
> John Ledys [*struck through*]
> John Lowge [*struck through*]
> John Wyllys
> John Clerk
> John Grygges [*struck through*]
> Laurence Herte [*struck through*]
> William Baker [*struck through*]

John [Coke Stra *struck through*] Stanforth
William Barnarde sworn serjeant of the said town [*added in a different hand*]

24. [f. 230v. N.D. ? 1459/60] Memorandum that Thomas Francis askyd and p[r]ayd the mayr of Qwenbroght at the reverene off gode and for Kyng Edwarde soule to have the ffranchis off the town of Qwenbroght a for saide.

25. [f. 229v. 18 Oct. 1460] Memorandum that at the View of Frankpledge held at Quenburgh on Monday immediately after the feast of St. Luke the Evangelist in the 39th year of the reign of king Henry VI it was ordered that whosoever shall come into the borough by boat and shall desire to make his dwelling within the same shall each pay to the mayor a (?) by each fourth part 4*d*. until he shall be admitted to the liberty and franchises aforesaid.

26. [f. 231v. N.D., *c.* 1460] Memorandum that Laurence Herte has bought from Thomas Benet the reversion on one messuage which Agnes the wife of Laurence holds for the term of her life. And upon this sale, on the same day, Agnes released and discharged all the right and title which she has in the same messuage, into the hands of the mayor aforesaid. And the said mayor gave and granted the aforesaid messuage to the said Laurence, to have to him and his heirs according to the customs of the said borough.

27. [f. 231v. N.D., (?) *c.* 1460] Remembranse that Thomas Polayn of Upcherche hade j costame at Quynborowe the xxviij day of Genaver' xiij^{xx} [260] quarterys barle price ... the quarter ijs. 6*d*.
Item iij barellys tallow price ... xxs.

28. [f. 231v. 11 Oct. 1462] Memorandum that at this View, forsooth held on the 11th day of October in the second year of the reign of king Edward IV, at Quenburgh [Thomas Bromfelde *written above*] came before William Brette sen., now mayor there and his fellows, burgesses, and he received from the same mayor and burgesses there a plot of land for one shamell [booth] fit for a butchery and situated in this same town opposite to the messuage of John Swalman to hold to the same Thomas [Branfelde *written above*] and his assigns, paying from thence yearly at the chapel of Holy Trinity there, 4*d*. that is, paying annually at the feast of Holy Trinity.

29. [f. 230v.]

William Brette sen., mayor.

In the third year of E[dward] IV [1453–4] It is ordered by common assent that the View of Frankpledge of this liberty shall be held for the future on Monday immediately after the Monday when the View of Frankpledge is held at Middleston after the feast of St. Michael and on the Monday called Hoke Munday after the feast of Easter and it shall not be varied except on account of the gravest cause. And that nothing shall be allowed or sealed with the common seal unless at an earlier council between the mayor and his neighbours it shall be sealed with the common seal and if the mayor or the keeper of the common seal shall intend, opposition being made by none. And if any inhabitant being a merchant shall sell or buy any goods or merchandise and shall not have been admitted to the liberty of the town by the will of the mayor, he shall never have a licence from the mayor.

30. [f. 230v. N.D., ? 1463] Memorandum the xxviij day of Aprell comyth William Benygton be for' the Mayr' and acsyth franchese.

31. [f. 230v. N.D., ? 1463] Memorandum the x day of May comyth John Jenvay and John Randall be for' the Mayer and acsyth ffranches.

32. [f. 231v. 16 April 1464] Memorandum that at a View of Frankpledge held at Quenburgh on Monday 16 day of April in the fourth year of the reign of King Edward IV, John de Wardroper, taillour[32] came before Alan Jacob now mayor there and took one messuage [with a garden as far as le ffleet *written above*] with appurtenances from the aforesaid mayor and Burgesses there and it was granted to him in the same Court to have [the same] to him and his heirs according to the custom of the same town paying annually at the chapel there on the feast of Holy Trinity − 4*d*. The same John afterward built another messuage within the town paying thence annually on the feast of Holy Trinity − 4*d*. at the foresaid chapel. And afterwards the said John Wardroper sold the said other messuage to Thomas Lemman to have to him and his heirs according to the customs, paying to the said chapel of Holy Trinity, he paid 4*d*.

33. [f. 227v. 15 Oct. 1464] Thomas Clement formerly of Rovchester was admitted to the liberty of the town, forsooth on the 15th day of October in the fourth year of the reign of King Edward IV, and was sworn.

34. [f. 229v. 13 Oct. 1466] At the View held at Quenburgh on Monday the feast of St. Edward the King[33] in the sixth year of the reign of King Edward IV, William Brette sen. now mayor of the town of Quenburgh came and purchased from Hugh Wallwyn and Cecilie his wife one messuage which the same Hugh recently built in the same town. And he owes to pay thence annually at the feast of Holy Trinity, 4*d*.

35. [f. 227v. 17 February 1467/8] Memorandum that Jon Perker of Newcastell mastir off the Cristofir langyng' to William Waxston the mayr off Newcastill came to Quenborought the xvij day of Fever3eir in the reyn off Kyng' Edward the fourt the vij 3eir with the schippe a fore sayde full of colys the xx day of the same monyth the sayde Jon Parker and Jon Asshburn' pursar of the fore sayde schippe came to William

Bret yonger the mair off Quenborught and asshyde frannchesse for savegarde off ther schippe and ther ffelysschippe and ther selfe.

36. [f. 227v. 21 May 1468] John Lyncoln formerly of Madynston was admitted to the liberties of the town of Quenborught 21 day May in the eighth year of Edward IV.

37. [f. 227v. 21 May 1468] William Fouler formerly of Ditton was admitted to the liberties of the town of Quenborught 21 day of May in the eighth year of Edward IV.

38. [f. 227v. 10 Oct. 1468] Thomas Knyght came here before William Bret sen. mayor, at the View of Frankpledge held at Quenburgh on Monday the 10th day of October in the eighth year of the reign of King Edward IV and sought to be granted and to be admitted to the liberties of this town. And it was granted to him.

39. [f. 229 16 April 1469] Memorandum[34] that on Monday 16th day of April in the ninth year of King Edward IV, Henry Smyth otherwise known as Henry Larkham formerly of the County of Somerset received from William Brette sen. mayor, one tenement newly built by himself lying in the same town opposite le Courthall to have to the same Henry and his heirs according to the customs of the borough. Paying annually at the chapel of Holy Trinity and on the feast of Holy Trinity, 6d.

40. [f. 229v. 15 October, (?) 1470] Memorandum that this day the xv day of October cometh Richard Pylgrym and certifieth the maier and the court of a bargayn made by twen hym and his moder that ys to wete he and his heyres shall bere to his said moder duryng the terme of here lyff—vjs. atte midsomer and myghelmas or ellys by xiiij nyghte after eche terme by evyn porciones to be payd this dun well and truly, then the sayd Richard Pylgrym shall have the masuage that he dwellyth for hym and to his heyres in fee withoute lettyng of his said moder or her assyn'.[35]

41. [f. 187v. 25 Nov. 1470] Rychard' Coole[36] came here before Wylliam Brete at the View of Frankpledge held at Quenborow on Monday the 25th day of November in the year of the reign of King Henry VI, from the beginning of his reign after the conquest, the 49th and from the reassumption of his royal power the first year.

42. [f. 227v. 25 Nov. 1470] Rychard' Yeldich came here before Wylliam Brete mayr at the View of Frankpledge held at Quenborow on Monday the 25th day of November in the year of the reign of King Henry VI, from the beginning of his reign after the conquest the 49th and from the reassumption of his royal power the first year.[37].

43. [f. 187v. (?) 4 or 14 January 1470/1][38] Herry Smeth oderwyse callyd Herry Larcum come be ffor the Wylliam Brette mayr and acsyd ffranchesse at Quenborow the fforte day of Jeniver in the yer' of Kyng Henry the VI ffro his comyng agayn of his rayne after the conqueste

xlix and his resavyng agayne of his Royall powr' the fryste yer'.

44. [f. 12v. 22 April 1471] Memorandum that at the View of Frankpledge held there on Monday commonly called 'Hokemunday' because it was a time of war, in the year of our Lord 1471, it is found by the grand jury, the names of which are William Brette, John Cokerell, John Stamford, William Estlow, Thomas Aleyn, Robert Brette, Simon Parker, John Cristian, Richard Rande, John Riggeman and Thomas Knyght, it is both recorded and stated by William Butte, Robert Brette, Thomas Aleyn and others of their neighbours that it was the wish of William Cokerell that Isabella his wife should have and hold for the term of her life a messuage of his in Queneborow caring for all repairs to the same messuage according to the customs of the said town paying both for (?) upkeep of the bonnds and for customary taxes there.

45. [f. 230v.] Names of the Burgesses now newly appointed in the 11th year of Edward IV [1471]

William Bret, sen.

William Brette, jun. [*struck through*, sen. *added in another hand*]

[*William Brette and all subsequent names are bracketed together and the word* jurati *added*]

Robert Knyght

John Clerk

Alan Jacob

John Bowle

John Stanfurth

Richard Pilgrym

William Butte

John Paynot

Thomas Benet

Robert Bret

Richard Rande

William Estlove

Thomas Aleyn [*The last three names in a different hand and Aleyn outside the bracket*]

46. [f. 228. 3 April 1473] Memorandum the iijd. day of April in the yere and Raygn of Kyng Edward the iiij the xiij yere of his Rayng comyt Roberd Lytle pryst and Thomas Coldbreth and acsyth Franches in Kyng Edwardes Name the iijd of Robert Knyght mayer of Quenborow and the franches ys grantyd to the said persons above sayd be the Mayer and his brederyn.

47. [f. 128v. N.D., (?) 1474] Marget Colyns and all her goodes cum before John Clerke then be mare and Rychard Rande and John Clerke yownger and Wylliam Clerke and Wylliam Bret and Robert Bret, Wylliam Laurens, Thomas Scrai to aske fransches of Qwynborow the xxvj day off August.

48. [f. 229. 30 May 1474]   Memorandum that on the thirtieth May in the fourteenth year of the reign of King Edward IV after the conquest Thomas Tannar came and sought frankpledge from me John Clerk mayor on the year and day aforesaid and my brethren, burgesses of the town of Quenborough, to which he was admitted.

49. [f. 229v. 18 Nov. 1474]   Memorandum that on the 18 day of the said month of November in the fourteenth year of the reign of King Edward IV after the conquest, John Dennam otherwise called John (?) Fooke came before us Richard Rande mayor and our brethren of the town of Queneborow and petitioned for the frankpledge of the aforesaid town to which he was admitted.

50. [f. 232. (?) 1474–5]   Item Thomas Bassem a freman of this towne by the Recorde of the mayer Recard Rand and his bretherne.

51. [f. 232. (?) 1474–5]   Item John Dygon ys freman of this towne by the Recorde of the mayre Recard Rond and alle his brotherne.

52. [f. 128v. (?) 1475–6]   Alan Jacobe has the papal bull and common seal
John Paynot has a casket made of leather with two charters
John Clerk has a casket 'de wyker' with one charter
Richard Pylgrime has a casket with one charter
Richard Rand has a casket with one charter
Robert Knyght has a casket with one charter
William Butte has a casket with one charter

53. [f. 187. 16 April 1576]   Mariorya, the widow of Edward Kyng came before us Alan Jacob, mayor of the town of Queneburgh and sought the privileges of our said town for the safety and welfare of her body and her goods and she was admitted and received by us on the 16th day of the month of April in the 16th year of the reign of King Edward IV.

54. [f. 187v. 30 April 1576]   Memorandum that on the last day of April in the 16th year of the reign of King Edward IV, Robert Harper formerly of Rethered [Rotherhithe], shipman, came before Alan Jacob mayor of our lord king's town of Qweneborough and sought admission to the franchises and privileges of the aforesaid town for certain causes between him and various men of London.

55. [f. 2v. (?) 1476]   In the matter of the boat of Philiberd Archer called the Mar' of Gerrand judgement was given on the 23rd December regarding 20 'mues' of salt.

56. [f. 230. 23 June 1478]   Memorandum that on the 23rd June in the 18th year of the reign of King Edward IV, Thomas Craske came before Robert Knyght, mayor, and his liberties and franchises, and he was sworn.

57. [f. 187v. 1478]   In the 18th year of the reign of King Edward IV, in the time of Robert Knyght.

Memorandum that Henry Smyght has newly built a house with appurtenances in the same town and it is granted to him and his heirs in perpetuity paying from this time annually at the chapel of Queneborow at the feast of Holy Trinity ... 4d.

58. [f. 231v. 3 July (?) 1480] Memorandum on the 3rd day of July comyth Thomas Gunne and acsyth franches of the mayer Roberd Knyght in the reverens of god and Kyng Edward.

59. [f. 231v. 11 Jan. 1480/1] Memorandum that on the 11th day of the month of January in the 20th year of the reign of King Edward IV after the conquest, Elizabeth Howell came and petitioned for frankpledge from Richard Rande then deputy mayor and from his bretheren burgesses of the town of Queneburghe in the year and on the day aforesaid, to which she was admitted.

60. [f. 231. 30 Dec. 1482] Houses alienated:[39] William Corneforth and Alice his wife entered into the franchises on the penultimate day of December in the 22nd year of the reign of King Edward IV.

61. [f. 187v. 13 Jan. 1485/6] Thomas Jacobe came before Richard Rande mayor at the view of frankpledge held at Quenborow on the 13th day of the month of January in the first year of the reign of King Henry VII after the conquest.

62. [f. 188. 11 August 1486] John Coper came before Richard Rande mayor of Quenborw on the 11th day of the month of August in the first year of the reign of King Henry VII for the franchises of Quenborw aforesaid. In witness thereof Richard Pylgrym, William Kokerell, William Barnard, John Rand and many others.[40]

63. [f. 186v. 30 August 1486] John Bedwyall, John Arnold, John Fysche citizens of London came before Richard Rand mayor of Quenborowh on the 30th day of the month of August in the second year of King Henry VII of England, after the conquest, for the franchises of Quenborw aforesaid. In ratification of which William Cokerell, Thomas Scraskke, Robart Brett, William Lawrensse and many others.

64. [f. 229. 12 March 1486/7] Memorandum that on the 12th day of March in the second year of the reign of King Henry VII, Robert Syred formerly of London, merchant, took from Richard Rande then mayor and his colleagues a tenement newly built by him himself, lying in the same town next to the water containing in length 60 feet and in breadth 40 feet, to have and to hold to him and his heirs perpetually paying thence an annual rent at the chapel of Holy Trinity at the feast of Pentecost 4d. [written above *ibidem* struck through] [Therefore he seeks privileges from John Raunde senior. *Added*]

65. [f. 233. 27 October (?) 1488] Thomas Blake of Feversham askyth the mayer Robert yn the kyngys name Harry the vijth ffre ffranchys to the saff gard of hys body and hys godys enterytt the xxvij day of Octobre'.

66. [f. 233. (?) 1488–9] The book [?] of the town of Quenesborough[41]

(?) *Rechardus solve*

The names of the barons of the Cinque Ports [? having] lands and tenements in the parish of the port town of Quenebor [? and] in divers parishes within the hundred of [? Milton] [? assessed] to a whole fifteenth and tenth granted to our lord king on the 9th day of the month of November in the third year of his reign and [?] to the 4th year of the same lord king and [?] to the ninth day of November in the 5th year of payment.

Inhabitants of the town of Queneborowe are allowed [? for land] existing within the parish of Minster.

Item John Northwood one of the burgesses of the town of [Queenborough] is allowed for his goods and chattels and is taxed in the parishes of Iwade and Bobbing, 51s.[42]

William Cockerell of Queneborough, item he seeks allowance, 4s.

William Barnard burgess of Queneborough seeks an allowance John Rand burgess of Queneborough is taxed 22s. 6d.

67. [f. 128v. 22 Jan. 1488/9] Thomas Crowland came with his ship called le George to William Cokkerell mayor of Quenebourgh and there were granted to the said Thomas Crowland with his ship and all his merchandise and his things all the privileges granted for the aforesaid town. Given this 22nd day of the month of January in the fourth year of the reign of King Henry VII after the conquest before these witnesses Richard Raund, John Lecche senior, Richard Bussard with others.

68. [f. 128v. 20 April 1489] Cowrt Frauncke came on Monday the morrow of the Sunday immediately before the feast of White Sunday at Queneborough in the fourth year of the reign of King [Henry] VII[43] when one and all the liberties and privileges of the same town were granted to him with all freedoms suitable by William Cockerell mayor of the said town with the agreement and common consent of all the free burgesses. These being witnesses Richard Raunde, Thomas Keteriche, Geoffrey Rolff, John Clerk with many others.

69. [f. 128v. 3 May 1489] Memorandum that William Hardyng of Malden in the County of Essex sold his boat called 'le Margaret' to John Keele of Antwerp in Brabant for 100 *li.* sterling on the day of the feast of Holy Cross in the fourth year of the reign of King Henry VII as appears in the deed of acquittance.

70. [f. 187. 16 July 1489] Thomas Smalwood of Middelton came before William Cockerell mayor of Queneborgh and sought the privileges of the town of Queneborgh for a defence and safe conduct of his body and his goods and he was admitted to the privileges and suffrages and was received by the aforesaid William Cockerell mayor and by all the burgesses on the 16th day of the month of July in the 4th year of the reign of King Henry VII.

71. [f. 232. 10 Sept. 1489] Memorandum that on the 10th day of the

95

month of September in the 5th. year of the reign of King Henry VII, John Northwode esq. came before William Cokerell then mayor of the town of Queneborough, Richard Rande, Robert Brett, John Leche and others, burgesses of the aforesaid town and was admitted to the liberties of the said town and was sworn.

72. [f. 2v. 17 April 1490] The 17th day of the month of April in the 5th year of the reign of King Henry VII, John Bolland formerly of Hornchurch came and sought the privileges from Richard Rand, mayor of the town of Quynborow which aforesaid privileges were granted to him with the agreement of all the burgesses of the said borough in all matters by those present.

73. [228v. 23 January 1490/1] Memorandum that on the 24th day of the month of January in the sixth year of the reign of King Henry VII after the conquest William Frebarn yeoman came and sought the frankpledge of the town of Quenborogh from me Richard Pilgrim mayor on the aforesaid day and my bretheren, to which he was admitted.

74. [f. 2. 7 February 1490/1] Memorandum that William Kyng and Rechart Davy hath axett ffranchys in the Kynges name of yngelond of the mayer of Queneborgh for the saffgard of thar lyffys and ther godys on the vijth day of February and in the yere of owre soveren lorde kyng Harry the vijth. vjth. yere.

75. [f. 227v. 20 December 1491] Richard Bern merchant of London came before Robert Brate sen. mayor at the View of Frankpledge held at Quenburgh on the 20th day of December in the 7th year of the reign of King Henry VII and sought the liberty and was admitted to the liberty of this town and to whom it was granted etc.

76. [f. 3v. 20 April 1527] Be itt knowyn to all men by theys presentes thatt I Rychard Rond of Quinborow mayer in the countey of Kent in the Ile of Shipy and I John Allan of the same towne byndys us and every one of us to other our heyers executors and assyns to a byde the wurde and arbytrement of Rychard Tayler, Robert Bolton, Thomas Hewet and Rychard Cockerell the elder burgesys of the same towne for all maner of causes de bayttes demandes and controversyes hade betwene the forsayd Rychard and John from the begynnyng of the world to the date here of on payne of forffitt xijli sterling to the partey that wyll nottabyde the arbetryment of the forsayd arbetrors and for the more suerty we the forsayd Rychard and John cherytably hathe sett to our (?) separate seylls & hand Rwytyng the xx day of Aprell the xviij yere off Kyng Harry the viij th.

By me Rychard Rond

By me John Aleyn [in a different hand from the rest]

77. [f. 189. 19 April 1543] Memorandum that Antoney Nevell hath purchased one Tenement in the Towne of Queneborowgh of theyres of

(?) Rand and hathe payd before the mayre William Robynson and other the Burges xiijs. ivd. to the churche of Queneborowgh the xix day of Aprell in the xxxiv year of the reign of King Henry viijth of England in full payement.

78. [f. 188v. *c.* 1543] Memorandum that John Pett of Queneborowgh hathe purchased one howse of William Robynson in Queneborowgh aforeseid lying to the [landes *struck through*] Kynges prysson weste to the Crycke South to the howse of Rycharde Skynner East and to the Kynges hygh strete northe and hathe payed in full Contentation and payment for the same – lxs. afore the mayre Thomas Robynson John Lytle and (?) Thomas Hewet with others.

79. [f. 190v. 1555–6] Be it knowen unto all men [? that] I Gylberde Anmre hath bothe on howse of on Gylberd Roberdes lyyng and beyng in the towne of Quynborowe lyyng agyns the howses of Tomas Wylsun on the west, the Kyng strete suthe, the comen paster northe, the howse of Tomas Jenwere on the este. I hathe payde in ful contentacyon and paymente afore the mayre John Sander and hys bredern £4 in the iijth yere of Phelyp & Mary by the grase of God of Ynglond, Franse and Yerlande Kyng & Quene.

Notes

1. KAO., Qb/JMs 1.
2. KAO., Qb/AZ 1.
3. See J. Harvey, *Henry Yevele* (1944), pp. 25–6.
4. KAO., Qb/I 9/4.
5. Stat. 43 Edw. III, c. 1.
6. There are *inspeximus* copies of Edward's charter dated 1399 and 1461. KAO., Qb/I 1,2.
7. The poem is omitted from this paper since it is hoped that it, together with other early poems found in the Kent Archives Office will be the subject of a paper to be published shortly.
8. K.A.O., Qb/JMs 1, f. 5.
9. See below p. 83.
10. The word used is *communicantes* presumably in the sense of the sharers.
11. Or for the larder.
12. Latham, *Revised Medieval Latin Word List* (1965) suggests 'shelf' or 'shell-fish beds'. Here the impression is either an allocation of shore line or perhaps of huts on the shore.
13. The word 'south' is inserted after the above Henry Cusakes in the original list.
14. Another word, illegible is interlineated above William and it is followed by the phrase 'et partes australis'.
15. The word 'jurates' is used but Queenborough never had 'jurats' the usual title in the Cinque Ports.
16. These names are no longer identifiable with certainty but probably Hollet is to be equated with Ladies Hole just west of Queenborough.
17. Latham, *op. cit.*, gives 'balinger' or 'whale boat', 1495.
18. This is the earliest freedom entry and is of special interest because of the detail and the inaccuracies which occur.
19. There is a difficult reading apparently *precibus* after *nostris*.
20. A scribal error for Edward III.
21. A scribal error for Nicholas V, 1447–55.
22. Presumably the list given in No. 1. p. 83.
23. A scribal error for Edward III.
24. The words *venerunt duo*, struck through follow Novembris.

25. There is a marginal gloss *edificavit de novo* and *scilicet* similarly added for No. 7.
26. The word 'purchase' is added in the margin.
27. This extraordinary and corrupt phrase must mean 'or by whatsoever other name he is known'.
28. A second 'and' is inserted in error.
29. 'frer' struck through precedes 'franches'.
30. Followed by 'dre°', *struck through*, 'd' and 'will'.
31. A second column of names for 1471 has been added—these are listed under no 45.
32. The words *de eadem venit* are added above.
33. The only feast of King Edward which can apply is 13 Oct.
34. 'Purchase' added in margin.
35. This entry is written over another order now illegible.
36. This entry is repeated in almost identical words on f. 227v, but is omitted here.
37. Entry in red ink.
38. Since the View was normally held on a Monday, 14 Jan. seems the probable reading.
39. These two words plainly do not relate to item 60 and should probably be associated with items 15 and 16 on p. 88. The whole of f. 231 is most confused and difficult.
40. The Latin of 62 is so corrupt that it includes 'venyth' for 'venit', and 'fracunsesse' for 'franchises'. Richard and William are spelt with an 'e'. In 63 the form 'venith coraham' appears.
41. This page is defective and it appears that the surface of part of the parchment has been removed so that the last word(s) of several lines is missing. The whole entry appears to relate to Cinque Ports 'advocantes' dwelling at Queenborough and to the exemption agreed between the Ports and Henry VII so far as fifteenths and tenths were concerned. The heading *Rechardus solve* is obscure.
42. Between the words *parochiis* and *Iwade* is a line of much earlier writing largely illegible but apparently beginning *Honorable hom et* ...
43. *Anno rr Regis septimi quarto.*

Appendix 1

Mayors of Queenborough whose names appear in the Statute Book

c. 1455	Thomas Cokerell
c. 1458–9	John Jacob
1459–60	John Swalman
1462–3	William Brette, sen.
1463–4	Alan Jacob
1466–7 ⎫ 1468–9 ⎬ 1470–1 ⎭	William Brette, sen.
1472–3	Robert Knyght
1473–4	John Clerke
1474–5	Richard Rande
1475–6	Alan Jacob
1477–8	Robert Knyght

1479–80	Robert Knyght
1480–1	Richard Rande [deputy mayor]
1485–6⎫ 1486–7⎭	Richard Rande
1488–9	William Cokerell
1489–90	Richard Rande
1490–1	Richard Pilgrim
1491–2	Robert Brette, sen.
1526–7	Richard Rand
1542–3	William Robynson
c. 1543	Thomas Robynson
1555–6	John Sander

Appendix 2

Index of persons named in the text. The references are to the actual entries not to pages, and all variants given are indicated.

Day(e), Robert, 1.
Dennam, John, 49.
Dyson, John, 51.

Estlow (Estlove), William, 44, 45.

Fooke (?), John, 49.
Fornareysyde, Anneys de (w. of John), 13;
John de, 12.
Fouler, William of Ditton, 37.
Francis, Thomas, 24.
Frauncke, Cowrt, 68.
Frebarn, William, 73.
Fysche, John of London, 63.

Glyn (?), John, 9.
Gold (?), John, 1.
Gossan, John, 11.
Gren(e)(Grean), John, 1, 9.
Grygges, John, 23.
Gunne, Thomas, 58

Ha[-], John, 1.
Hardyng, William of Maldon, 69.
Harper, Robert of Rotherhithe, 54.
Hayward, Robert, 17.
Henry, Tomand, 19.
Herte, Agnes, 26; Lawrence, 23, 26.
Hewet, Thomas, 76, 78.
Hokeday, Richard, 1, 9.
Hoo, William of, 9.
Howell, Elizabeth, 59.
Howlot (Howlet), Ralph, 1; Robert, 1;
William, 1.

Jacob(e), Alan, 1, 23, 32, 45, 52, 53, 54;
Henry, 1, 9; John, 10, 11, 16; Thomas,
61.
Jenvay, John, 31.
Jenwere, Thomas, 72.
Jude, Roger, 1.

Keele, John of Antwerp, 69.
Kegewyn, Robert, 21.
Keteriche, Thomas, 68.
Knyght, Robert, 45, 46, 52, 56, 57; Thomas,
38, 44.
Kokerell see Cokerell.
Kyng, Edward, decd., 53; Marioya (wid. of
Edward), 53; William, 74.

Larkham (Larcum) alias Smith, Henry, 39,
43; see also Smith.
Laurens (Lawrensse), William, 47, 63.
Led(c)he, John, 67, 76.
Ledes (Ledys), John, 1, 16, 23.
Legyly, John, 1.
Lemman, Thomas, 32.
Lowge, John, 1, 23.
Lyncoln, John of Maidstone, 36.

Lyte, Roberd, priest, 46.
Lythefot, Ummfryd, 18.
Lytle, John, 78.

Man(e), Thomas, 1, 9.
Marchall, John, sen., 1; Richard, 1.
Mondford, Rechartt, 11.

Nete, John, 1; Thomas (jun.), 1.
Nevell, Antony, 77.
Norman, John, 9; William, 1.
Northwod(e), John, esq., 1, 66, 76; [-], 23.

Parker, Jon of Newcastle, 35; Simon, 44.
Passhele, Henry, 1.
Paynot, John, 45, 52; Robert, 1.
Pelhocke, Thomas, 16.
Pett, John, 78.
Petyr, Adam, 5
Polayn, Thomas, 27.
Poore, Nicholas, 1.
Pylgrym [Pilgrim], Mrs. (w. of Richard), 40;
Richard, 40, 45, 52, 62, 73.

Ran [-], Raff, 11.
Rand(e) (Raunde, Rond), John, 62, 64, 66;
Richard, 6, 8, 44, 45, 47, 49, 50–2, 59,
61–4, 67, 69, 71, 72, 76.
Randall, John, 31.
Rede, Jermyne, 14.
Reginald, John, 22.
Riggeman, John, 44.
Roberdes, Gylberd, 79.
[-], Robert (mayor), 65.
Robynson, Thomas, 78; William, 77, 78.
Rogger, Henry, 5.
Rolff, Geoffrey, 68.

Sammesby, John, 4.
Sander, John, 79.
Schyrbourne, William, 1.
Scrai, Thomas, 47.
Scraskke, Thomas, 63.
Skalsfyn, John, 1.
Skynner, Richard, 78.
Smalwood, Thomas of Middleton, 70.
Smyth (Smeth, Smyght) alias Larkham,
Henry, 8, 22, 39, 43, 57; see also
Larkham.
Spaldyng, John, 1.
Stanforth (Stanford, Stanfurth), John, 23, 44,
45.
Style, Henry, 1.
Sumner, Robert, 1; see also Sumpter.
Sumpter (Sumptor), Robert, 9; William, 1, 9;
see also Sumner.
Swalman, John, 1, 7, 23, 28.
Syger, John, 1; Richard, 1.
Syred, Robert of London, 64.

Tannar, Thomas, 48.
Tayler, Rychard, 76.
Thedman, John (sen.), 1.
Thomas, Laurence, 1.

Walesby (Walysby)(de), John, 1; Richard, 1;
   Robert, 1.
Walwyn, Cecilie, 34; Hugh, 34.

Warde, John, 1.
Warderope(r), John, 15, 32.
Waxston, William (mayor of Newcastle), 35.
Wellys, John, 9.
Werner, Edmunde, 20.
Willes (Wyllys), John, 1, 23.
Wylsun, Thomas, 79.

Yeldich, Richard, 42.

THE VIEW AND STATE OF THE COMMANDERY OF SWINGFIELD
AND ITS APPURTENANCES IN 1529

L. R. A. Grove and S. E. Rigold

INTRODUCTION

I. *The Document.* This came from the Folkestone manorial estate office and was deposited on loan on May 11th, 1950, by the Earl of Radnor with the Kent County Council Archives, where it was remounted and indexed as U 270 Q3. It consists of 22 folios of laid paper, each about 28.5 by 20.0 cm., bearing a watermark, about 10.5 cm. overall, in the form of an animal, apparently a fox, with a long snout and bushy tail, and is contained in a cover of the same paper, torn away to a fragment at the front and endorsed in a late seventeenth-century hand, "The State of the Commandrie of Swingfield 20 Hen: ..." It is written in black ink on both sides of every folio save the verso of 22, almost entirely in a single, variable but fairly formal and legible late-medieval cursive hand, presumably that of the notary, William Wilcockes. A few additions and corrections are in another hand, presumably that of the auditor, Guthlac Overton. In two places only, those abbreviated below as sections A and B, the initial ı is ornate. It bears no other year than "20 Hen. VIII" and the month in the first entry is lost but the contract which concludes the document is dated 5th April of the same regnal year, which ended 21st April, 1529. Since the survey has every appearance of a swift and businesslike tour by officials from Headquarters, including the urgent arrangement of the said contract, the whole may safely be dated in the early part, March and April, of 1529, New Style.

II. *Textual Editing.* The MS was exactly transcribed by L.R.A.G., reproducing line-divisions, contractions and suspensions, and this transcription, collated with the original by S.E.R., forms the basis of the text printed hereunder. However, with the agreement of the general editor, it was decided to employ three distinct standards of presentation:

1. The bulk of the text is printed in entirety save for the "carried over" page-headings ("Adhuc the hall", etc.), with spelling unaltered but contractions expanded and normalized (the conventional plural termination always read as "es"). Lineation within the items is ignored but the folios are indicated in the margin. Defects, as far as possible, are supplied within square brackets. Punctuation, of which the MS has very little, is not supplied.

2. Certain passages concerning lands and woods, lettered A to G in the printed text, are repetitious in the original ("xvi acres, called xvi acres,

ST. JOHN'S, SWINGFIELD
From NNW. Unsigned Watercolour Drawing, 1794

ST. JOHN'S, SWINGFIELD

From SE. Drawn and engraved by G. Cooke, 1806

(*The Beauties of England and Wales*)

ST. JOHN'S, SWINGFIELD

From SE. Watercolour Drawing in Petrie Collection, 1807

ST. JOHN'S, SWINGFIELD

containing xvi acres") and are abbreviated and printed in continuous, not tabular, form.

3. The final contract for a barn is printed, as far as typography allows, in facsimile.

III. *The Importance of the Record.* This far exceeds any purely local interest as the terrier of a small and scattered estate, albeit one probably little changed since the thirteenth century. In general, the parts of the record in this category are those that have been chosen for abbreviation (standard 2, above). Of much wider interest are the parts that form the inventory of a minor, if specialized, religious house a decade before the dissolution and with no explicit thought of surrender, and the last part, which is a hitherto unrecorded building-contract of a utilitarian kind, at a critical moment in the history of vernacular architecture when the use of brick in cheap structures was just becoming widespread. The former is principally an inventory of contents: few dimensions of the capital buildings are given and information about them must be cautiously extracted from the tour of the interior. Nevertheless, these buildings, though altered subsequently, still stand in part and are in process of consolidation and examination by the Department of the Environment.[1] There are also four drawings and engravings showing the surviving range before its west end was truncated in the middle of last century. These are reproduced (Pl. 1–4).[2]

Three commentaries by S.E.R. are appended to the text. The first is a provisional review of the lands, including the dependencies, in the light of their apparent present condition. The second considers the buildings in the triple light of documentary, archaeological and graphic evidence, but must again be regarded as provisional, since no excavation has yet taken place and the only part of the structure yet completely dissected is the roof. The third examines the building contract, which is for a barn, together with the less complete descriptions of other barns and similar buildings found in the text. [There has now been some excavation. S.E.R. 1979]

IV. *Other Records of the Hospitallers in Kent.* Beside the famous report to the Grand Master in 1338, edited by the effective founder of our Society,[3] many of these are conveniently covered in *Kent Records* and earlier volumes of *Archaeologia Cantiana* that include a "record" function and, where suitable, reference will be confined to these sources. True, J. F. Wadmore, "The Knights Hospitallers in Kent"[4] and Charles Cotton, *A Kentish Cartulary of the Order of St. John of Jerusalem*[5] are mainly summaries and repetitions of published material, with not always accurate translations, but both include previously unprinted material, in particular, for our purposes, the post-Dissolution documents from the Exchequer Minister's Accounts of 1547[6] and the Patent Roll of 1558.[7]

V. The Occasion of the Survey. The "View and State" is not an instrument of dissolution, nor, like the Account of 1547 or the entry in the *Valor* of *c.* 1535,[8] is it primarily a valuation. It is a minute enquiry into physical conditions, which does not, in fact, cover all the spiritual and temporal assets of the Commandery, or Preceptory, of Swingfield, and where concerned with money it is with actual gains and losses rather than with notional and "fossilized" assessments.

It is an internal report by two officials of Sir William Weston, last Prior of England,[9] neither of whom were local men (Guthlac Overton, to judge from his name, came from Lincolnshire), and was evidently to conclude a period of abuse and misappropriation, all of which is tactfully laid at the door of "my lord of Kilmayne", Sir John Rawson,[10] who is described as having been, though not necessarily throughout the time of peculation, Commander of Swingfield. "About four years past", i.e. *c.* 1525, he had sold timber at Oare, intended for another purpose, and as recently as Midsummer 1528 he had sold more and given movables away. He had ordered a weather-vane for the house at Swingfield bearing his own arms, which were also displayed in a window of the church there.[11] It will be argued that he was probably responsible for the "Lord's new chamber", encroaching on the chapel. Though at some time (*c.* 1524–5 ?) he had duly held the command, he treated the whole estate, and for a longer time, like a private manor. Yet, there is internal evidence that both Swingfield and Oare were then normally at farm and other evidence that the command and revenues of Swingfield were sometimes shared between two knights on service in the Mediterranean, where a pair met their deaths soon after appointment, to be replaced by two more on May 8th, 1528,[12] the very day that Weston was allowed livery of his temporalities and began to put the whole Hospitaller house in order.

Rawson belonged to the "top brass" of the Order, the peer, and no doubt the rival, of Weston and far more secure—if anyone was secure, in the favour of his Prince. Though he seems to have been present at the defence of Rhodes in 1522, his temper and abilities were those of his mercantile origins in London. With a brief interval he was Prior of Kilmainham, and thereby of Ireland, from 1511–12 until 1540, when he exchanged it for a lay viscountcy and the enormous pension of 500 marks. He turned nearly all the dependencies to his own advantage and that of his household. He served as Treasurer of Ireland more than once from 1517 and was one of the commission of three that exercised the office of Deputy from August 1529.[13] Cringing to Wolsey and the King, whose ablest instrument of Ascendancy he was, overbearing and managing to everyone else, his wood-mongering in Kent (or that of his servant Anthony) must have been small business but all grist to the mill of the "pecuniose" Prior. His presence was required in England as well as Ireland, particularly in the critical years between 1524 and 1528, for part of which, no doubt, he enjoyed the command of Swingfield as a convenient residence, or staging-post to the Continent, but could not resist turning it to good account. From the autumn of 1529 he was safely in Ireland and, as far as is known, remained there.

TEXT

1. The Viewe and State of the Commanndrie off Swyngfeld with all and singler membres lordshippes maners landes and tenementes pastures medowes and wodes as well tymber as underwodes to the saide Commanndrie bel[ongy]ng and apperteynyng viewed sene and taken [by Guthlacu]s overton auditor to the right honorable [Sir William] Weston knyght prior of thospitall of seynt [John of Hi]erusalem in England and William Wilcockes [notary] auttorised servant to the seid prior the vjth day [---]s xxti yere of the Reigne of king Henry [viij]

The hall

Imprimis the hall their is in leyngth xlij fote and in brede xxx fote Item within the said hall their is a cupborde of waynescot old Item ij syde bordes dormant verray feble the on of them is in leyngh xxiij fote and in brede ij fote

Item the other is in leyngh xv fote and in brede on fote & di Item ij formes to the same tables accordyng to the leyngh of aither of them

2. Item an old benche at the hygh dease with a borded bakk nygh a yard dypp Item iiij peces of bay steyned verray feble conteynyng in leyngh ix yardes and in brede ij yardes

Item on wyndow on the E[ast ? of] the saide hall with leves therto without any barres

Item on the oder syde be [ij wyndowes] the on with xiiij barres and [the oder with] iiij barres verray old and [feble]

Item in the Rofe a litle [---]

Item the said hall is of [----] facion covered with tyle the [most ?] wherof is good and substanciall [----] tyles must be rypped and new layed

Item on the west side of the same hall ther is a metly good dorre with lock and key and a bolt of Iron to the same

Item at the hall dorre in the porche their be a payre of old stockes

3. The Newe parlor

Item within the same an old borde varray old and feble conteynyng in leyngh xvj fote and in brede iij fote di

Item ij old formes to the same the on [-- f]ote long and the other xiij fote

Ite[m] a c]upborde of waynscot metly good

Item ij wyndowes well glased & furnysshed with [bar]res

Ite[m] a p]ortall of waynscot with ij dorres [---] the iiij boltes iiij staples of Iron [an]d ij cachys ij good handilles [on t]he owt side and ij rynges of [Iron] insyde the saide portall

4. The chambor ovyr the saide parlor

Item the seid chambor is called the lordes new chambor
Item therin is a standyng [---] a troclebed and a forme
Item a litle old borde for a presse with ij trestylles
Item a chymney and ij [andi]rons ther unto belongyng and a fyre shovell
Item a forme
Item a portall of waynnescot after the order and maner of the portall in the said parlor
Item ij Stone bottelles with wikeres for wyne
The galary their
Item in the galary betwixt the said chambor and the chappell on ladder to go up to the uppur galary ovyr the saide chambor
Item within the galary v hopys of Iron for a Bucket and iij hyngys
5. Item a fane of Iron with Sir John Rawson Armes lord of Kilmayne
Item on cultre for a plugh
Item a barre of Iron a glasse wyndowe a [fot]e & di long
Item ij lasser barres of Iron of the same length for glasse wyndowes
Item ij Iron cheynes for oxen
Item an old trevet of Iron verray feble and [not] worthe kepyng
Item an old payre of great steroppys of the old facion not worthe kepyng
Item ij brasse pottes the on conteynyng [--] gallons and the other ij gallons metly goode
Item ij pothokes of Iron
Item an old brasse panne conteynyng ij gallons
Item ij sydes of a bed new
Item ij Iron rackes Aither of them conteynyng in leyngth v fote
Item an old fyre fork of Iron cont in leyngh iiij fote di
Item on flesshe hoke
Item ij great hevy bylles verray old
Item a lock without a key
Item a square spyt of Iron of viij fote long by estimacion
6.   A studie by the saide galary and chapell
In primis a chest with evidens
Item a vestiment with floures of goldwerk and selk
Item an Albe without amys
Item a Tenacle and stole of the saide werke
Item a masse boke of parchyment grayles offitories and post comynes in playne song
Item ij Antifenars of parchyment in playn song
Item an old Ordynall in parchyment
Item an old Saulter in parchyment
Item an old masse boke in parchyment
Item a grayle in parchyment

Memo. that all the said parcelles and every of them so old and feble and not used nor worthe keping

Item a case of Iron for wyndow new within the said studie

7. **The Chappell**

Inprimis within the same a chalys with a paten of Selver parcell gilt

Item a corporas case

Item a text and a masse boke

Item a canapy of chaungeable red sarcenet with iiij knappys and terselles of selke

Item a Net that the pix hangith in

Item an Albe of white fustian branchied with red and grene selke and spanged

Item iij Aulter clothes the on of drap broken most par[t] and-the other ij playn

Item an Aulter clothe of canvas to covyr the said aulter clothes

Item ij brasse candilstyckes of a fote of length and ij tapurs of a handful leyngh uppon them

Item complete hangynges for the rerdose and curtens for the same aulter of ledder wrought with branchies like clothe of tyssis of the gift of Mr Rawson lord of Kylmayn

Item iij Irons for the ryredose and curtens ffor the said Aulter.

8. Item ij crosses with the pyctor of Crist in the on of them is stones of glasse and the other without stones and ther uppon is a towell of selke of iij quarters of a yard leyngh by estymacon bawdekyn werk that cam from the Rhodes

Item a pyx for the sacrament of copur and iij crownes broken whiche shuld be opon the top of the canapy

Item a doble paxe and ij other paxes all old and litle worthe

Item on candilstyck of Iron of vj fote leyngh

Item a cofyr with a lyd without lock and key

Item ij steyned clothes old and feble for the same aulter

Item an old Cruet not worth keping

Item ther be vj pycters on of our lady ij of saint John Baptest on of saint Blase Another of Mary Mawdelen and another of seynt John Evangelist old picters except ij of them whiche be ungild or paynted

Item an old boxe before saint John Baptest old and feble

Item x wyndowes glased and barred old and feble

9. Item a feyre quere of kervyng werke and well burded under fyt and within the said quere hangith iij tables whiche ar copies of bulles written ther uppon

Item a pew for Mr Commannder to syt or knele in and iij rygalles of Iron to draw curtens abought the same

Item vj tapurs iij before seint John Baptest and iij before seint John the Evangelist

Item the said Chappell is well paved within the quere and without and a pyctor of Crist in the top of the quere

Item in the bodye of the Chapell be the copies of ij bulles uppon ij tables on in englishe and another in laten

Item a forme within the said chappell

Item ther ar ij belles hangyng ovyr the churche porche besides the studye chambor and ij dorres to the same the on with lock and ij boltes and the other dorre barred

Item a dorre going out of the chappell in to the hall bolted with on bolt

10. The parlor on the Sowth end of the saide hall

In primis therin a table old and feble conteynyng in leyngh xiij fete & di and in brede ij fote and iiij qarters with ij old trestylles to the same

Item an old forme cont in leyngh xij fote

Item the store underfote burded old & feble

Item a portall of waynscot with ij dorres with ij lachys and ij cachys of Iron ij rynges ij boltes iiij stapuls with ij rynges on the Inneside and ij handilles on the owteside

Item the wyndow in the west ende wel glaced & well bared and ij levys with hynges and hokes to the same and a lynyng of waynscot to lene uppon

Item another wyndow therin wel glaced and well barred

Item for the same wyndow ij bordes nayled togeder to lene uppon.

The pantry

Item therin ij shelffes of bordes the on vij fote in leyngh and the other xiij fote and therunto belongith a steyned clothe of v fote and di in length

Item a table conteynyng in leyngh ix fote and in brede ij fote and iiij Inches

11. Item ij trestelles [to] the said table

Item an old chest to put in bred conteynyng in leyngh vj fote and in brede ij fote and iiij Inches

Item an old wyndow with ij trestylles cont in leyngh v fote & in brede ij fote or ther opon

Item to the same pantry a dorre with ij leves ij peyre of hokys & ij peyre of hynges toward the parlor

Item into the hallward owte of the same pantry a dorre with ij levys to serve bred and ale into the hall

Item within the same a wyndow barred with Iron old and feble

The Buttry

Item therin ij shelffes of oken burdes cont in leyngh either of them xij fote and in brede on fote & more

Item ij old quarters to ley uppon Ale and bere conteynyng in leyngh xiij fote

Item to the same a dorre with a bolt

Item by the same a litle Rome to ley in wyne

Item therin a shelff conteynyng in leyngh iiij fote and iij Inches and in brede a fote & ij Inches

12. The litle Buttry

Item therin an old mustard querne within the stock and iij fote to the same

Item ij shelffes to put these uppon and the on side quarter borde by cause the walls be broken

Item ij dorres with ii lockes and on key

Item an old quevyr broken covered with leder nothing worth

The pasterye

Item therin a knedyng trough with a table to mowld bred uppon conteynyng in leyngh x fote and in brede iij quarters

Item a shelf to set bred uppon conteynyng in leyngh ij yardes and in brede a fote & more

Item an old dorre to the same with a lache and ij ryngges that the dorre hangeth uppon

The Kechyn

Item to the same a dorre with ij levys with lock and key a bolt of Iron and a stay of Iron to hold the dorre to

13. Item a dressyng borde dormant of iiij Inches thyck with ij postes to lye upon

Item another borde dormant with ij postes within the grond

Item ij great brasse pottes unset but at large whereof on of them hathe a great hole conteynyng xiiij gallons & the other is sownd whiche conteyneth xviij gallons

Item a Rack of Iron to hang iij pottes togeder over the fyre

Item a litle burde to put mete uppon

Item ij barres of Iron to set pottes uppon every of them conteynyng iiij fote leyngh

Item within the said kechyn is iij ovyns the great conteyneth by estimacon vij buscels another iij bs and the iijde ij buscels

Item ther is a fayre Chymney cont in leyngh xxij fote and ther unto belongith on wyndow and a place to serve out mete at

A galary beyende the same kechyn at the

Est side for the Chaplen and other s(er)vantes

In p(ri)mis a chambor at the steyer hed whiche the prist lieth in wherin is an old broken federbed and to the same a bolster and a pelow old & feble al not worth the [kep]ing

14. Item to the said chambor for the bed ther a good coverlet red and yolow and a payre of shetes

Item a cupborde & ij formes

Item to the said chambor belongith a dorre a lock and a key & a chymney

The ijde chambor ther

Item therin lieth the servantes of the place

Item within the same chambor is a bedstede ij burdes for shelffes a drawyng wyndow and a dorre with lock & key

Item an old hawkys perche and the wall on the on side of the chambor broken

The iijde chambor

Item therin a bedstede a wyndow a dorre without lock and key and the chambor metly good

15. The iiijth chambor

Item the same chambor hathe a dorre with a claspe of Iron and ij panys of the wall is broken

The vth chambor

Item the said chambor is without dorre & wyndow

Item at thende of the saide galary is house of easement & therin is iij setes to chite in

Item the bordes of the same galary under fyt ar old & broken mony of them

The galary under the said chambors

In primis a chambor with a dorre and a back dorre by the same next to the steyer fote openyng on the wodeyerd

The ijde chambor

Item the said chambor now is a larder house and therin a trough to powder flesh

The iijde chambor

Item a chambor and a dorre to the same

The iiijth chambor

Item the walles ar broken & no dorre to the same

16. A larder agenst the saide galary other wise called a sclaughter house

Item anout the said galary is a longhouse conteynyng in leyngth lx fote and in brede ix fote in the whiche house ther is a Rome for a sclaughter house and iij other Romes for Swyne the walles be all broken and the tyles most part gon and the tymber therof roten for lack of coveryng which must nedes be new made or elles it wil fal down

The entre from the yemens galary

Item an entre from the yemens galary to go through by the kechyn unto the hall and a dorre in the middst of the said entre with a lache and no lock nor key and the on side of the entre is borded with ij bordes brede

17. The chambor ovyr the old parlor by the pantry

In primis therin a bedstede

Item a kervyd chest the on ende broke and gonne without lock and keye

Item ij wyndowes well barred and wel glaced with foldyng wyndowes
Item a dore therunto without lock and key havyng a bolt and therin is a
chy(m)ney old and must be repayred

The hall porche chambor

Item ovyr the porche ther is a closed a dorre with lock and key and a
ryng of Iron to the same dorre
Item the wyndowes wel barred and glaced
Item a chambor by the draught and therin a bedstede
Item iiij wyndowes wel barred with Iron the on half glaced feble with
certen armes upon them
Item to the same chambor belongith a house of easement and a dorre to
it and ij other dorres besides with bolt and rynges
Item at the steyer hed a dorre with lock and key and a ring of Iron

18.   The chambor at the steyer hed

Item by the same is a chambor whiche the maydyns lieth in called the
Red chamber with a bedstede & a troclebed
Item a forme and a dorre to the same chamber
Item iiij wyndowes wel barred ij be glaced and ij without glasse
Item a chymney within the said chamber
Item within the forsaid chambor is another chambor and therin ij sydes
of a bed and a house of easement and a wyndow well barred without
glasse

A galary alias a chambor

Item besides the steyer hed ther is a galary with a dorre whiche is a
chambor where the whete is therin now
Item at thende therof ther is a chambor with a dorre and the wall
broken
Item at the steyer fote a good strong dorre with lock and key

19.   The Southe side by the old parlor

Item a house old and feble and the loft is broken and therin standith a
kylne to dry malt and the steyer is broken
Item the said house hathe a dorre with lock and a claspe

The Malthouse

Item a querne to grynd malt
Item an old chese presse
Item a dorre with lock and key
Item ij old tubbys
Item the maltloft is wel tymbured and the walles feble and broken
Item in the said maltloft is iiij Romes for whete and malt
Item to the said loft is a fallyng dorre with ij hynges and ij hokes & a
claspe of Iron
Item the steyer old and broken
Item at thende of the saide malthouse is a deyry with a chymney of
wood old and feble and ij small chambors aloft and on bedstede the tyle

ovyr hed broken

20. Item beneth under that on chambor
Item in the deyry house is ij old trestylles
Item an old cupbord with iij florys
Item to the seyd deyry belongith iij dorres the on hathe lock & key

The store house

In primis old glasse with the led for wyndowes
Item old Iron barres for wyndowes
Item on syde of an old bedstede
Item a chynesate with a staf
Item iiij brases of tymbor of litle valure for a house
Item diverse peces of tymbor as doithe appere ther of smal valure
Item an old barre of Iron for a wyndow
Item a trase for a cart
Item a yoke with ij Iron hokys
Item iij kynderkyns nothing worthe but to the fyre
Item an old broken tubbe very feble
Item an old stand for Ale
Item a markying Iron with saint Johns crosse metly good to marke bestes

21. A stable

Item next the said storehouse is a stable of on bay unplanched

The barne annexed to the said stable

Item next the seid stable is a barne called the hey barne with a great yate to the same with ij leves the said barne is of iiij bayes and therin is saint Johns frary cart without any wheles
Item a banner of black clothe with a white crosse and a bell belonging to the said frary cart
Item the tymbor of the barne is good the walles broken and the barne lackith thackyng
Item at thende of the same barne is a mylne house without any mylne under the said Rofe the tymber beyng good and the walles broken ffrom the said store house unto the said mylne al as under on Rofe whiche conteyneth in leyngth C^m & xx fote and in brede xxx fote

22. The great barne

Item the tymber of the great barne is good and substanciall and the Rome therin is of viij bayes the barne covered with straw which conteneth in leyngh vj^{xx}xvj fote and in brede xxx fote
Item to the same barne belongith ij great gates covered with tyle
Item to the said barne belongith v dorres and the walles borded verray feble the groundsylles not good and the underpynnyng must nedes be amendet

The doif Cote

Item ij doif cotes under on Rofe and on quarter therin is al down

Item on the westside of the same the plates ar rotted and uncovered at thende of the said cote is covered with tyle verray feble and the walles broken

Item to the same belongith ij dorres havyng no lock nor key but lached

23.   An orchard annexed to the said dof cote

Item an orchard and a garden belonging to the same conteyniyng by estymacon di. acr whiche orchard is paled round abought

A pynfold

Item by the said garden is a pynfold verray feble palyd abought & therin a bore stye

The great gate cumyng into the place

In p(ri)mis a great yate whiche is broken and a posterne by the same with a dorre hole

Item ovyr the same yate is a chamber and a steyer belongyng to hyt opon the top wherof standith a fane the said lackith tylyng and the walles therof broken and feble

24.   A long house with a stable next the said gate

In primis a stable very evyll plancked and a chambor next it

Item iij houses of offices under the same Rof whiche house with the premisses afore said conteyneth in leyngh lxxxxiiij fote and in brede xix fote the wall on the on syde is of stone and the other ar of erthe feble and old

The horse pond

Item afore the said house is a pond and by the same lieth iij old trowes of stone

Item from the yate to the same pond is paled metly well

25.   A garden

Item a garden called the holme standyng sowth and by sowthe Est paled abought and most part broken

(Lands: the next two sections are catalogued in tautologous fashion and summarised hereunder. P = pasture: M = meadow; A = arable ("herable"); ac. = acres; yrs. = years' growth of woodland, all young coppice)

A. "The demeanes belongyng to the fermor of Swingfeld", viz: 1, "A close called the holmes", from the south to the east sides—6 ac. of which 3 ac. P and 3 ac. tree-grown (ashes); 2, "Churchfeild"—9 ac., A; 3, "old mede"—7 ac., M; 4, "dowlettes"—5 ac., P; 5, ditto—2 ac., A; 6, ditto—1 ac., P; 7,

26.   "Stochamfeld" (Stockham)—26 ac., A; 8, "mawnsys grond"—7 ac., A; 9, 20 ac., P, "lye for medow this yere"; 10, 16 ac., P; 11, "parke hole"—7 ac., P; 12, "beside boynton crosse (Boyington) within my lady fenys[14] grond"—2 ac., P; 13, "Coldesoland"—5 ac., A; 14, ditto—2 ac., M; 15, "bromfeld"–8 ac., P; 16, "old Mede" (cf. no. 3)—1 ac., P but containing oaks and ashes; 17,

"the heremytage"—14 ac., A; 18, "Stretfeld"—8 ac., P; 19, ditto, on other side of street—1 ac., P; 20, "horeswiche"—6 ac., P.

27. B. "Woodes within the ferme of Sylstyd belonging to the same demayne", viz: 1, "on brow of the great pastur" (Swingfield Minnis ?)—4 ac., at 6s. 8d. per ac.; 2, on "side of the hyll on the west side joynyng to my lady peytons pastur"—6 ac., 7 or 8 yrs., at 10s per ac.; 3, "begynwod" (Biggin Wood)—3 or 4 yrs., not otherwise estimated; 4, 5, two woods called "belchaster", the springs of both "distryed with catell"—one 1 or 2 yrs., the other 7 or 8, not otherwise estimated; 6, "dowlettes"—2 or 3 ac., at 12s. per ac.; 7, "lywod" (possibly Lyoak), "belonging to the lordship of Swyngfeld"—4 or 5 ac., 2 yrs., not valued.

28.

The channcell of Swyngfeild

Item the said channcell is covered with tyle the tymber wherof is old and metly good and the Rofe lackith Reparacon and ther unto belongith vj wyndowes the particion of on is broken and without help wil shortly fall down

Item before the high Aulter ther is a front of satten of bruges grene and yolow

The parsonnage at Ewelme

In p(ri)mis ib(ide)m an old barne underpyned and the ground sylles feble cont in leyngh lxxij fote and in brede xxviij fote & di the said barne standith in a close called parsonnage medow

Item the p(ar)sonnage medow cont acres by estymacon ij

Item a close called glebeland cont acres herable iiij

29.

The maner at Ewell called the Temple

Item ther belongith to the same manor lyeng within hitself acres herable landes pasture and woodes to the Nombre in all as heraftre foloweth

(These are summarised as in sections A and B, above)

    C. 1, in the parish of "colred" (Coldred)—7 ac., P; 2, "westlese"—20 ac., P; 3, two closes—30 ac., A; 4, "the court closes wher the walles and a long barne stand covered with straw the tymber metly good the coveryng most be amended"—7 ac.; 5, two closes "called the Estlese"—80 ac., 6, a close between the same—40 ac., A; 7, "a wood called the Temple wood"—16 ac., 8 or 10 yrs.; 8, by the barn—5 ac., M; 9, a close "Est from the wood"—

30.   20 ac.; 10, "ground lyeng at large out of closure"—60 ac., A; 11, "in Shiplese ther at large uppon the downes—300 ac.; 12, "oxenhyll" s12 ac., P.; 13, 14, 15, three woods, "derwald", "cart busshes" and "medilhurst", lying and reckoned together—26 ac., 3 or 4 yrs.

31. Item ther is in the same parreshe (Ewell) ij mylles under on Rofe the on

for whete and the other for malt now beyng in the tenure of Thomas Townley the milne stones ar woren and of litle value and the mylne is verray old and fallyng down and the milner is an old poure man whiche is bownd to bere all charges & rep(ar)acons if he were able—
iiijli

32. The manor of bonyngton
(summarised as in sections A, B, C, above)
D. 1, "a wood called cort wood"—7 ac., 8 yrs; 2, "another wood called strode nygh the fryghe" (Aldington Frith)—6 ac., 10 yrs; 3, (prefixed "Rentes Landes and pastures ther") 26 ac. at 20d. per acre (60s.); 4, 10 ac. at 3d. per acre (2s. 6d.); 5, 112 ac. at 2s. per acre 40 4s.); 6, "the Rentes of Assise", 46s. 6d. yearly; 7, "the certaynte and other presettes of courtes", annual value not entered.

33. Woodes sold
Md that there was sold at Ester anno xx° R h viii by my lord of kylmayn S John Rawson to Snachebull fermor ther and to other p(er)sons xxiiij great okys (xlviij s, above) and xl or 1 great Elmes and asshes (iiijli iijs iiijd, above) in ij closes abought the churche ther whiche were worth vjli xjs iijd
Item the personnage ther is at the gift of the Commannder of Swyngfeld and is worth by estimacon toward the chargies xx marcs

34. Woodes sold abought Sylsted
(These and the following sections are abbreviated: the woods are reckoned in acres or "yards" (yd.) of a quarter of an acre and the value sometimes said to be paid)
E. 1, "certayn hedgerowes of Elmes okes and other woods", at Midsummer, 20 Hen. VIII, to George Marsshe of Alkrygg (Acrise) and Robart Jenkyn of Alham (Alkham), "the spryng wherof is clyrely distryed for default of closure", for 40s; 2, 12 elms in "the close called xx acres" (A, 9 ?), to R. Jenkyn, for 20s; 3, 1 yd. "under the wood of skegyn (or stregyn (?), perhaps Biggin Wood), to Andrew Manger for 3s. 4d.; 1 ac. and 1 yd. "in the close where the court of Sylstede is kept", to John Stacy for 15s.

35. Woodes felled at Mydlast and sold
F. 1, to William William of Dover "by Antony M Rawson servant sens Cristomas was twelvemoneth Anno xix°h viij" for 5s.; 2 (this and the following all to men of Ewell), ½ ac. delivered by Thos. Master to Thos. ffawkener, for 8s.; 3, ½ ac. to Richard Salmon for 8s.; 4, 1 ac. to [--] bacheler for 16s.; 5, 1 yd. to Robart Sawyer for 4s.; 6, ¼ yd. to John Fryre for 2s., 7, ditto to Edward Mylton.

Woodes sold owt of lywood Menys

(Initial date as in section F; woods from which timber is taken generally named)

36.

G. 1, to John ffysher of Alkham, not named or valued; 2, Curbushe, 1 yd. to R. Sawyer, of Ewell (as the four following), for 4s.; 3, ditto, ½ yd., to Robart Hamond, at same rate, as all the following; 4, ditto, 1 yd. to Henry Tachebe; 5, ditto, ½ ac., but valued as ½ yd., to Nicholas Hony; 6, ditto, ½ yd. to William Clerck; 7, "the lodge", 1 yd. to John Mount, of Lydden (as the three following); 8, "the Shave", ½ yd. to Thos. Water; 9, ditto, ½ yd. to William Taylor; 10, ditto, 1 yd. to the Vicar of Lydden; 11, Lywood Menys, to Rauf [--] of Alkham, not valued; 12, ditto, to William Golfynche of River, not valued.

Houshold stuf and Implementes delivered and geven out of Swyngfeld by Sir John Rawston (sic) lord of Kylmayn to dyverse persons at mydsomer as herafter foloweth Anno xx h viij viz To John Elles of Dovor Thomas fawkener of Ewell & to Christofer del of Canterbury

ij fayre cheyers of waynscot kervyd and joyned stoles vj or vij of waynscot a fayre standyng cubbord with ij awmburies lokyd

Item a tyll a chest whiche was veray ponderowse & weyghtie supposed to be Impleted with pewter vesselles and other stuff

37.

The Names of Woodes belonging to Waltham ferme

In p(ri)mis a wood called buttrwood conteynyng by estimacon acres v

Item another wood called covert conteynyng by estimacon acres (blank)

Md that John barnes of petham coliar hathe bought of M Gutlace Overton Auditor to the right honourable Sir Willm. Weston knyght prior of saint Johns ij acres wood standyng of the North part of Shawdell als. butt wood within the ferme of Waltham anno xxº R h. viij for xls to be paid at Midsomer and Michelmas next cummyng by equal porcons al ys Reserved to the lord or Commander of Swyngfeld—This beyng witnes Thomas Court

38.

Ore

First ther is a barne coveryd with straw of lxxviij fote on leyngth & xxxiii fote in brede very old feble & fallyng down wheroppon no cost nor charge was doon by the space of xxiij yeres past as it is said and nedes a newe barne must ther be made

Item ther is another house to kepe in calves and shepe conteynyng in leyngth lvj fote and xvj fote in brede wherof the tymber is good and it is covered with strawe metly well but the walles must be amended

Item ther be iiij acres of pastures of the demeanes by est. within the Circuyt wher the Mancion place orchard and garden hertofor hathe ben enclosed within on hedge

Item ther is on close of herable land of the demeanes lyeng est of the said barne and house cont. v acres

Item ther is another close of herable land of the said demeanes lyeng North and sowthe of the said houses cont. xl acres

Item ther be by estimacon xlvj acres of pasture whiche were somtyme in vj closes called Corte closes and now they lye at large except on cont. by est. xvj acres whiche is inclosed & was aired and sowen within iiij yeres past

39. Item ther be ij acres by estimacon that were latly medow and now be lost by the salt water and they lye at thende of the Golet toward the salt m(ar)sshe whiche if they were Inned & kept from the salt water wil be worthe vjs viijd by yere

Item ther be abought lx or iiij^{xx} acres of salt m(ar)sshe whiche is litle worthe and if they were enclosed and saved from the salt water ev(er)y acre wil be worthe yerely ijs And it is supposed that xl or lli wil s(er)ve to Inne and close it

Item ther be meny faire Elmes and div(er)se okes growing in hedgerowes about the said landes and pastures whiche wil suufice and s(er)ve for to maynteyn & kepe the reparacons and buyldinges of the said barne and house and the shredinges of them will serve for hedges and closures of the said Landes and most part of the pastures but now to be sold for the lordes Armitage and other woodes ther be now ther

Item every acre of Land is estimate to be worthe yerely ijs and every acre of pasture ijs iiijd

40. Item my lord of Kylmayn S John Rawson late Comaunder of Swyngfeld about iiij yeres past felled and sold lx or above of the best and farest Elmes that grewe on the demeanes for vjli or x marc as it is reported whiche were felled to have newe made the seid berne

Item Willm Bromfeld occupiethe the ferme of the said landes pastures and m(ar)sshes at the lordes pleasure without any lease and payeth yerely xijli xiijs iiijd and he takith the profettes of the cortes and he recevyth of the tenantes lxxvjs ijd in Rentes cc^{mi} iiij^{xx} xvij egges and xij hennes and j cocke and he paieth the Surveyers and stewardes costes at his own charges

For the Berne
at ore

41. Md that I have covenãted and made
a bargen the vth day of Aprill Anno xx^{o}
R 'H viij w^{t} Richard Ryvet of Fevshme
Carpenter that he shal make or cause to
be made anew frame of Elmen tymber
and oke for a Berne in the Rome and
place wher the old berne doith stand of
lxx fete of assice in length and xxiiij
fete in brede and of xij foote in hight

117

betwene the Groundesell and the syde
Reasones and that he shall fel cut and
sawe square al man of tymber that to
the said frame shal sve and belong
and al the same frame w^t great large
dorris and on lesse dore and al other
that to the werk of a carpenter and sawyer
doith belong and appteyne at his own
ppre costes and charges and that he shall
set up in all the said frame well & substancially
or cause to be set up and don betwene
this and the last ende monethe of

42. Julye next comyng for the whiche
bargen well and truly & substan
tially to be made and don in
man & forme beforsaid the said
Richard shal have of the lord and
his successours of the Comanndre of
Swyngfeld for the tyme beyng
viij^{li} vj^s viij^d on redy money and
a cote clothe or elles x^s in money
for the same cote thies being
present and witnesses at and to this
Bargen John Elles of dovo^r stuard
of the co^{r}tes S'Will^{a}m Iresby preshe
prist of ore Will^{a}m Bromfeld
fermo^r of the Mano^r ther Will^{a}m
Wilcockes svaunt to my lord of saint
Johns notary and divse other moos   viij^{li} xvj^s viiij^d

p me Guthlacū ovton

43. Item Richard atkynson of Fevsh^{a}me
tyler doithe report and saye that
xxxiiij^{ml} Tyles by estimacon will   v^s
sve to cover all the seid Berne and
evy m^l will cost redy brought home v^s
Item that lyme and Sand asmoche as
will sve for the same wil stand and   xxvj^s viij^d
cost by estimacon xxvj^s viij^d
Item the Rof tyles and corner CCC di   viij^s
tyles will cost by estimacon viij^s
Item the underpynnyng will cost   vj^s viij^d
by estimacon   vj^s viij^d

118

Itm the said Richard will and doithe ⎫
pmese to ley evy m^l tyle for xij^d and ⎪
the R of tyle to be pcell and rekened   ⎬   xxxvij^s vj^d
in the Nombre if tyles and for evy   ⎪
C corn tyles viij^d ⎭
Itm as for tyle pynnes the seid Richard
will make w^{t}out any thing taking for the same
Sm^a—xxj^{li} v^s vj^d ov
and besides tymber for the
seid work whiche wilbe
worth by est if it shuld
be bought—x m^{a}rc

COMMENTARIES

I. *Lands and Woods*

Those surveyed comprise four small manors, in effect the demesnes and their woods, farmed in one or two units, with little mention of incidents and none of commons. These are: 1, Swingfield with Selstead, extending into Denton; 2, Ewell, derived from the Templars; 3, Bonnington, on the edge of Romney Marsh; 4, Oare, near Faversham, even further away. Of Waltham, another former Templar manor, only the woods are counted, between 3 and 4. The assessment is frank and fresh, taking little from ancient valuations, and the arrangement is probably in order of visitation. In the report of 1338 the order is quite different: only Bonnington is treated with Swingfield: Oare, though already associated with it, is taken with Stalisfield as a separate Hospitaller endowment, and the two ex-Templar houses are listed together and apart. These were not all that was administered from Swingfield. The exchequer account of 1547[15] includes numerous tenements which the officials did not bother to inspect, either because the farm-rents were paid without trouble or because they were fragmented, uneconomic or only existed on paper. Soon after 1547 anything of any size had been disposed of and what remained—dozens of small rents, perhaps unchanged for centuries, totalling only a few pounds and hardly worth the trouble of collecting—was duly enrolled in Philip and Mary's grandiose charter of 1558 re-establishing the Hospital in England.[16] Thus were the bulwarks of Christendom to be reinforced with left-overs! They need not trouble us any more than they troubled the realistic Guthlac Overton, save in one point of topographical interest.

Among them the aforementioned documents of 1547 and 1558 list, in identical order and valuation, Wyngmere (Wingmore) and Blodbeame (the Blood-tree, softened to Bladbean), hamlets each with five tenements which still remain in the upper Elham valley, then nine tenements, mostly of cottage size, in Bilchester, or Belchester, and finally the single, larger yeoman's homestead of Gatehurst (Gatteridge) in Denton. Belchester exercised Wallenberg as an apparently "false" *chester* name, the site of which is lost.[17] If it could be found the descriptions would make it just big enough to qualify as a deserted medieval *village*. It was certainly in the Hundred of Folkestone, and Wallenberg, while suggesting Beachborough as a possible location, provisionally puts it in Hawkinge. However, the order of the aforementioned documents suggests that it should lie between Denton and the Elham valley and the name occurs in the "View and State", not as a place of habitation but twice in folio 27 (see summary "B") among the woods on the farm of Selstead, where the adjacent Butcher's and Billets woods may preserve the name in a corrupt form. It may well be that the cottage rents were still being paid in the sixteenth century for plots that had reverted to woodland.

Most of the demesne farm of Swingfield was comprised in a compact holding between the preceptory and the church. The small, squarish fields can be identified with varying probability from the nineteenth-century Ordnance Survey and from the obviously ancient hedgerows, which are being progressively eroded. Thus, the 9 acres of Churchfield, which must be O.S. no. 150 (9 ac. 6 p.) have since been thrown into a larger field and another, perhaps Old Mede, dovetailing into it, had already gone before the O.S. was made. Other old fields can be recognized on both sides of the lane leading to the church, while those to the north-west, towards Stockham, look like recent enclosures and "Stochamfeld" can no longer be identified. There were also outliers, including the enclave beside Boynton (i.e. Boyington) cross, but there is no evidence that the Hospital had interests in the remaining sub-manors of Swingfield, North Court and Boyington (which Wadmore confused with Bonnington).[18] Apart from Lywood, which may be identical with Lyoak and have lain towards Ewell, the demesne woods were all in Selstead, where Biggin Wood and perhaps Belchester (see above) can still be located, and where the occurrence of the word "dowlettes", found also on the demesne farm, suggests that other patches, too, may have reverted to wood. These woods were ash-coppices and the like, surprisingly young, and, here as at Oare, it is arguable that Rawson, having sold much of the timber-trees had planted for a quick crop that might have been very well in Ireland but appeared in Kent as a form of asset-stripping. Without the woods the demesne formed a good mixed farm of about 150 acres, at least twice the size of a typical larger Wealden yeoman's holding, and befitting a great aisled barn, 136 feet long and a capacious hay-barn, though there is no mention of byres as such. At the final count it contained 63 acres of arable, 80 of pasture and meadow (hayfield) and perhaps four of orchard and garden.

Temple Ewell, in contrast, was an upland estate, again apparently at farm in one unit without complaint, containing at least 130 acres of arable and a vast extent of sheep-runs (much of both "at large", i.e. unenclosed) but with less of intensive pasture than Swingfield. The woods probably lay south-west of Lydden and Watling Street, towards Ewell Minnis and bordered on Swingfield at Lyoak. The individual woods, such as Mydlast or Medilhurst, are hard to trace. They were probably scrubby and neglected but found many takers at 4s. for a "yard" of a quarter-acre. Again, Rawson may have been genuinely intent on replanting and "improving".

The two small marsh-side manors of Bonnington and Oare had much in common. Here, it was large timber rather than coppice that was misappropriated: at Bonnington the farmer Snachebull (?Knatchbull) made a bargain with 48 great oaks, to say nothing of elms, at 2s. each, when a tie-beam was often conventionally valued at 13s. 4d.[19] The valuation of Bonnington is very close to that of 1338:[20] the rents of assize had risen but much marsh-meadow is still reckoned at 2s. an acre (the potential worth of the worse sort at Oare if it were to be reclaimed) and the rest is even poorer. At Oare, if this inundated marsh-meadow is ignored, the arable, including that recently "aired" (eared, ploughed), is nearly twice as much as the pasture. The whole, including rents and incidents, is at farm for 19 marks (probably what it had rendered in 1338) and is neglected, especially the Court Lodge site and buildings, where nothing obviously medieval is now to be seen. The name of the farmer, Broomfield, is preserved today by a house on another site. The wharf and fishery, which saved Oare from utter decay, are not mentioned. It says well for Overton that he thoroughly inspected these two shrunken settlements.

II. *The House at Swingfield*

Only two structures mentioned stand today: A, the greater part of a flint-built east–west range, with the obvious termination of a chapel in fine Early English work,[20] and B, running beside the road, a little north-west of A, a flint wall with a slight central projection, which is now just under 94 ft. long but until lately formed the back wall of a shed about 19 ft. wide and almost certainly represents the "Long House" beside the gateway.

Less than 150 ft. west of the original west end of A there stood, at least until the 1930s, obliquely orientated and on ground by no means level, a square farmyard of which the south-west range was a great barn, agreeing in size and very probably identical in substance with that described in the "View". The substantial and slightly longer south-east range may well have included the hay-barn and the single-bay stable, but the storehouse linking them with the main building had gone.

Range A, as it now stands, is 27 ft. wide and 62 ft. from the east end to where it was truncated at the west in the mid-nineteenth century, when a flimsy wing, now demolished, was added on the south and the truncation sealed with a tile-hung wall. On the north side, at the present extreme west is a flint porch, probably a medieval addition, with a chamber over it, which suggests that when it was added there was access from an upper floor. Subsequently, the entire range was divided into two storeys and a large internal chimney-breast of seventeenth-century aspect, now has flues east and west on either floor.

The precise date of the mid-nineteenth-century mutilation has not been ascertained, but it entailed the destruction of the western third of the range, not more than 10 m. long (as shown by a sudden fall in the ground), and of outshots on the south side, but of no transverse wing, as well as a crude re-gothicization of the north side by making bogus lancets in hard cement, not in the place of the original ones and still lighting two floors. It left intact a fair extent of old rendering coloured to resemble brickwork. The previous state of the building is known, not yet from excavation, but from four independent views, of which copies (or in one case an original water-colour drawing) are in the K.A.S. collections and which are all reproduced here. These are:

A, the original drawing, unsigned, dated 1794, from N.N.W.;[21]

B, the engraving in Brayley and Britton, *The Beauties of England and Wales*, 1806, from S.E.;

C, another water-colour, in the Petrie collection, but feeble by the standards of that splendid series, dated 1807, also from S.E.;[22]

D, a sparely, perhaps amateurishly engraved, but convincingly drawn, view found in the Colyer-Fergusson collection, signed G.J.K., undated but from the tree-growth apparently a generation or so after the others, from N.E.

The only view hitherto reprinted[23] is of no value—a crude, romanticized lithograph obviously based on B. The north views show two tiers of square-headed windows. These were perhaps inserted at the same time as the internal chimney-stack, only a short distance to the west of which rose the now demolished western part, with its roof-ridge not much higher than that of the rest, but clearly a two-storey chamber-block, buttressed on the south between the lean-tos, but with a big, two-flue chimney-breast of Tudor type on the north, just west of the porch.

Previous attempts at interpretation have assumed that the porch was a hall-porch, implying a short hall between the chapel and the chamber, roughly co-extensive with the hall of the later farmhouse. Since this odd series—chamber, chamber, hall, chapel, can be found in hospitals and infirmaries it might also have been used by the military orders at an early, and less "domestic", period. It has also been suggested for the comparable but no less altered Sutton-at-Hone.[24] The document makes clear that, at least at Swingfield, this interpretation is wrong. The porch must be the chapel (or "church") porch that carried two bells, and the *Chapel*, considered structurally, must extend over the whole surviving building. Only thus can its ten windows be accounted for: the eastern oculi were certainly already blocked[25] and all the others remain in part or whole—three on the north, three on the east and four on the south, of which two were above the outshot roof.

The *Hall*, the only part for which dimensions are given, was contiguous with the Chapel but ran north from the chamber-block, which contained its "service", in normal fashion, and matched the width of 30 ft., which suggests that it was an aisled hall. This and the absence of a chamber beyond the dais are consistent with its having been as old as the Chapel. It had a porch of its own on the better-lighted west side. Though it has long been utterly demolished its physical relations are quite unequivocal.

To follow the itinerary of the inventory in the logical way that such things are usually arranged leads from the Hall to the *New Parlour* and to the *Lord's New Chamber* above it, which had an unlighted, two-stage gallery between it and the Chapel, adjoining the *Study* which was evidently a very small room. Though the New Parlour was big enough to hold a 16-ft. table, all these, except perhaps the last, must surely have been won out of the space at the west end of the Chapel or just west of it. The only difficulties are in accounting for the two windows of the parlour, or indeed for its lighting at all, unless they were borrowed lights, and in the fireplace to the upper chamber. It seems that their construction began the process of flooring across the Chapel[26] and that the perpetrator may have been Rawson. The internal "portal" is a typically early-Tudor feature, and one floor-beam survives, apparently undisturbed, together with a quantity of re-used flooring and parts of a moulded wall-plate, all bearing mouldings consistent with this date. The inventory leads thence into the Chapel and back again into the Hall by a door in or adjoining the porch. It is possible that the study is in fact the chamber over the porch and certain that the inserts did not penetrate much further eastward into the Chapel. Between them and the sanctuary there was room for a "fair quire", i.e. a few quire-stalls, screened-off, and the Master's pew.

From the Hall the inventory leads into the ground-floor of the chamber-block to the south of it. Even if it was fractionally wider than the Chapel this pressed a good deal into a space less than 30 ft. square and its outshots; it included the *Old Parlour*, lighted from the west, the *Pantry*, lighted from the south, the *Buttery*, unlighted, other service-rooms, probably in the outshots, and no doubt a passage to the *Kitchen*. This last was probably free-standing, to the south, and east of it ran, probably further southward, the *Yeomen's Gallery*, a range of timber-framed lodgings for menservants, including the Chaplain (!), ending in a garderobe. This had formerly had access from a continuation of the kitchen-passage, and probably formed one side of a kitchen-court.

The next room examined is the *Chamber over the Old Parlour* (and perhaps over the service too), which suggests that its access was by an external staircase, either from the kitchen-court or from the west. This must have been the original great chamber; it was neglected, but had glazed and shuttered windows in good order and a fireplace, perhaps in the wall towards the hall, where the great chimney-breast was later built. It apparently had direct access to the chamber over the hall-porch, immediately north, but no further; steps must be retraced to the outside stair, whence extended three more lodgings: one by a garderobe (draught, or house of easement), another for womenservants, with its own garderobe, and a third, reduced to storing wheat. Adjoining these were two more neglected, two-storey timber-framed buildings, perhaps once inhabited but invaded by farm uses, one for a malt-kiln, the other for a malt-loft and dairy, containing a timber (and plaster) chimney-hood. The survey then moves south-west to the farmyard proper along a range comprising *Storehouse, Stable, Hay-barn and Mill-house* (? for a horse-mill). This was probably the south-east range, the range opposite being not yet built, and the *Great Barn* was at right angles to it. The *Dovecote* perhaps lay beyond the Barn, where the nineteenth-century Ordnance Survey still marks a building. The circuit ends at the *Gatehouse*, with chamber over, probably timber-framed, of the type once common and still seen, for example, at Nettlestead,[27] and beside it the *Long House* of which one wall remains.

III. *Barns*

Six barns are described,[28] to a more or less degree, in the document:

(1) The Hay Barn at Swingfield—the central four bays, including a waggon-door, out of a range of seven or eight, 120 ft. long and 30 ft. wide throughout. This would appear to have been an aisled grain-barn, with a single, central midstrey, in the older fashion, subsequently subdivided.

(2) The Great Barn at Swingfield, 136 ft. long and 30 ft. broad (i.e. aisled, but not of great section), in eight bays, with two midstreys and two "gates", which must be projecting or overhanging porches to the waggon-doors, since their roofs are separately covered. The two midstreys and generally good condition suggest that it was then not more than about 150 years old,[29] though in need of some repair.

(3) The relatively small barn at Ewell Parsonage, 72 ft. by 28½ ft., but still probably aisled on both sides.

(4) The Long Barn at Temple Ewell, dimensions not given.

(5) The Old Barn at Oare, condemned as unserviceable, 78 ft. long and 33 ft. wide, i.e. probably with relatively wide aisles and genuinely very old.

(6) The New Barn to be built at Oare to replace no. 5. This was to be aisleless and completely different from the others in fabric and structure. The site was probably at the Court Lodge, where no barn or trace of one remains or is shown by the Ordnance Survey. At Pheasant Farm, however, just south of the church, is a fine late specimen of an aisled barn, very conservative but clearly dated 1734 on the jowl of one of the main posts. This happens to be about the same length, 70 ft., as the New Barn and nearly as wide as the old one.

Apart from the last and that at Ewell Parsonage all the forementioned are described as thatched, or covered, with straw. At Swingfield the sides were boarded, and probably so at the others, but the possibility that the walls might have been daubed or that the straw covering might have extended to the sides, as sometimes in the Netherlands, should not be excluded. The covering, the ground-sills (sole-plates) and underpinnings (ground-walls) are often defective but, except at Oare, the main frame is never found unsatisfactory. Again with the exception of the New Barn at Oare, only at the Great Barn of Swingfield, and here only the waggon-porches, is any part of the roof described as tiled. Straw covering is still characteristic of arable east Kent, but tiles may have already been more usual in mid-Kent and the Weald.

As far as described, the other barns seem "normal" enough, but the specification for the New Barn, though quite detailed, raises almost as many questions as it answers. The carpenter's part is not especially remarkable. The frame is a relatively cheap one, including elm, and the supply of timber is left undefined. The general form, however, sounds typical of a widespread series of ultimate medieval and early post-medieval aisleless barns, of which a few, in Kent, still have crown-post roofs but the majority have clasped side-purlins.[30] The ties, which are often of elm, are relatively long; the walls commonly, as here, about 12 ft. high, have a half-height rail, to which, in Kent, the heads of the posts are normally braced. The type is assumed to be familiar to the carpenter. The only technical term that might be unfamiliar is "side-reason", meaning wall-plate.

This frame is evidently expected to be self-supporting, as though to be boarded or daubed in the usual manner, but it clearly was not so treated. The tiler's share of the contract is more costly than that of the carpenter, and of this the underpinning, no doubt the ground-wall for the frame, and the covering of the roof, materials included, are remarkably cheap. The bulk of the outlay, nearly as much as the whole carpenter's bill, is in the 34,000 "tiles" estimated as sufficient to "cover" the barn, which are quite distinct from the roof-tiles and "corner-tiles" (hip and ridge tiles) and, in any case, are far more numerous than would be needed to cover a roof, hipped or gabled, for a building of the given dimensions, more indeed than would be needed if all the walls were tile-hung, a practice for which there is no evidence until at least a century later. It seems inescapable that they must be some form of "wall-tile", i.e. brick; but this usage, familiar enough in the fourteenth and early-fifteenth centuries, seems most old-fashioned for 1529.[31] Moreover, the trade of "bricklayer" had long been so-called and that of a tiler generally restricted to laying floors and roofs. It may be a matter of trade "demarcation", and when a tiler entered into the bricklayer's business he may have adhered to the usage of less specialized days: certainly, there is an instance of "wall-tile" in York as late as 1510.[32] The huge estimate of 34,000 works out very well in terms of bricks about 9 in. long if they are no more than 2 in. thick and laid, not as a single nogging within the frame but as a double-thickness "nine-inch wall" completely enclosing it. Alternatively, if they were only 1 in. thick, or small "Flemish bricks" of half the volume by any other reduction, a single-depth nogging could be contrived. The York document just cited suggests an answer, since the price, 5s. a thousand, is that charged at York for "single wall tiel" (whatever that means), other wall-tiles being more costly. Nothing of this huge quantity of sixteenth-century bricks or tiles, whatever their size, could be seen at the Court Lodge or elsewhere in Oare.

Notes

1. The remaining range, derelict after long use as a farmhouse, and threatened with demolition, was compulsorily purchased by the Kent County Council in 1969. The contribution of the Department of the Environment is in the consolidation, with the intention of guardianship when completed, which is still in progress. Cf. *Arch. Cant.*, lxxxiv (1969), xlix–l. The Kent Archaeological Society sustained the campaign for preservation over twelve years and made a donation towards the purchase.
2. See plates 1–4 between pages 102 and 103.
3. Lambert B. Larking and J. M. Kemble, *The Knights Hospitallers in England* (Camden Society, no. 25), 1857.
4. *Arch. Cant.*, xxii (1897), 232–279 (includes plan and elevation of east end and general view of Swingfield), and xxiv (1900), 128–138.
5. Kent Records, vol. xi (1930).
6. *Arch. Cant.*, xxiv (1900), 129 ff.
7. C. Cotton, *op. cit.*, 142–167.
8. *Valor Ecclesiasticus* (Record Commission, IX), i (1810), 86; a single-page entry, totalling £104 gross, without "reprises", for the whole tenure with dependencies, of which Swingfield itself only accounts for £23. It has little in common with the "View" save one or two fixed assessments, such as Ewell mill at £4.
9. See entry in *D.N.B.*
10. See entry in *D.N.B.*
11. Hasted, *History of Kent*, quarto ed., viii, 125. The first and fourth quarters (az. a castle sa.) are Rawson's paternal coat.
12. C. Cotton, *op. cit.* in note 5, xxix, *sub voce* James Babington.
13. F. M. Powicke *et al.*, *Handbook of British Chronology* (1961), 157.
14. Lady Feneux in the *Valor* (cf. note 8).
15. cf. note 6.
16. cf. note 7.
17. J. K. Wallenberg, *The Place-names of Kent*, Uppsala, 1934, 447.
18. cf. note 4; *Arch. Cant.*, xxii (1897), 238.
19. e.g. L. F. Salzman, *Building in England down to 1540*, Oxford, 1952, p. 208, shows tie-beams (trabes) at 13s. 4d. in 1442, but the same account shows twice that for two "dormands" of the same length, and two tie-beams might be taken from one tree.
20. The extreme east end forms the measured drawing in *Arch. Cant.*, xxii (1897), Pl. opp. 260.
21. In the Brain Collection, "Kent Drawings"; the artist can hardly be T. Fisher, who did many of the drawings in this collection, since he was only 12 in 1794.
22. A series of water-colours, mainly of churches, made for, and in some cases by, the antiquary H. Petrie (1768–1842), covering Kent, Sussex, Surrey and parts of Hants. and Northants. Photographs of the Kent portion are in the Society's collection, but the whole series has been re-photographed by the National Monuments Record, by courtesy of whom the present reproduction is made.
23. Cotton, *op. cit.* in note 5, Pl. opp. 61.
24. For the east end, *op. cit.* in note 20, Pl. opp. 258.
25. One is obstructed by the later medieval crown-post roof: *op. cit.* in note 5, Pl. opp. 67.
26. The two-storey ante-chapel or western chamber, either built as such or created by partial flooring of a chapel, is familiar in hospitals (cf. Milton Chantry, Gravesend) and small houses of the Military orders (cf. *Arch. Journ.*, cxxii (1965), 119–121 and fig. 10).
27. *Arch. Cant.*, lxxxi (1966), 1–30, "Some Major Kentish Timber Barns", esp. p. 28.

28. The terminology is generally that of *op. cit.* in note 27.
29. *ibid.*; the second strey, even in very long barns, seems to be an innovation of the later fourteenth century.
30. *ibid.*, p. 28, where the type is briefly described.
31. *op. cit.* in note 19, 98, 140–1, 145, 454 (all references before 1434).
32. *ibid.*, 144.

A SIXTEENTH-CENTURY MS OF PRECEDENTS OF INDICTMENTS

R. E. A. POOLE

The MS has come down to us in two fragments, both in the archives of the Kent County Council at Maidstone. The first, catalogued as U419 01, consists of 14 pages of text, bound up in the nineteenth century with a list of contents and a translation. It was transferred to the County Archives from the Gravesend Public Library in 1954. The second part, catalogued as U4, was presented to the County Council in 1934 by the late Dr. F. W. Cock, of Appledore, and consists of 18 pages.

The paper bears the watermark of a flagon with one handle, with a fleur-de-lys on the body of a vessel and a small quatrefoil above the lid. This is almost certainly the watermark numbered 12,759 in C. M. Briquet, *Les Filigranes* (1968 edition), where it is stated to have been found at Grevenbroich in a document dated 1546, in Düsseldorf (Staatsarchiv II.4) in records from 1537 to 1546, and in a Russian MS of 1544. According to Briquet, the paper with this watermark was probably manufactured in Normandy, but more recent research has suggested an origin in Auvergne or Champagne, the association with Normandy being that large quantities of the paper were transported to Paris, and from there to other parts of the Seine valley. It has also been contended by Louis Le Clert, in a work entitled *"Le Papier, notes pour servir à l'histoire du papier principalement à Troyes"* (1926) that the quatrefoil is the especial mark that the paper was manufactured at Troyes.[1] In any case, a French origin of the paper appears certain. The only substantial difference from the illustration in Briquet is that this bears the initials "I V", whereas the watermark of the MS clearly has "I I I". Briquet himself, however, mentions that the letters can be taken for three little vertical lines, and as the letters "I V" were almost certainly the initials of the manufacturer, the difference is probably due to repairs; it is therefore likely that the paper was made when the watermark had already been in use for some time. As we shall see, a date within a year or two of 1545 is consistent with the text and such other clues as we have as well.

The handwriting is a typical legal hand of the middle of the sixteenth century, very much like that given as Alphabet No. 17 in H. Jenkinson, "The later court hands in England from the 15th to the 17th Century" (1927).

Part of the MS has certainly been lost, for the last page ends in the midst of a sentence. Most of the pages must have fallen apart at an early date, but it has been possible to put them into their proper order with almost complete certainty by using the clues provided by the continuity of the text from one page to another, by comparison of the position of the watermark, and in one or two cases by changes in the colour of the ink and by correspondences between blots, due to the book having been closed while the ink was still wet. Reconstruction by these means shows that the 32 pages must have been made up from four sheets of paper, each 31 by 41 cm. (exactly the size mentioned by Briquet), folded into four so that they could be stitched together into a note book.

The text consists of a collection of specimens of indictments presented to Justices of the Peace by grand juries, in respect of offences alleged to have been committed in Kent, and it seems likely to have been made by, or for the use of, the Clerk of the Peace for this county, by copying a selection of indictments from actual cases. In the MS, the specimen indictments were not numbered, though each had a heading with a frame round it; the numbers by which I shall refer to them are my own, based on the reconstruction of the text as already described.

The indictments are arranged in an order which, though not strictly logical, has a certain coherence. On the whole, those of a similar nature are grouped together, and occasionally there is a transition from one group to another; it is almost as if the person who made the collection, having come upon an indictment which related to an offence with two aspects, was then reminded of others having the second aspect, and followed this up rather than the first. We can, therefore, arrange the indictments in groups, subject to allowing for these transitions:

Group I. Homicide (Nos. 1 to 4). This falls into two sub-groups: Nos. 1 and 2 relate to the killing of newly-born infants, and Nos. 3 and 4 to the killing of adults.

Group II. Keeping a suspect house, and playing unlawful games (Nos. 5 to 8). Here again, there is a kind of subdivision. Nos. 5, 6 and 7 all relate to the keeping of some kind of premises in which unlawful activities were carried on, and in No. 6 it is quite explicit that the house was used as a brothel, while in Nos. 5 and 7 the charge is rather that of keeping a gaming house. This leads on, however, to No. 8, where the offence alleged is playing games which were forbidden by statute, without any allegation of keeping premises for the purpose.

Group III. This consists simply of No. 9, a charge of selling unwholesome meat.

Group IV. This also has only one indictment, No. 10, for enticing servants to leave their employment.

Group V. Lying in wait by the highway (Nos. 11 to 14). In Nos. 11 and 12 the primary motive was highway robbery, while in Nos. 13 and 14 it seems to have been rather the commission of an assault for purposes of revenge.

Group VI. Riotous assembly (Nos. 15 and 16). In No. 14, the assault was made by a fair-sized gang, and so there is a natural transition to the activities of armed gangs generally; more specifically, breaking into houses.

Group VII. Assaults upon women (Nos. 17 to 19). Here again, there is a transition. In No. 16, the gang attacked a woman in her bedroom, and this seems to have led on to No. 17, where the accused is said to have beaten a woman, and to Nos. 18 and 19, which are cases of attempted rape.

Group VIII. Trouble-makers (Nos. 20 and 21). The theme of breaches of the peace is followed up by these two charges of trying to induce them by words.

Group IX. An assault upon a man (No. 22).

Group X. Trespass to land (Nos. 23 and 24). No. 22 was, from the legal point of view, a trespass to the person, and so there is again a transition to trespass to land.

Group XI. Unlawful assembly (Nos. 25 and 26). In No. 25 the purpose of the assembly is not stated, but in No. 26 it was a trespass of the same kind as in Group X, so that there is again a continuity.

Group XII. Interference with public rights (Nos. 27 and 28); in the one case, a watercourse, and in the other a public right of way.

Group XIII. Extortion (Nos. 29 and 30). In No. 28 there was an element of extortion, in that the person who obstructed the way tried to claim a toll from persons using it. Again, there is a transition from this to charges against public officers of misusing their powers to extort money from members of the public.

Group XIV. Rescue of persons under arrest (Nos. 31 to 37). The victim in No. 30 had to pay to be released from a unlawful arrest, and so we pass to a group of charges of using violence to release someone from a lawful arrest.

Group XV. Disobeying a lawful summons (No. 38). This follows from No. 37, with the difference that the disobedience to a summons did not take a directly violent form.

Group XVI. Refusing lawful employment (Nos. 39 and 40). Even here, there is a kind of continuity, in that the offence in No. 39 consisted essentially in failure to comply with a lawful command to enter into employment. As this carried the implication that the accused were getting a living by begging or thieving, it carried on to No. 40, where the charge was of harbouring such persons.

Group XVII. Poaching (Nos. 41 and 42). The theme of dishonest means of gaining a livelihood is continued. The MS, as we have it, breaks off after the first few lines of No. 42. As it is to be hoped that the missing parts are still in existence, I shall discuss later how the text would probably have continued, so as to facilitate recognition of them.

The collection is of very much the same kind as the comparable, though more extensive, collection of specimen indictments, mostly from Yorkshire and dating from the early Elizabethan period, which were printed in the second part of William West's *Symboleography* (1601), and it therefore seems worth while to quote those parts of the introduction to the printed collection, as a more or less contemporary account of the matters which the compiler of the present MS would have had in mind:

"An indictment is a bill or declaration made in form of law (for the benefit of the commonwealth) of an accusation for some offence, either criminal or penal, exhibited unto jurors, and by their verdict found and presented to be true, before an officer having power to punish the same offence. And such an indictment is made to the end to compel the party accused to answer thereunto.

"In every indictment two things seem principally to be considered: first, the very offence, for reformation whereof the indictment is framed; and then the right form of the indictment itself, according to the distinct quality of every several offence. Wherefore ... I have thought good briefly to unfold the sundry natures of offences and defaults, and how they bind the offender, and then to lay down the doctrine and several forms of indictments concerning the same ...

"The slaughter of man is called homicide, which is every taking away of life from any person bond or free, by man done with violence by which the soul is severed from the body, by what manner of means so ever it chance, whether by sword, staff, or other weapons, or by venom or poison, the cause of death be given. Homicide is either voluntary or casual. Homicide voluntary is that which is deliberate and committed of a set mind and purpose to kill ... Homicide voluntary of malice proceeding ... is termed murder, and is the felonious killing through malice prepensed of any person living in this realm under the Queen's protection ...

"Robbery is a felonious taking away of another man's goods, from his person, or presence, against his will, putting him in fear and of purpose to steal the same goods; and this robbery is sometime termed violent theft, because the party is in the law thereby terrified ...

"And those offences which are achieved with force, are done by true force, or by force after a certain sort. Those offences which are finished by true force, are either done by men assembled, or without men assembled; and force with men assembled is private or public. Private force is when any with weapons by men assembled, doth invade the goods or body of another, as trespass by entering into ground, or taking his cattle, or other goods, imprisoning of a man's body, or beating him with one's fist, or rescues of a trespass, pound breach, or otherwise without weapon and such like. Public force is that violence which is done by any men assembled with any kind of weapon whatsoever, as by forcible entry, keeping of possession of ... houses, or lands, or offices, unlawful assemblies, routs, riots, rebellions ... etc ...

"An unlawful assembly is the meeting of three or more persons together, with force to commit some unlawful act, and abiding still, not endeavouring the execution thereof, as to assault or beat any person, or enter into his house or land etc. A rout is an assembly of three persons or more, going on about forcibly to commit an unlawful act ... A riot is the forcible doing of an unlawful act by three or more persons assembled together for that purpose ...

"It followeth how force may be committed without a multitude. This kind of force comprehendeth every harm, hurt, damage, loss, hindrance, and danger besides death, happening to any good, quick or dead, movable or unmovable, or to men, either ... negligently or unwittingly, or guilefully or of set purpose ... also breaking of prisons, to escape thence, breaking of houses to steal something thence, or to do some felony there ... In this rank also may be placed the pulling up or removing of meres, bounds or marks, set for the dividing of one man's land from another's, and many other such trespasses wherein in none apparent force or terror, as to hawk, hunt, fish, or fowl, or to cut, eat, tread or soil grass in another man's soil unlawfully ...

"Hitherto of offences done by true force indeed: now of such as are not properly done with force and violence, but by intendment of the law only: of which sort be bribery, extortion, exaction, private imprisonment, and certain other like misdemeanors. Those offences of bribery, extortion, and exaction, are committed when any for fear of his judgment, office, or other power, or authority, or for any other terror exacteth, extorteth, and wringeth money or other things from another man, as sheriffs ... bailiffs ... or other officers whatsoever ...

"To this crew as it seemeth, may be referred the exaction of unlawful usury ... and all unlawful games, which be all games, but shooting ... and every other taking of more than is due by colour or pretence of right ...

"Thus have we rather slightly shadowed, than perfectly portrayed, the ugly shape of such enormous offences, as with their deformity most blemish the body of our beautiful, (otherwise flourishing) common wealth. Now therefore we are to show the ways how to prepare remedies for the same, which must be done by indictments ... In the form of every indictment, besides the ordinary words of form, precise certainty to every intent is to be ... warily looked unto ...

"This certainty consisteth, first in the name and surname of the party indicted, both principal and accessory.

2. In the certain name and surname of the party offended.

3. In the certainty of time, wherein the offence is done, as the certain day, years, yea, and many times the very hour is expressed.

4. In the place where the offence is perpetrated.

5. In the very matter of the fact, and nature of the offence committed, as whether it be treason, felony, trespass, deceit, penal statute etc.

6. In the name and value of the thing, in which the offence is done.

"Unto the name of the party indicted must be united the addition of his estate, degree, or mystery,[2] and the shire, and town, hamlet or place of his then, or late dwelling ... The addition of the degree or mystery must be such, as the party hath at the very time of the indictments: but he may be termed *nuper*[3] of any place whereof he hath been at any time before, but it is best to name him of the place of which he is or last was, thus: *Iurator' pro dña reg' present' qz I.S. nuper de D. in com Essex*,[4] husbandman etc. And further, the time of the offence committed must be thus set down, as in personal actions *5. die Feb. anno regni dñae nostr̄ Eliz. dei gratia Angl'*[5] etc. And in some indictments, as of murder, and burglary, the very hour is to be expressed, as *hora 6. ante merid'* (if it were before noon) and *post mer̄* (if it were after) *eiusdē diei* ...[6] The place is thus to be set down *apud B. in com C.*[7] For it is not good to say *in com praedict'*[8] referring to the name of the county written in the margent of the indictment: and the place of the offence is sometime more specially set down thus, *apud B. in com C. in quodam loco ibidē vocat*[9] the northclose etc.

"The names of things in which the offence is committed ought also to be certainly mentioned ... And the value of those things in which offences are committed is usually comprised in indictments, which seemeth necessary in theft to make a difference from petty larceny, and in trespass, to aggravate the fault and increase the fine ...

"The very manner of the fact or deed itself, and nature of the offence, must also be mentioned in the indictment, as in escape, for prison breaking, must be expressed, for what felony the offender was apprehended, and imprisoned ... And in murder and manslaughter, the stroke whereof death ensued ... And for entry, into house, land or tenements must be expressed, what manner of house, lands or tenements, as a messuage, a cottage, arable land, meadow, pasture, or wood. And where in any indictment, several acts be said to make up the offence which may be done at several times and places, both the times and places must be certainly expressed, as in murder and manslaughter, the assault and the striking, as *apud B. in comitatu E. &c. in quendam I.S. insultum fecit, & ipsum I.S. cum quodā gladio precii &c. adtunc et ibidem felonice, & ex malitia sua praecogitata percussit & murdravit* ...[10] And an indictment against an accessory, must shew what felony the principal committed, and that knowing it, received the felon feloniously.

"Touching the several natures of several offences, it is to be noted, that in indictments of treasons the fact must necessarily be said to be done, *proditorie*:[11] of murder, *murdravit*:[12] and of manslaughter, and all other felonies, the deed must be said to be done *felonice*, and in burglary, *burglariter*,[14] or *intentione ad feloniam sive murdrum faciend' &c.*,[15] in rape *felonice rapuit*,[16] in theft, *felonice cepit & asportavit*,[17] if it be a dead thing: if living, *abduxit*,[18] or *felonice furatus est*.[19] In petty larceny and mayhem, must also be said, *felonice*.

"And notwithstanding the statute of 37 H8. ca.8. it is not amiss in every indictment containing felony or trespess, to use the words *vi & armis viz gladiis, baculis, cultellis &c* ...[20] And in an indictment found upon statutes, it seemeth not needful to recite the statute verbatim ... but fully and certainly to describe the offence against the tenor of the same statute, and then conclude with these words, *contra formam statuti in hum̄di casu provisi et aediti*,[21] if there be only one statute of that offence: but if there be diverse concerning the same, then the conclusion must be, *contra formam diversorum statutorum in hum̄di casu aedit & provisorum &c."*[22]

The indictments are in Latin, of much the same abbreviated kind as that in the examples already quoted from West. This remained the practice until 1731, when the statute 6 Geo.2 c.14 required all such documents from thenceforth to be written in English. The decision to publish the MS in translation, rather than in the original language, has been taken not only on the grounds of making it intelligible to the general reader, but also because, although in most cases it would be simple enough to expand the abbreviations into normal Latin, there are some ambiguities. These usually affect only the grammatical form, and not the general sense of the words, and were probably deliberately designed to enable forms to be used by a clerk with only a modest knowledge of Latin. For the names of places, the surnames of persons, and English words actually cited, such as the words spoken by the robbers in No. 12, I have followed the spelling of the original, putting the words in italics. After some hestitation, the same practice has been followed for the occupations or descriptions of the persons, where these are given in English in the original. For Christian names, however, the modern English equivalent has been used, as these are normally given in the text in a Latinised form. Where there is a reference to a statute, I have followed the English wording as set forth in the 1618 edition of Rastall's *Statutes at Large*, though with modern spelling.

As this was a collection of precedents for future use rather than a record of past events, the copyist normally omitted information which was peculiar to the actual case, where its inclusion would have meant repeatedly writing out a standard formula. This applies particularly to the regnal year in which the events are alleged to have happened, but fortunately, in eight cases, the date has been preserved because there was a reference to it also in the body of the text. Two of the indictments. Nos. 31 and 38, can be shown in this way to relate to events in 1528, and five, Nos. 1, 4, 32, 34 and 37, to events between 1536 and 1542. The remaining date is 1518, in No. 28; but this relates to the commencement of an interference with a public way, which had evidently been continuing for several years. None of the indictments shows any influence of the reforms introduced by the statute 37 Hen.8 c.8 (1545–6), already mentioned in one of the passages cited from West's *Symboleography*, but West's own comments show that the statute had little effect, so that it does not provide us necessarily with a terminal date for the compilation of the MS.

As this passage from West also shows us, not all the statements are to be taken as literally true. This applies not only to allegations of the degree of force used (we can hardly suppose, for instance, that in No. 19 William Wylson was really using swords, clubs and knives, in the plural and all together, when he was trying to rape Joan Payne) but also to accompanying allegations that the injuries inflicted were so severe that someone's life was despaired of. Where, however, the words depart from the common form, as in No. 1, it seems reasonable to suppose that the instruments mentioned were really those used.

Consistently with the use of the indictments as precedents, the copyist occasionally saved himself trouble by giving only the initials of persons or places. Even where a name purports to be given in full, however, it cannot be taken for granted that it is the true name of the person mentioned in the original indictment. For purposes of example, sixteenth-century lawyers often used the names of imaginary persons, John at Style being an especial favourite. This is probably the reason why West, in two of the examples just quoted, uses the initials "I. S." to represent a name, and why the same initials are given for the murdered baby in Indictment No. 1 of the present set. In that case, the initials must almost certainly be fictitious, since it is hardly imaginable from the circumstances that the child had been baptised or had a name. The possibility of "John Style" being the name of a real person cannot of course be altogether excluded, just as there may have existed at some time a soldier whose name really was "Thomas Atkins". Indeed, it seems reasonable to suppose that the name of the first defendant in No. 8 was John Style, seeing that the text shows no other sign of fictitious elements. The case is rather different in No. 16, however, for in that text we have not only the name "John Style" but also the place-names "Dowe", "Hedlyng" and "Godeham" which (with the possible exception of the lathe of Hedling which roughly covered the area between Sandwich and Dover) cannot readily be identified in Kent, the place-name "Dowe" and the personal name "Nowe" which have the same endings as the name "Crowe" in Nos. 14 and 15, and the name of William Sylly whose wife is called Agnes Dyte. The most probable explanation of this discrepancy is surely that the copyist intended to replace all the real names with fictitious ones, but that the true name of Agnes Dyte was allowed to remain in the text by an oversight. The name "William Crowe" is also occasionally met with as a fictitious name in legal examples, and this may explain its occurrence as the name of one of the victims in both No. 14 and No. 15. Another case in which a name may have to be treated with suspicion is that of Thomas Abell, *clericus*, in No. 36. A priest named Thomas Abell was chaplain and confessor to Katharine of Aragon, and was one of the persons attainted by the statute (1534) in consequence of his having given credence to the prophecies of Elizabeth Barton, the "Holy Maid of Kent", concerning the matrimonial adventures of Henry VIII. He is believed to have been executed in 1540 after a long and wretched imprisonment, and as no other priest of that name seems to be recorded in Kent for the period, it is very possible that the copyist substituted his name, as someone who was then in the news, in place of the true name of the accused. In short, although we cannot say for certain that a name is fictitious, we must exercise caution in accepting the names in the texts, whether of persons or of places, as they stand.

Certain of the indictments refer to statutes, and it will be convenient to discuss these not only for their legal implications, but also because they may provide a clue for the date of the events. I shall deal with them in the order in which they are mentioned in the text:

No. 3: poisoning. This is almost certainly a reference to "An act against poisoning", 22 Henry VIII c.9 (1531). As the events which gave rise to this statute, as recited in the preamble, concerned persons living in Kent, it may be of interest to set them forth in some detail. On 28 February of that year "one *Richard Roose,* late of Rochester in the County of Kent, cook, otherwise called *Richard Cooke"* put poison into a vessel in the kitchen of the Bishop of Rochester at Lambeth Marsh, with the result that seventeen members of the bishop's household, and a number of poor people who were fed at his door by way of charity, were poisoned. Benet Curwin, a gentleman of the household, and Alice Tripit, a poor widow, died of it, and Parliament thereupon passed the statute, providing that from thenceforth wilful poisoning was to be punished with death as high treason, and that Roose himself was to be boiled to death. Coke, in Book III of the *Institutes,*[23] tells us that under this statute a young woman named Margaret Davy was attainted of high treason for poisoning her mistress, and that some others were boiled to death in Smithfield on 17 March of the same year, but that the Act was "too severe to live long". It was, along with all other statutes deeming something to be high treason although not actually treasonable, repealed immediately after the death of Henry VIII by the statute 1 Edward VI c.12. We may be sure, therefore, that the indictment now under discussion was framed between 1531 and 1547, and its inclusion in the MS indicates that the MS itself is unlikely to be later than 1547.

Nos. 5, 7 and 8: idlers, playing unlawful games. Two themes of early Tudor legislation become intermingled in these indictments. On the one hand, statutes were passed for the discouragement of vagrancy and the return of vagrants to their place of origin; this was more particularly the subject of 19 Henry VII c.12 (1504), and 22 Henry VIII c.12 (1531). On the other hand, there were statutes designed to promote the practice of archery, upon which (with a fine disregard for contemporary military technology) the defence of the realm was supposed still to depend; the principal statutes concerning this were 3 Henry VIII c.3 (1512) and 33 Henry VIII c.9 (1542). Since idlers have to pass their time somehow, and games such as "tables, tennis, dice, cards, bowls, cloish, coiting and logating" tended to distract the common people from passing their spare time with bows and arrows, all these statutes, with the exception of that of 1531, contained provisions regulating the circumstances in which the lower orders were to be permitted to engage in such pastimes.

No. 39: labourers. The relevant provisions of the Statute of Labourers, 23 Edward III, c.1 to 8 (1349), passed in an attempt to regulate the changes in supply and demand for labour by reason of the Black Death, are set forth almost verbatim in the indictment.

No. 40: harbouring vagabonds. The statute 19 Henry VII c.12 (1504) has already been mentioned in connection with Nos. 5, 7 and 8. It contained a provision that sheriffs, constables and other public officers were to "make due search and take or cause to be taken all such vagabonds, idle people, and suspect persons, living suspiciously, and them to take and set in stocks, there to remain by the space of one day and one night, and there to have none other sustenance, but bread and water ... and if any person or persons give any other meat or drink to the said misdoers, so being in stocks in form aforesaid, or the said prisoners favour in their misdoing, or them receive or harbour over one night that then they forfeit for every time so doing 12d." This seems to be the explanation for the reference in the indictment to giving any "other" meat or drink, (*alt' aliquā cibū aut potū*) although none has previously there been specified. There appears also to be a reference, though not express, to another statute, 22 Henry VIII c.10 (1531) "An act concerning outlandish people calling themselves Egyptians" which sought to expel the gypsies from the realm on the ground, among others, that they had "used great subtle and crafty means to deceive the people, bearing them in hand that they by palmistry could tell men's and women's fortunes".

No. 41: killing a hare in the snow. The statute referred to is 14 & 15 Henry VIII c.10 (1523), aimed at preserving hares for the "disport and pleasure" of the king and the nobility in hunting them. It provided that "no person or persons of what estate degree or condition they be, from henceforth trace, destroy, and kill no Hare in snow with any dog, bitch, nor otherwise", under a penalty of 6s. 8d. for each offence.

No. 42: poaching. The statute 13 Richard II c.13 (1390), in Rastell's translation, provided that "no manner of artificer, labourer nor other lay man, which hath not lands or tenements to the value of 40 shillings by year, nor no priest or other clerk, if he be not advanced to the value of £40 by year, shall have nor keep from henceforth any greyhound, hound, nor other dog for to hunt, nor shall they not use ferrets, hays, nets, harepipes, nor cords, nor other engines for to take or destroy deer, hares, nor conies, nor other gentlemen's game upon pain of one year's imprisonment."

This is the last of the indictments in the MS as we have it, and breaks off at the end of the page. The words of the MS so closely follow those of the statute that it is possible to make a plausible reconstruction of the passage which would follow at the top of the next page, and in the hope that this may enable the missing text to be identified, if it still exists, I shall give the Latin text as we have it, with a conjectural version of the continuation:

(Existing text)

137

Indictamentum de venatoribus contra formam Statuti.

Jurati &c. quod Cum in Statuto in parliamento domini R. nuper Regis Anglie secundi aput Westmonasterium anno regni sui tercio decimo tento editum inter cetera contineatur quod nullus laborator nec aliquis laicus homo qui terra et Tenementa ad valorem xl s. per annum non

(Conjectural continuation)

habet ullum canem venaticum vel leporarium venari haberet seu custodiret nec ullis venariis vocatis *Firrets* vel magnis retibus vocatus *Hayes* vel retibus vocatis *Harepipes* vel cordis aut allis engenis quibuscunque ad capiendum aut destruendum feras lepores aut cuniculos uteretur ...[24]

U 419
(Page 1)

1. *Indictment for the murder of a baby*

Kent

The jurors present, on behalf of our lord the King, that M. Q. , lately of T in the aforesaid county, Spynster, desiring to conceal and intending to hide the foul and secretive cohabitation, and the detestable lust, which J. W. , lately of T aforesaid in the aforesaid county, cleric,[25] had been having and practising for a long time with A(lice) S. , his maidservant, on the 25th day of May in the 30th year of the reign of Henry VIII,[26] by the grace of God king of England and France, Defender of the Faith, Lord of Ireland, and on earth supreme head of the Anglican church, by force and arms, namely with knives and skewers,[27] at T aforesaid in the aforesaid county, of malice aforethought feloniously killed and murdered a certain J S , a baby delivered and born of the body of the said Alice, and newly and recently come forth from within his mother's womb, against the peace of our said lord the King; and that the aforesaid J W , lately of T aforesaid in the aforesaid county, cleric, knowing that the aforesaid M had feloniously done and perpetrated the aforesaid murder and infanticide in manner aforesaid, on the aforesaid 26th day of May in the above mentioned 30th year of the reign of our said lord the present King, at T aforesaid in the aforesaid county, harboured, fed and comforted the aforesaid M in his own house after the felony and murder had been so done and perpetrated, and about the tenth hour of the night of the same 25th day of May at T aforesaid in the aforesaid county, he secretly and privily buried and inhumed the baby, who had been killed and murdered as before set forth, against the peace of our aforesaid lord the King etc.

(Page 2)

2. *Indictment for the murder of an infant*

Kent

The jurors present, on behalf of our lord the King, that Alice M , lately of Eltham in the aforesaid county, *Spynster*, being lately pregnant, on the 5th day of November in the   year of the reign etc., at Eltham aforesaid in the aforesaid county, gave birth to a certain infant; and afterwards the aforesaid Alice, and a certain John Martyngdale lately of Eltham aforesaid in the aforesaid county, *yoman*, and Margery his wife, immediately after the aforesaid birth and before any baptism had been administered to the same infant, on the day and in the year abovementioned etc., at Eltham aforesaid in the aforesaid county, by the instigation of the devil, with force and arms etc. then and there feloniously killed and murdered the aforesaid infant, against the peace of our aforesaid lord the King that now is, etc.

3. *Indictment for poisoning a man*

Kent

The jurors present, on behalf of our lord the King, that John K   , lately of Stone in the county aforesaid, *Husbandman*, and M   his wife, on the 10th day of September in the   year etc., at Stone aforesaid, then administered a certain drink with a certain venom and certain other kinds of poison,[28] and gave it to the aforementioned T   B   to drink; which said T   then and there drank of the same drink and poison; and was then and there poisoned by the same drink, so poisoned; and so J(ohn) K   and M   poisoned the aforesaid T   B   at Stone aforesaid in the county aforesaid, against the peace of our said lord the King, his crown and dignity, and against the form of the statute lately issued and provided in that behalf etc.

(Page 3)

4. *Indictment for premeditated murder*

Kent

The jurors etc. that Morgan W   , lately of Cowden in the aforesaid county, *Laborer*, on the seventh day of September in the (31st) year of the reign of Henry etc., of malice aforethought made an assault upon a certain R   S   at Cowden aforesaid in the aforesaid county, being then and there in the peace of God and our said lord the King, with force and arms, namely with a certain dagger of the value of 6d which the aforesaid Morgan then and there held in his right hand; and then and there feloniously struck the same R   with the aforesaid dagger upon his head; and gave to the same R   six mortal blows, with the aforesaid dagger, upon his head, by which some blows the head and brain of the aforesaid R   S   were then and there altogether broken; of which some mortal blows the same R   then and there instantly died; and so the aforesaid jurors say that the aforesaid Morgan W feloniously killed and murdered the aforementioned R   B   [29] on the day and in the year, place, and county aforesaid, against the peace of our said lord the King, his crown and dignity; and further, the aforesaid jurors present upon their oath, on behalf of our lord the King, that a certain Richard G , lately of Cowden aforesaid in the aforesaid county, *laborer*, on the aforesaid seventh day of September in the above mentioned thirty first year of the reign of our said lord the King,[30] at Cowden aforesaid, feloniously comforted, maintained, fed and assisted the aforementioned Morgan W in committing the aforesaid felony and murder in manner aforesaid, against the peace of our said lord the King, his crown and dignity.

5. *Indictment for keeping a suspect house*

Kent

The jurors etc. that William Cutler, lately of Downe in the aforesaid county. *Laborer*, practising the common sale of beer[31] and other victuals to the subjects of our lord the King, on the 15th day of December in the year of the reign etc., in the night time of the same day.

(Page 4)

and also at divers other days, nights, times and occasions, as well before as after, kept his house suspiciously at Downe aforesaid in the aforesaid county, to harbour therein sundry idlers and other suspect persons, playing at cards, dice, and other games and pastimes,[32] unlawful and prohibited by the law of this realm of England, to the pernicious example of other evildoers; and against the form of sundry statutes and ordinances lately issued and provided in that behalf, and against the peace of our aforesaid lord the King that now is, etc.

6. *Indictment for keeping a suspect house*

Kent

The jurors present, on behalf of our lord the King, that Joan Lyme, the wife of John Lyme, lately of W in the aforesaid county, Spynster, on the fourth day of July in the year of the reign etc. and on sundry days and occasions before the same day, and continuously thereafter on sundry occasions, has kept, and keeps to this day, that is to say the day of the taking of this inquisition, a suspect house, commonly called *a Bawdry Howse* at W aforesaid in the aforesaid county, receiving therein, both by night and by day, sundry persons, both women of evil behaviour and men, both clergy and laity, of like behaviour, using carnal copulation in the aforesaid house both by night and by day, and with the support of the aforesaid J(oan) in manner aforesaid dealing suspiciously with those keeping company with them, and perpetrating it there on sundry occasions, to grave harm and pernicious example, and against the peace of our said lord the King that now is, etc.

(Page 5)

7. *Indictment for keeping a suspect house*

Kent

The jurors etc. that J   A   , lately of H   in the aforesaid county, widow, on the 10th day of N(ovember) in the   year of the reign etc., and on sundry days and occasions as well before as after at H   aforesaid in the aforesaid county has kept, and still keeps a certain suspect house, in consequence whereof many servants,[33] of both sexes, of sundry subjects of our lord the King, and of the neighbours being there, and many other persons of evil condition, disposition and governance, not known to the aforesaid jurors, resort to and frequent the same house by day and night, and sundry times have stayed up all night in the same house, and have then and there for many whole nights played at unlawful games and pastimes, namely *tables, dyce, cards* and many other games prohibited by the law of the land, by occasion whereof the said servants have been unable duly to do and perform the service for their masters as is proper, on account of their inability to keep awake, and their inordinate governance, and so the same masters have lost the services of their servants, to the evil example of other subjects of our lord the King, and grave harm, and against the form of sundry statutes and ordinances lately issued and provided in that behalf, and against the peace of our aforesaid lord the King that now is, etc.

8. *Indictment for unlawful games*

Kent

The jurors present, on behalf of our lord the King, that whereas unlawful games and pastimes, which do not promote the defence of the realm of our lord the King of England, are prohibited by the laws of this realm of England, as more fully appears by sundry statutes and ordinances made in that behalf before this:

(Page 6)

nevertheless a certain John Style, lately of Darteford in the aforesaid county, *laborer*, and William Hawpeney, lately of Dartford in the aforesaid county, *Glover*, little heeding the aforesaid statutes and ordinances, on the 12th day of July in the   year etc., and on sundry days, times and occasions as well before as after, at D(artford) aforesaid in the aforesaid county, have unlawfully assembled with sundry other persons unknown, and played at bowls,[34] and each one of them played in contempt of our lord the King that now is, and against the form of the aforesaid statutes and ordinances etc.

9. *Indictment for the sale of unwholesome meat*

Kent

The jurors present, on behalf of our lord the King, that Henry Codde, lately of E.   in the aforesaid county, *Bocher*, is a common retailer of meat, and that he on the 10th day of S(eptember) in the   year of the reign etc., at E   aforesaid in the aforesaid county, under colour of his trade as a slaughterer, killed a certain pig, called *a porkyer*, which was putrid and corrupt, and unwholesome for the human body, and then and there falsely and deceitfully exposed and sold it to sundry subjects of our said lord the King, living thereabouts, to the deception, inpoverishment and destruction of the people of our said lord the King who tasted or ate of it; to the grave harm of the subjects of our lord the King, a pernicious example, and against the peace of our said lord the King that now is, etc.

(Page 7)

10. *Indictment for the procuration of servants*
Kent

The jurors etc., that W   W   , lately of Folkestone in the aforesaid county, *yoman*, on the fifth day of S(eptember) in the   year etc., abetted, incited and procured a certain Alice P   , the servant of a certain Thomas Long, being then in the service of the same Thomas, to go away and to withdraw from the same service; in consequence of which procuration the same Alice P   then and there withdrew; and that the same W   W   is a common procurer of the servants of sundry subjects of our said lord the King, who are often disquieted in performing their work in such service; and that the same W   W   has continued such incitement and procurations from the day and year abovementioned until the day of the taking of this inquisition; in contempt of our lord the King that now is, to the grave (harm) of the subjects of our said lord the King, and against the peace of our aforesaid lord the King etc.

11. *Indictment of highway robbers*
Kent

The jurors present on behalf of our lord the King, that N   J   , lately of A   in the county aforesaid, *laborer*, on the fifth day of June in the   year etc., about the seventh hour after the noon of the same day, of malice aforethought and as a highway robber,[35] with force and arms, namely with swords, clubs and knives, lay in wait for Thomas One, upon the King's highway going between the town of Wy and Assheforthe, and made an assault upon the same Thomas at Asshefoth aforesaid in the aforesaid county, and then and there beat, wounded and illtreated him, with the intention of despoiling the same Thomas of his goods and money; so that his life was despaired of, against the peace of our said lord the King etc.

(Page 8)

12. *Indictment of highway robbers and those assisting them*
Kent

The jurors present on behalf of our lord (the King) that Henry Man, lately of Feverssham in the aforesaid county, *laborer*, and William Grove, lately of Feversham in the aforesaid county, *lab-*, on the 10th day of August in the year etc., lay in wait for the purpose of killing a certain Laurence Somer and made an ambush for despoiling him of his goods, at Newynton in the aforesaid county, by the highway there, at a place called Moriscrosse, about the seventh hour after the noon of the same day, by the procuration, incitement, and abetting of a certain Mary Hunt, lately of Feversham aforesaid in the aforesaid county, widow, and then and there made an assault upon the same Laurence, and illtreated him, saying in English words, *Stond styll*, and moreover they stretched forth their hands to take hold of the bridle of the horse upon which the same Laurence was then and there riding, so that the same Laurence only by good fortune narrowly escaped death and spoliation then and there, by the liveliness and swift running of the aforesaid horse; against the peace of our said lord the King that now is, etc.

13. *Indictment of highway robbers*

Kent

The jurors present etc. that W   T   [36] on the 17th day of September in the   year etc., with force and arms, namely with a certain sword drawn from its sheath, at M   [37] in the aforesaid county, at a certain place called Petynden Hothe, then and there made an assault upon a certain William Nowe and then and there gave sundry blows against and at the said William Nowe,

(Page 9)

with the aforesaid sword which the said John then held in his right hand, by reason whereof the same William feared for his life and the mutilation of his limbs, against the peace of our lord the King that now is, etc.

14. *Indictment of highway robbers and their accessories*

Kent

The jurors present, on behalf of our lord the King, that Thomas Ken, lately of Tong in the aforesaid county, *laborer*, and Richard Godderd, lately of Dodynton in the aforesaid county, *Smyth*, having gathered to themselves several other evildoers and disturbers of the peace of our lord the King, not known to the aforesaid jurors, to the number of seven persons, arrayed in warlike manner, on the tenth day of November in the   year etc., about the tenth hour after noon, and after sunset of the same day, with force and arms, namely with swords, clubs, shields, daggers, bows and arrows, like rioters or routers and in the manner of disturbers of the peace of our lord the King in the recent insurrection, assembled unlawfully and riotously at Tong aforesaid in the aforesaid county in the house there of a certain William Kene, and secretly lay in ambush with the intention of killing a certain William Crowe of the same town and county, *laborer*, and afterwards made an assault upon the same William and beat, wounded and illtreated him very gravely, and gave him a certain wound on his head; so that his life was despaired of; and that the aforesaid William K(ene) abetted and comforted them in his house, unlawfully and against the peace of our aforesaid lord the King that now is, etc.

(Page 10)

15. *Indictment against rioters and routers, and disturbers of the peace*
Kent

The jurors, etc., that William Browne, lately of Challock in the aforesaid County, *laborer*, on the tenth day of June in the   year etc., about the tenth hour after the noon of the same day, having gathered to himself several other evildoers to the number of six persons, not known to the aforesaid jurors, and disturbers of the peace of our lord the King, arrayed and armed in warlike manner, with force and arms, namely with swords, bills, shields, bows, arrows and knives, broke and entered the house of William Crowe at Chalocke aforesaid in the aforesaid county, and broke the doors and windows of the house, and with the force and arms aforesaid made an assault upon the aforesaid William Crowe and a certain William Dodde, the servant of the aforesaid William Crowe, then and there being within the peace of God and of our said lord the King, and beat, wounded and illtreated them, against the peace of our aforesaid lord the King that now is, etc.

16. *Another indictment against rioters, routers and disturbers of the peace*
Kent

The jurors present, on behalf of our lord the King, that John Style lately of Dowe in the aforesaid county, *laborer*, and John Nowe, lately of Hedlyng in the aforesaid county, *laborer*, on the tenth day of September in the   year etc., with force and arms, namely with swords, bills, shields, bow, arrows and knives, about the tenth hour after the noon of the same day, having gathered to themselves several other evildoers and disturbers of the peace of our lord the King, arrayed and armed in warlike manner, to the number of six persons, with the aforesaid force and arms, riotously and routously, broke and entered the house of William Sylly at Godeham in the aforesaid county,

(Page 11)

and broke the doors, both of the hall and of one room, of the aforesaid house, in which room Agnes Dyte, the wife of the aforesaid William, lay, the same Agnes then being pregnant; and entered into the aforesaid room with their swords drawn, and with the force and arms aforesaid, and riotously, made an assault upon the aforesaid Agnes, being then within the peace of God and of our said lord the King, and put the same Agnes, then being pregnant, in peril of death, against the peace of our lord the King that now is, etc.

17. *Indictment for making an assault upon a woman*

Kent

The jurors present, on behalf of our lord the King, that John Oldman, lately of London, *yoman*, on the tenth day of July in the   year etc. with force and arms, namely with swords, sticks and knives, made an assault upon a certain Dorothy the wife of Edward Bar of B   in the aforesaid county, at B   aforesaid, and then and there beat, wounded and illtreated her; and then and there afflicted her with such injuries, grievances, assaults and affrays that the life of the same Dorothy was then and there despaired of; and inflicted other enormities upon the same Dorothy, to the grave harm of the said Dorothy and against the peace of our said lord the King.

(Page 12)

18. *Indictment for trespass with intent to rape the wife of a certain man, and not being able to carry out the intention*

Kent

The jurors present, on behalf of our lord the King, that Ed(ward) Clerk, lately of Charyng in the aforesaid county, *Smythe*, on the fifth day of September in the   year etc., with force and arms, namely with swords, clubs and knives, broke and entered the close and house of Richard Barker at Charyng aforesaid in the aforesaid county, and then and there seized Joan, the wife of the aforesaid Richard Barker, with the intention of raping and carnally knowing her, and when the same Ed(ward) was unable to carry out his intention to rape her, he then made an assault upon the aforesaid Joan with the aforesaid force and arms, and then and there, beat, wounded and illtreated her; so that her life was despaired of; and inflicted other enormities upon her, to the grave harm of the same Richard Barker, her husband, and of the said Joan his wife, and against the peace of our said lord the King.

19. *Indictment of a man seeking to rape a certain man's daughter, and he was not able to carry out his intention*

Kent

The jurors present, on behalf of our lord the King, that William Wylson, lately of Feversham in the aforesaid county, *laborer*, on the sixth day of June in the   year etc. by force and arms, namely with swords, clubs and knives, broke and entered the close of John Payne at Feversham aforesaid in the aforesaid county, and finding then and there Joan, the daughter of the same John Payne, he took her and dragged her away and flung the same Joan to the ground with the intention, if he could, of raping and carnally knowing her, and when he was unable to carry out his

145

intention of raping her then he then and there by the aforesaid force and arms made an assault upon her,

(Page 13)

and then and there beat, wounded and illtreated her; so that her life was despaired of; and inflicted other enormities upon her against the peace of our said lord the King etc.

20. *Indictment of a common barrator*[38]

Kent

The jurors present, on behalf of our lord the King; that Alice S   lately of Bersted in the aforesaid county, *Spynster*, on the tenth day of July in the   year etc., and also on sundry days and occasions both before and after, in a public lane at Bersted aforesaid, openly, wickedly and maliciously made and uttered malicious and perverse words to her neighbours, inciting and procuring discords, lawsuits, quarrels and strifes between the aforesaid neighbours, not only to the perturbation, disquiet and trouble of the aforesaid neighbours, but even to the pernicious example of others in totally misbehaving, and against the peace of our said lord the King that now is, etc.

21. *Another indictment of a common barrator*

Kent

The jurors present on behalf of our lord the King, that Nicholas Godwyn, of Shorn in the aforesaid county, *laborer*, on the first day of September in the   year etc. and on sundry days and occasions both before and after, at Chalock in the aforesaid county, and also in other parishes and places adjoining the aforesaid parish, and daily from the aforesaid day and year until the day of the taking of this inquisition, has been and is a common barrator, a most a most wicked, seditious and unlawful procurer and waylayer[39] of many of the inhabitants, both of the aforesaid parish and of sundry parishes and places adjoining the aforesaid parish, to sundry discords, strifes, lawsuits, quarrels, pleas, suits and conspiracies,[40] and not only to the disturbance of the peace of our aforesaid Lord the King, and the disquieting and trouble of peaceful and honest persons, and of the inhabitants, and of those living thereabout, but also to the most pernicious example to such persons to offend in the future, and against the peace of our said lord the King that now is, etc.

(Page 14)

22. *Indictment for making an assault on a man*

Kent

The jurors present, on behalf of our lord the King, that Henry Shape, lately of Hadlo in the aforesaid county, *Taylor*, on the 10th day of October in the   year etc. with force and arms, namely with swords, clubs and knives, made an assault upon Ed(ward) Curle at Boxeley in a certain place there called *the Leparke*, and then and there beat, wounded and illtreated him, so that his life was despaired of; and inflicted other enormities upon him, against the peace of our said lord the King that now is, etc.

23. *Indictment for depasturing grass*

Kent

The jurors present, on behalf of our lord the King, that Adam Abell, lately of Godeherst in the aforesaid county, *lab-*, on the 10th day of July in the   year etc. broke the close of John T   at Godherst in the aforesaid county, and depastured, trampled and consumed his grass, to the value of one hundred shillings, lately growing there, with certain animals, namely horses, oxen, cows, pigs, sheep, geese and ewes;[41] the aforesaid Adam continuing the aforesaid trespass, including the depasturing, trampling and consumption of the aforesaid grass, from the 10th day of July in the above mentioned year until the day of the ordering of this inquisition, and on sundry days and occasions, to the grave harm of John, and against the peace of our said lord the King etc.

(Page 15)

24. *An indictment for trespass.*

Kent

The jurors present, on behalf of our lord the King, that N   M lately of B   in the aforesaid county, *yeman*, on the 10th day of October etc., with force and arms, namely with swords, clubs and knives, broke and entered the close of J   M   at B   aforesaid in the aforesaid county, and depastured, trod down and consumed his wheat, namely two acres of corn, with certain cattle, namely horses, oxen, cows, pigs and sheep,[42] against the peace of our lord the King that now is, etc.

25. *An indictment for unlawful assembly.*

Kent

The jurors present, on behalf of our lord the King, that Thomas B   of M   in the aforesaid county, *Draper*, having gathered to himself sundry other malefactors, to the number of sixty persons, on the third day of June in the year etc. with force and arms, namely with swords, clubs and knives, arrayed in warlike manner, at M   aforesaid in the aforesaid county, they unlawfully assembled and gathered together, to the disturbance of divers subjects of our lord the King then and there being. to the evil, and most evil, example of all other malefactors then and there dwelling, and against the peace of our said lord the King etc.

147

26. *Another indictment for unlawful assembly.*

Kent

The jurors present, on behalf of our lord the King, that W   M   lately of D   , with other persons unknown to the number of six persons, unknown to the said jurors, on the 10th day of July in the year etc., with force and arms, namely with swords, clubs, knives, daggers, cudgels, shields, bows, arrows, and other arms both defensive

(Page 16)

and offensive, arrayed in warlike manner, unlawfully assembled at L in the aforesaid county, and there and then riotously and routously broke and entered the close of J   C   at L   aforesaid and cut down and carried away the grass of the same J   then and there growing, namely 14 acres of grass aforesaid to the value of three pounds; And inflicted other enormities upon him, to the grave loss of the same J   , and to the most iniquitous example of other malefactors, and against the peace of our lord the King etc.

27. *An indictment for diverting a common watercourse.*

Kent

The jurors present, on behalf of our lord the King, that T   P   , lately of Godeherst in the aforesaid county, yoman, on the 10th day of J   in the year etc., with force and arms etc. diverted a certain common watercourse which ought to run, and was accustomed to run since a time whereof the memory of man knows not to the contrary, through and between the lands now belonging to a certain Thomas Cowden called *le brokes* in Godherst aforesaid in the aforesaid county, from its ancient frequented and rightful course, and procured it to run through and between the lands of the same Thomas Cowden, and did this to the grave nuisance and loss of the aforesaid Thomas Cowden, and to the evil example of others offending in like case, unless a suitable remedy be provided in that behalf, and against the peace of our lord the King that now is, etc.

28. *An indictment for extortion, for the obstruction of the common highway*

Kent

The jurors present on behalf of our lord the King, that whereas all the subjects of our lord the King have had and have been accustomed to have, since a time whereof the memory of man is not extant,

(Page 17)

a certain highway, both on horseback and on foot, at all times convenient to them, to go and come by and beyond a certain common wall called *le Sewall*, extending from a certain place called the Chapel of St. Alphege in Sesalter in the aforesaid county, up to a certain other place called Graveneygutt in Graveney in the same county, and from thence up to the town of Feversham in the aforesaid County, and which for the whole of the

aforesaid time the said subjects, and all the tenants of the marsh lands there called *Graveney mersche* have had, and have been accustomed to have, a common highway by and beyond the aforesaid wall, for carrying, drawing and bearing, with carts, horses and men, all and singular such things as might be necessary or opportune for the supportation, maintenance and repair of the aforesaid wall, for the defence of the aforesaid marshes, at times convenient and opportune to them, until lately; a certain Edward Menge, lately of Graveney in the aforesaid County, maliciously scheming to impede the aforesaid liege people from the aforesaid highway by and beyond the aforesaid wall, and to impoverish the same subjects of our lord the King by grievous extortion, by the taking of divers fines, on the 28th day of July in the year etc., with force and arms, namely with swords, clubs and knives, made and installed two wooden gates called *Stokegates*, firmly locked, and other enclosures, beside the aforesaid wall at Graveney aforesaid in the aforesaid county, whereby all the subjects of our said lord the King have been altogether impeded from going, returning and passing on horseback by and beyond the aforesaid wall, from the aforesaid 28th day of July in the aforesaid tenth year[43] until the day of the taking of this inquisition, and are still impeded, and on this pretext the aforesaid Edward has taken by extortion, and now retains, divers fines from certain persons unknown, subjects of our said lord the King, for their way and passage on horseback by and beyond the aforesaid wall, on the first day of August in the tenth year above mentioned, at Grav(ene)y
(Page 18)
aforesaid in the aforesaid county, and he still has not desisted from taking and retaining by extortion such fines from the subjects of our said lord the King, to the grave loss, nuisance, impoverishment and inconvenience of the subjects of our lord the King and against the peace of our lord the King that now is, etc.

29. *Another indictment for extortion.*

Kent

The jurors present on behalf of our lord the King, that William Dean, lately of Stansted in the aforesaid County, *yoman*, bailiff of our lord the King within the hundreds of Chetham and Gyllyngham in the said county of Kent, setting at naught the prosperity and common utility of the same hundreds and of the kingdom, received by extortion several gifts, benefits and rewards from a certain John Long and Thomas Hone, and divers other persons, highly suitable and of the greatest substance, gravity and discretion, dwelling within the said hundreds, on the sixth day of January in the year of the reign of Henry VIII etc. and at divers times and places, both before and after, at Chetham aforesaid in the aforesaid county, and elsewhere in the same county, and has retained them, with the intention that the same bailiff should not impanel such suitable and substantial persons in any inquisitions or juries whatsoever; and then and there, by pretext of the matters aforementioned, the same William Dean unlawfully promised to the same suitable and discreet persons, that he would keep them indemnified from being impanelled or returned, from any inquisition, summons or jury whatsoever during the term for which he the said William Dean should be bailiff of the aforesaid hundreds, and advised and permitted them to remain at home,

(Page 19)

and then and there caused to be impanelled and summoned sundry poor persons, dwelling within the aforesaid hundreds and being of little discretion, to enquire on behalf of our lord the King about and upon certain articles of the peace and concerning the law of our said lord the King, and compelled and coerced them to appear before the Justices of our said lord the King for preserving the peace in the said county of Kent, and also assigned to hear and determine divers felonies, trespasses and other misdeeds committed in the same county, at Maydeston in the aforesaid county, held on the aforesaid Tuesday next before the feast of St. James the Apostle last past, against the peace of our lord the King in the year etc.

30. *Another indictment for extortion.*

Kent

The jurors etc., that William Capon of Woodchurche in the aforesaid county, *Taylor*, on the first day of August in the year etc., with force and arms, namely with swords, extortionately and with misprision, in contempt of our said lord the King, and for the purpose of extortion, came to a certain William Hope at Woodchurche aforesaid, in the aforesaid county, and asserted to him that he had a warrant directed to him from the court of our lord the King, to arrest the same William Hope; and then said to him, "I will arrest you unless you will give me three shillings and fourpence"; and thereupon the aforesaid William

(Page 20)

Capon, not having any power or authority of our said lord the King, and not having directed to him any warrant or precept from any minister of our same lord the King, but of his own extortion and power, then and there arrested the aforementioned William Hope, and kept him in prison for the space of one hour on the aforesaid first day of May, and he to obtain his deliverance then and there gave to the aforesaid William Capon three shillings and fourpence in silver, to the great impoverishment of the same William Hope and against the peace of our said lord the King that now is, etc.

31. *An indictment for a rescue.*

Kent

The jurors present on behalf of our lord the King, that whereas

150

Alexander Culpeper, esquire, sheriff of the aforesaid county, by virtue of a certain writ of our lord the King directed to him, by a certain warrant of his, sealed with his seal, composed and directed by him to a certain William Belser, required of the same William that the same William should take a certain William Lyall, lately of Gravesend in the aforesaid County, Taylor, to the purpose that he should have his body before the Justices of our lord the King for preserving the peace in the aforesaid county, and also assigned to hear and determine divers felonies, trespasses and other misdeeds committed in the same county, at Maydeston in the aforesaid county on the Tuesday next after the feast

(Page 21)

of the Epiphany of our Lord next following, then and there to stand (trial) upon the outlawry against him, at the suit of our said lord the King that now is, for certain trespasses, whereof the same William is indicted in the said county of Kent; in consequence of which warrant the aforesaid William arrested the same William Lyall on the sixth day of November in the year etc. at Gravesend aforesaid in the aforesaid county, and detained him under arrest by occasion of this until the same William Lyall and a certain John Grove of Sythyngbourn in the aforesaid county, yoman, and John Wilson of S   in the aforesaid County, *Baker*, with force and arms, namely with swords, clubs and knives, riotously made an assault upon the same William Belser on the aforesaid sixth day of November in the aforesaid twentieth year,[44] at Gravesend aforesaid in that county, and there and then beat, wounded and illtreated the same William Belser, so that his life was despaired of, and then and there riotously rescued the same William Lyall, being thus in the custody of the same William; and the same William Lyall, being thus in custody as is aforementioned, of his own free will then and there escaped from the same custody of the same William, against the peace of our aforesaid lord the King that now is, etc. and in most evil example to others offending in like case, unless due remedy be applied speedily in this behalf.

(Page 22)

32. *Another Indictment for a Rescue.*

Kent

The jurors present on behalf of our lord the King, that whereas Henry Vane, sheriff of the county of Kent, by virtue of a certain writ of our lord the King directed to the same sheriff of Kent, of which the date is at Maydeston the 12th day of January in the thirty third Year of the reign[45] (lately), by warrant of the same sheriff, authorised by the same writ, he some time past required and commanded Henry Hogett, itinerant bailiff of the same sheriff in the aforesaid county, that, any liberty notwithstanding, he should not fail to take William Prowde the younger, of Waltham in the aforesaid county, and should keep him in safe custody to the end that he

should have his body before the Justices of our lord the king for preserving
the peace in the aforesaid county, and also assigned to hear and determine
divers felonies, trespasses and other misdeeds committed in the same
county, at Canterbury on the Tuesday next after the Sunday after Easter
next following, to answer to our lord the King concerning certain
trespasses, rescues, contempts and enormities whereof the same William
has been indicted; by virtue of which warrant the same Henry Hogett
afterwards, namely on the third day of April in the year etc., at Waltham
aforesaid in the aforesaid county, was arresting the aforementioned
William; whereupon the same William and a certain John Peers of
Waltham aforesaid in the aforesaid county, *laborer*, together with other
malefactors unknown to the number of five persons, immediately after the
aforesaid arrest made in form aforesaid, on the day and in the year above
mentioned, at Waltham aforesaid in the aforesaid county.
(Page 23)
with force and arms, namely with swords, clubs and knives, rescued the
aforementioned William from the aforementioned Henry Hogett, in
contempt of our said lord the King, now etc., and in most evil example to
other malefactors, and against the peace of our said lord the King that now
is, etc.

33. *Another indictment for a rescue.*

The jurors present on behalf of our lord the King, that Edward Porle, lately
of Chart in the aforesaid county, gentleman, on the 9th day of March in the
year etc. at Waltham in the aforesaid county, distrained a certain John
Prowde, his lessee, within the fee of the same Edward at Waltham aforesaid
in the aforesaid county, for three pounds sterling owing to him (by seizing)
divers cattle, namely six cows and four bullocks[46] of the same John Prowde,
by William Maycott and Thomas Hone, servants of the same Edward;
William Prowde of Waltham in the aforesaid county, *yoman*, and Richard
Porte of Waltham aforesaid in the aforesaid county, *yeman*, the day, year,
place and county aforesaid, with force and arms, namely with swords,
clubs, and knives, made an assault upon the aforesaid William Maycott and
Thomas Hone, and then and there imposed such and so great threats to
their lives, and of the mutilation of their limbs, against the same William
and Thomas, that their lives were despaired of, and rescued the aforesaid
cattle, being then and there under the distraint of the same Edward, taken
by the aforesaid William and Thomas in form aforesaid, with force and
arms as aforesaid, against the peace of our lord the King that now is, etc.

(Page 24)

34. *Another indictment for a rescue.*

Kent

The jurors present, on behalf of our lord the King, that whereas Clement

Wyllyamson and William Kyng on the third day of October in the year etc. at Boxeley in the county aforesaid, in a certain place there called *Lexpark*, took there certain animals, namely four horses called *geldynges* of divers colours, of Anthony Knyvett, esquire, and in accordance with the law and custom of the kingdom of our said lord the King of England impounded these animals in the pound of our said lord the King; and that William Fyssher, lately of London, *yoman*, with force and arms, namely with swords, clubs and knives, on the said third day of October in the thirtieth year above mentioned,[47] at Boxeley aforesaid in the aforesaid county, there and then broke that pound, and there and then took and drove off these animals out of the pound, against the peace of our aforesaid lord the King that now is etc.

35. *An indictment for a rescue.*

Kent

The jurors present, on behalf of our lord the King, that whereas John Baker, Knight, seneschal of our Lord the King of his manor of Wy[48] in the county of Kent, by virtue of a certain warrant directed and composed by the same John Baker out of the court of Wy aforesaid to Edward Wood and William Bedworth, bailiffs of our said lord the King, to take William Beer of Westwell in the county aforesaid, *Carpynter*, and to keep him in safe custody to the end that they could have his body before the said John Baker or his deputy at the next

(Page 25)

court at Wy aforesaid, namely to be held on the twelfth day of February next following, to answer to Nicholas Tomson concerning a plea of trespass; by virtue of which warrant the aforesaid William Bedeworth on the tenth day of February in the year etc., at Westwell aforesaid in the aforesaid county, took and arrested the aforementioned William Beer and sought to place him in safe custody according to the exigence of the aforesaid warrant; and thereupon the same William Beer then and there with force and arms, namely with swords, clubs and knives, made an assault upon the aforementioned William Bedworth, and then and there beat, wounded and illtreated him, so that his life was despaired of, and took himself out of the custody of the aforesaid bailiff and escaped against the peace of our lord the King etc.

36. *Another indictment for a rescue.*

Kent

The jurors etc., that whereas our Lord the King, by his brief directed to the sheriff of Kent, to take and arrest Thomas Abell of Halstowe in the aforesaid county, cleric, if he should be found in the bailiwick of the aforesaid sheriff, and to keep him in safe custody, to the end that he could have his body before the Justices of our said lord the King fifteen days after

Easter day, wheresoever he might then be in England, to give satisfaction to Peter Nynne, a citizen and merchant of London, and to John Edmew, *Waterman*,

(Page 26)

both concerning a bond for sixteen pounds which the same Peter and John recovered against him in the court of our same lord the King, before the aforementioned Justices at Westminster, and also concerning sixteen shillings and four pence which was adjudicated to the same Peter and John, for their damages which they had sustained by occasion of the detention of his debt, whereof he was convicted as more fully appears by the aforesaid writ; by virtue of which writ a certain John West, Knight, sheriff of the county of Kent,[49] had made a certain warrant to Henry Fyll, bailiff of our said lord the King and of the same sheriff, to take the aforesaid Thomas Abell and keep him in safe custody, to the end that the aforesaid sheriff should be able to have the body of the said Thomas before the aforementioned Justices of our said lord the King, fifteen days after Easterday next following, wheresoever they might then be in England, to give satisfaction to the said Peter and John concerning the aforesaid plea of debt according to the form and tenour of the aforesaid writ; by virtue of which warrant the aforesaid Thomas, on the twentieth day of February in the year etc., at Halstowe aforesaid in the aforesaid county, arrested the aforesaid Thomas Abell and sought to keep him in safe custody according to the exigencies of the aforesaid warrant; and the same Thomas Abell and a certain John Beneflower lately of Halstowe aforesaid in the aforesaid county, *Bocher*, then and there made an assault upon the said bailiff with force and arms, namely with swords, clubs and knives, and took and rescued the aforesaid Thomas out of the custody of the aforesaid bailiff, against the peace of our said lord the King that now is, etc.

(Page 27)

37. *For a rescue.*

Kent

The jurors present, on behalf of our lord the King, that Thomas Terre, bailiff of our lord the King, by virtue of a certain warrant bearing date the 27th day of S(eptember) in the year etc., by Christopher Hales, Knight, John Hales and Walter Hendley, Justices of our said lord the King, for preserving the peace in the aforesaid county, and also assigned to hear and determine divers felonies, trespasses and other misdeeds committed in the same county, (which) was directed and delivered to the same Thomas Terre, bailiff of our lord, that he should attach a certain William Amersley of Godherst in the aforesaid county, *Fuller*, to the intent that he should keep the peace towards our said lord the King and all his people; and that he should be of good behaviour until the next general session of the peace, next to be held at Maydeston in the aforesaid county; which said bailiff, by virtue of the aforesaid warrant, on the 12th day of October in the year etc., at Godherst aforesaid, in the aforesaid county, sought to arrest the aforesaid William Amersley but the same William Amersley on the aforesaid 12th day of October in the above-mentioned 28th year,[50] with force and arms, namely with swords, clubs and knives, made an assault upon the aforesaid Thomas Terre, and rescued himself then and there from the custody of the same bailiff, against the peace of our said lord the King that now is, etc.

(Page 28)

38. *An indictment against men (summoned by) a warrant from the Justices of our lord the King.*

Kent

The jurors present on behalf of our lord the King, that whereas Richard Payne, one of the Justices of our lord the King for preserving the peace in the aforesaid county, and also assigned to hear and determine divers felonies, trespasses and other misdeeds committed in the same county, directed a certain warrant for surety of the peace to Thomas Hope of Wrotham in the aforesaid county *yeman*, a constable of our Lord the King for the hundred of Wrotham aforesaid, and to Richard Wescotte of Wrotham aforesaid in the aforesaid county, *yoman*, reeve[51] of the township of Wrotham, and to each of them, to arrest a certain William Wyllyamson and John Awsnell, to the end that they the aforesaid William Wyllyamson and John Awsnell should find sufficient security of the peace for their good behaviour toward our lord the King and all his people and in particular toward Richard Collyn, against whom the said William and John were wantonly and openly threatening his life and the mutilation of his limbs, whereof the same Richard Colyn had sworn his corporal oath before the aforesaid Justice; which same warrant the aforesaid Richard Colyn delivered to the aforesaid Thomas Hope and Richard Wescotte in execution of due form of law on the 26th day of November in the year etc. at Wrotham aforesaid in the aforesaid county; but the said Thomas Hope and Richard Westcott, setting at naught the warrant and command of the Justice of the peace of our said lord the King,

(Page 29)

and intending altogether to bring to nothing the laws of our said lord the King of England, so much as in them lay, they then and there sought not to obey or observe the aforesaid warrant in any way, but have altogether refused to observe that warrant according to due form of law, from the aforesaid 26th day of November in the aforementioned 20th year until now, at Wrotham aforesaid in the aforesaid county; in consequence of which refusal and disobedience the said Richard Colyn has not dared to go about openly without the greatest danger to his life and of mutilation of his limbs, nor yet dares do so up to the present; to the great contempt of our lord the King and in most evil example to other malefactors, to offend in like

155

manner, unless due remedy is applied speedily in this behalf, and against the peace of our lord the King that now is, etc.

39. *An indictment of labourers against the form of the statute.*

The jurors present, on behalf of our lord the King, that whereas in the statute in the parliament of the lord E(dward) III, formerly king of England, held in the 23rd year of his reign, published for the benefit of the common weal of the same realm, among other things it stands ordained and established that every man or woman, of what estate or condition he be, free or bond, able in body, and within the age of threescore years, not living in merchandise,

(Page 30)

nor exercising any certain craft, nor having of his own whereof he may live, nor having proper land, about whose tillage he may himself occupy, and not serving any other; if he in convenient service be required to serve, he shall be bounden to serve, taking only such and so much salary and wages as are specified in the aforesaid statute, under certain penalties specified in the same statute; nevertheless, a certain William Rose, lately of Rodmersham aforesaid in the aforesaid county, *laborer*, and William Awdeley lately of Rodmersham aforesaid in the aforesaid county, *laborer*, not heeding the aforesaid statute, who are able in body for labour, and within the age of threescore years, not living in merchandise nor exercising any certain craft, nor having of their own whereof they may live, nor having proper land, about whose tillage they may themselves occupy, and not serving any other; and nevertheless when they and each of them, on the 3rd day of March in the   year of the reign etc. and also on divers other days and occasions, both before and after, were required by sundry subjects of our lord the king at Kyngeston in the aforesaid county and divers other places in the aforesaid county, to serve them according to the form of the aforesaid statute, they there and then refused to serve, and each of them so refused, to the contempt thereby of our lord the King, contrary to the form of the statute and against the peace of our lord the King that now is, etc.

(Page 31)

40. *An indictment under the statute concerning the harbouring of vagabonds.*[52]

The jurors present, on behalf of our lord the King, that whereas it is among other things provided, stablished and ordained in a statute in a parliament of our lord H(enry) VII lately King of England, at Westminster in the 19th year of his reign, by authority of the same parliament, that if any person gives any other meat or drink whatsoever to any vagabond, idle people, and suspect persons, living suspiciously, or favours them in their misdoing or receives them, or harbours them over one night, that thereupon the same person shall forfeit, for every time so doing, 12d., as in the aforesaid statute is more fully contained; nevertheless a certain William Darte, lately of D in the aforesaid county, *yoman*, not taking heed of the aforesaid statute, on the 21st day of February in the year of the reign etc., received seven men, and three women, (idle vagabonds living suspiciously, being strong and able in their bodies to work, but not known to the aforesaid jurors, feigning themselves to have knowledge in physiognomy and palmistry, and by pretext thereof deceiving very many of the people of our lord the King) into the house of the same William at D aforesaid in the aforesaid county, and there and then received, harboured and fed the same men and women for the night then next following, and for the days and nights of Saturday, Sunday and Monday then next following,

(Page 32)

and there and then assisted and favoured both them and others who gathered to them there in their aforesaid misdeeds, in contempt of our said lord the King, that now is, etc., and against the form of the statute published and provided in this case etc.

41. *An indictment against a man for destroying a hare in the deep snow.*

The jurors etc. that Thomas Abell of Dunstable in the aforesaid county, *Laborer*, and William Johnson of D(unstable) aforesaid in the aforesaid county, *Laborer*, on the twelfth day of December in the year etc. in the deep snow lying upon the ground there at D(unstable) aforesaid in the aforesaid county, traced, pursued and tracked down two hares; and in the midst thereof they there and then chased and killed the same hares with certain greyhounds, against the form of the statute published and provided therein etc.

42. *An indictment against hunters against the form of the statute.*

The jurors etc. that whereas it is among other things contained in a statute published in a parliament of our lord Richard II lately king of England held at Westminster in the thirteenth year of his reign, that no labourer or other layman who   (End of MS.)

Places, with Ordnance Survey grid references.

Ashford	TR 0142, 11
Bearsted	TQ 8055. (3 m. E. of Maidstone), 20
Boxley	TQ 7759. (N. of Maidstone, and near Penenden Heath), 22, 34
Canterbury	TR 1557, 32
Challock	TR 0149. (4 m. N. of Ashford; only the church remains at the original site), 15, 21

Charing	TQ 9549. (5 m. NE. of Ashford), 18
Chatham and Gillingham (Hundreds)	29
Chart (Great)	TQ 9842. (2 m. W. of Ashford), 33
Cowden	TQ 4640. (7 m. W. of Tunbridge Wells), 4
Dartford	TQ 5474, 8
Doddington	TQ 9357. (5 m. SE. of Sittingbourne), 14
"Dowe"	(not identified), 16
Down	TQ 4361. (4 m. S. of Bromley, near Biggin Hill), 5
Dunstable	(see Tunstall).
Eltham	TQ 4274. (Site of a royal palace, and now among the suburbs of London), 2
Faversham	TR 0161, 12, 19, 28
Folkestone	TR 2336, 10
"Godeham"	(not identified), 16
Goudhurst	TQ 7237. (9 m. E. of Tunbridge Wells), 23, 27, 37
Graveney	TR 0562. (3 m. E. of Faversham), 28
Gravesend	TQ 6473, 31
Hadlow	TQ 6349. (4 m. NE. of Tonbridge), 22
Halstow (Lower)	TQ 8567. (4 m. NW. of Sittingbourne), 36
"Hedlyng"	(not identified, but Dr. Felix Hull tells me that there was a lathe of Hedling which roughly covered the area between Sandwich and Dover), 16
Kingston	TR 1951. (5 m. S. of Canterbury), 39
London	17, 36
Maidstone	TQ 7656, 13, 31, 32, 37
Newington	TQ 8665. (on the A2 road between Chatham and Sittingbourne), 12
Penenden Heath	TQ 7757. (N. of Maidstone), 13
Rodmersham	TQ 9261. (2 m. SE. of Sittingbourne), 39
Seasalter	TR 0964. (2 m. SW. of Whitstable), 28
Shorne	TQ 6971. (4 m. NW. of Rochester), 21
Sittingbourne	TQ 9163, 31
Stansted	TQ 6062. (7 m. NE. of Sevenoaks), 29
Stone	TQ 5774. (2 m. E. of Dartford), 3
Tonge	TQ 9364. (2 m. E. of Sittingbourne, and about a mile N. of the A2; the site is now almost deserted except for the church), 14
Tunstall	TQ 8961. (2 m. S. of Sittingbourne; Hasted, "History of Kent" 2/571 records that in his time (1782) it was pronounced "Dunstall", and it is therefore likely to be the "Dunstable" of the MS; see also J. K. Wallenberg, "The Place-names of Kent", p. 271), 41

Waltham	TR 1148. (6 m. SW. of Canterbury, and 7 m. NE. of Ashford), 32, 33
Westwell	TQ 9947. (4 m. N. of Ashford), 35
Woodchurch	TQ 9434. (4 m. E. of Tenterden), 30
Wrotham	TQ 6159. (8 m. W. of Maidstone), 38
Wye	TR 0546 (5 m. NE. of Ashford), 11, 35

Notes

1. I am indebted to the Conservator of the Municipal Library, Rouen, for the information in this paragraph which supplements that given by Briquet.
2. i.e. profession or occupation.
3. "lately".
4. "The jurors present, on behalf of our lady the Queen, that I.   S.   (or J.   S.   ), lately of D.   in the county of Essex ..." Here, and in the other extracts from West's Symboleography, I have given the Latin with abbreviations, as it stands in the printed text. It closely resembles the forms in the MS also.
5. "on the 5th day of February in the   year of the reign of our lady Elizabeth, by the grace of God, of England ..."
6. "at the 6th hour before the noon (or, after the noon) of the same day ..."
7. "at B.   in the county of C   ."
8. "in the aforesaid county".
9. "at B.   in the county of C.   at a certain place there called ..."
10. "at B.   in the county of E.   ... he made an assault upon a certain J.   S.   , and then and there, feloniously and of malice aforethought, struck and murdered the same J.   S.   with a certain sword of the price of ..."
11. "traitorously".
12. "he murdered".
13. "feloniously".
14. "burglariously".
15. "with the intention of committing a felony or murder ..."
16. "he feloniously seized".
17. "he feloniously took and carried away".
18. "he led off".
19. "he feloniously stole".
20. "with force and arms, namely with swords, clubs, knives etc ..."
21. "against the form of the statute in such case provided and published".
22. "against the form of sundry statutes in such case published and provided".
23. 4th edition (1669), 48.
24. I have followed, as closely as possible, the wording in the corresponding indictment in West, 299.
25. *clericus.*
26. 1538.
27. *cultellis et perforariis.*
28. *quodam veneno ac quibusdam aliis speciebus intoxicacionis.*
29. *Sic.*
30. 1539.
31. MS. *servicie* appears from the context to be a scribal error, said to be of common occurrence, for *cervisie*. The nineteenth century translator of this part of the text took the same view of this as I do.
32. *diversos vacabundos et alias personas suspectas ad cardas, aleas et alia ioca et lusa illicita ... ludentes.*
33. MS. *veriusque sexus* appears to be an error for *utriusque sexus*. In the hand of the MS, "u" and "v" are more or less interchangeable, and "t" and "e" are very similar to one another when joined to the preceding letter by a ligature.
34. *ad globulos.*
35. *insidiator viarum.*
36. Although the initials of the accused are given here as W.   T.   , his Christian name is

later given in full as John. Here, and in the similar case of the initials in No. 4, it seems rather more likely that the form which comes later in the text is the true one, than that the form is correct at the beginning, because of the tendency of a copyist, who has inserted a fictitious set of initials at the beginning, to lapse into copying the actual form before him.

37. Evidently Maidstone.

38. Rastell, *Les Termes de la Ley* (1641 edition, fo. 38v.) defines a barrator as "a common mover and stirrer up, or maintainer, of suits, quarrels, or plaints, either in courts or in country: ... In Country, in three manners; first, in disturbance of the peace; secondly, in taking or detaining of the possessions of house, lands, or goods etc., that are in question or controversy ...; thirdly, by false inventing and sowing of calumnies, rumours and reports, making discord and disquiet to rise between his neighbours."

39. *insidiator.*

40. *conventicula.*

41. *cum quibusdam averiis videlicet equis bobis vaccis porcis ovibus anceribus et bidentibus.*

42. *cum quibusdam averiis videlicet equis bobus vaccis porcis et bidentibus.*

43. 1518.

44. 1528. Alexander Culpeper, of Bedgebury in Goudhurst, was however sheriff in 15 and 22 Henry VII and 6 Henry VIII, not in 20 Henry VIII.

45. 1542. Here again, there is discrepancy with the name of the sheriff. Henry Vane, of Tonbridge, was sheriff in 23 Henry VII and 17 Henry VIII, not in 33 Henry VIII.

46. *boviculos.*

47. 1538. Hasted, *History of Kent,* 2/103e, informs us that Henry VIII, by a lease dated 21st July, 1542, let to William Smith of Maidstone, yeoman, "Le Parke, late in the occupation of Sir Anthony Knevet, Knight, but then in the occupation of the said William Smith. "Lexpark" appears to be a scribal error of a kind hardly possible for a copyist familiar with the locality. The date 1538 seems consistent with a forfeiture by Sir Anthony Knyvett between then and 1542.

48. The manor of Wye was held by Battle Abbey until its dissolution, being seized by the Crown in 30 Henry VIII (1538–9) and retained until 1551. It had been let to Roger Twisden in 25 Henry VIII (1533–4) for 40 years.

49. I have been unable to identify any sheriff of Kent at this period whose name was Sir John West.

50. 1536.

51. *prepositus.*

52. *vacabundos,* i.e. idlers. "Vacabond" and "vagabond" seem, however, to be treated as interchangeable in the statutes of the period.

Appendix

Persons

A   , J   of H   , widow, 7

Abell, Adam, of Goudhurst, labourer, 23

Abell, Thomas, of Halstow, cleric, 36

Abell, Thomas, of Dunstable (Tunstall?), labourer, 41

Amersley, William, of Goudhurst, fuller, 37

Awdeley, William, of Rodmersham, labourer, 39

Awsnell, John, of Wrotham, 38

B   , T   , 3

B   , Thomas, of M   , draper, 25

Baker, Sir John, seneschal of the manor of Wye, 35

Bar, Dorothy, of B   , wife of Edward Bar, 17

Bar, Edward, of B   , 17

Barker, Joan, of Charing, wife of Richard Baker, 18

Barker, Richard, of Charing, 18

Barte, William, of B   , 40

Bedworth, William, bailiff, 35